The POLYNESIAN TATTOO Handbook

Volume 2

An In-Depth Study of
Polynesian Tattoos and of
Their Foundational Symbols

Roberto Gemori

TattooTribes.com
2018

TattooTribes Ed.

ISBN-13: 978-8894205657

ISBN-10: 8894205657

chapter 3 photo:

© Thomas Andrew - 1890

chapter 4 watercolor:

© Jules-Louis Lejeune - 1825

chapter 5 photo:

© Madame S. Hoare - 1880

chapter 6 drawing:

© Jacques Arago - 1819

chapter 7 portrait:

© Gottfried Lindauer - 1878

All images by the author based on traditional motifs

TABLE OF CONTENTS

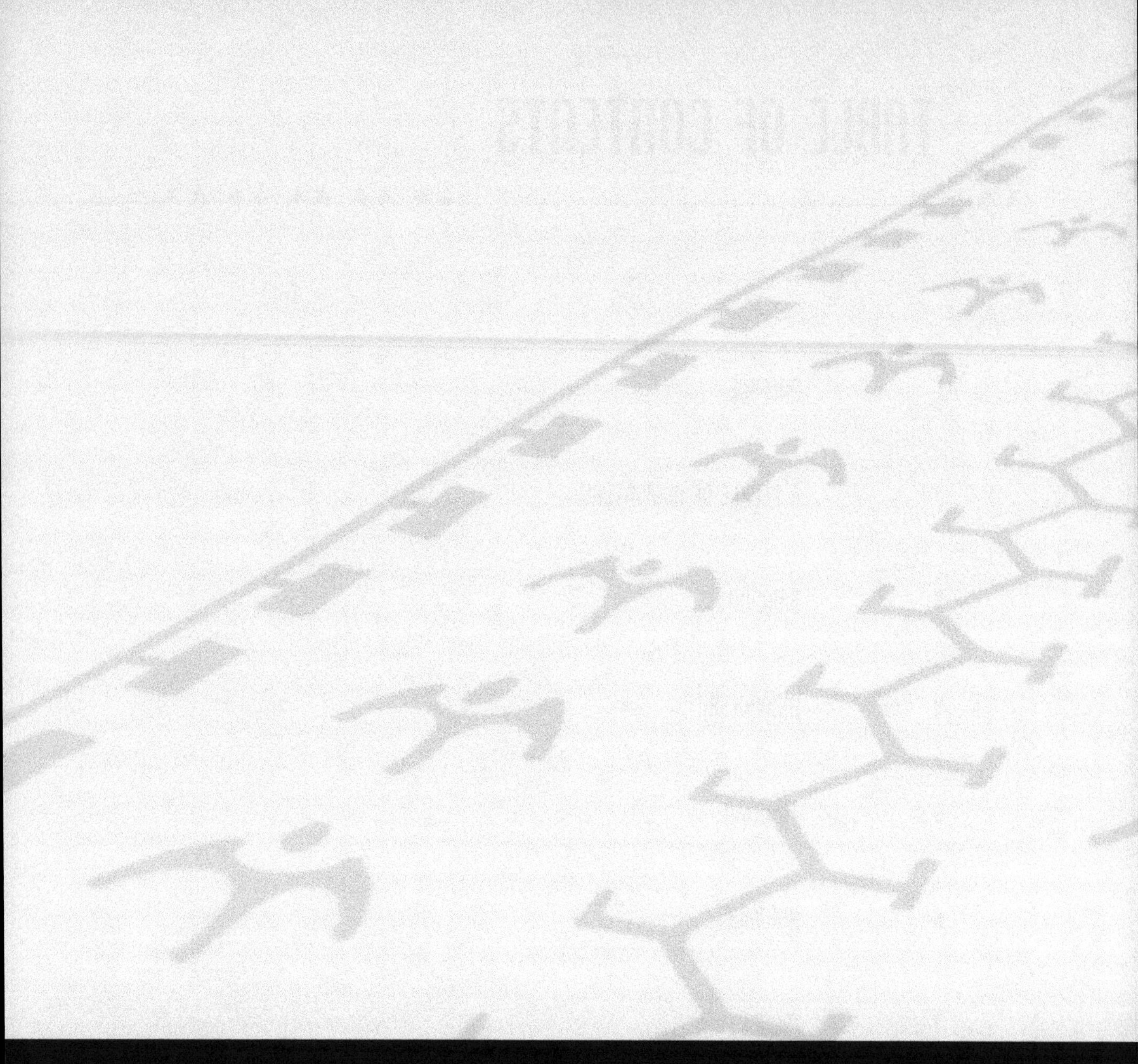

O le ala i le pule o le tautua

"The way to authority is through service."

1 PREFACE

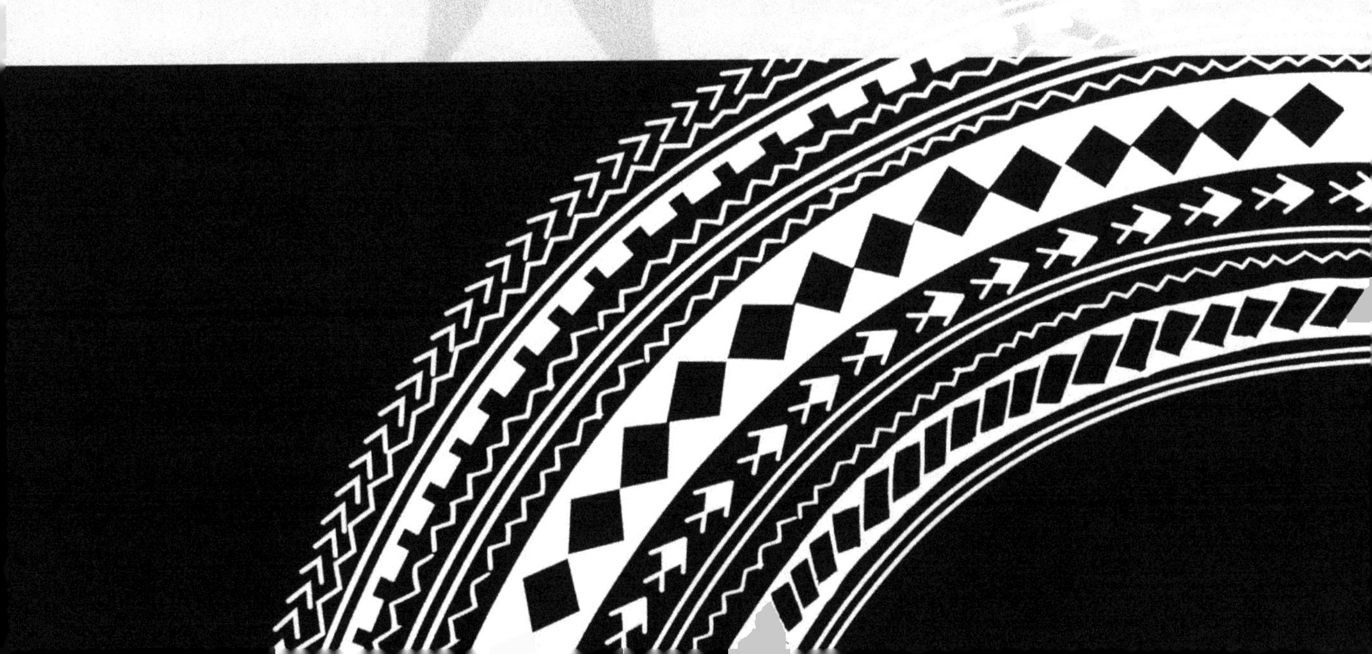

"O le ala i le pule o le tautua."
—***The way to authority is through service.***

On our mission to share our passion for Polynesian cultures and traditions, this book is a follow-up to *The Polynesian Tattoo Handbook* (2011), which was an introduction to Polynesian tattoos, to their basic symbols, and to how the elements could be selected and positioned to create meaningful designs.

While we suggest that book as a comprehensive introduction to the world of Polynesian tattoos, this one represents an unprecedented resource for those who wish to take one step further and delve deeper into the styles, elements, and meanings of this art. *The Polynesian Tattoo Handbook, Volume 2* collects over 400 symbols and variants from the five main Polynesian styles: Samoan, Marquesan, Tahitian, Hawaiian, and Maori.

Each main chapter is divided into three sections: a general introduction to the style, with its origins, features, and purpose; a list of symbols, along with their names and meanings, and insights on the origin of some of them; and a design section where three original tattoos are deconstructed into their building blocks and explained thoroughly in order to clarify why those specific elements were chosen to create them and what decisions led to the placement of each single element.

A bonus chapter shows how the styles can be mixed and even coupled with non-Polynesian elements to create intriguing new designs.

Whether you are just approaching the world of Polynesian tattoos as a novice, or you are already an experienced artist, this book will enrich your understanding of this complex and intriguing art form.

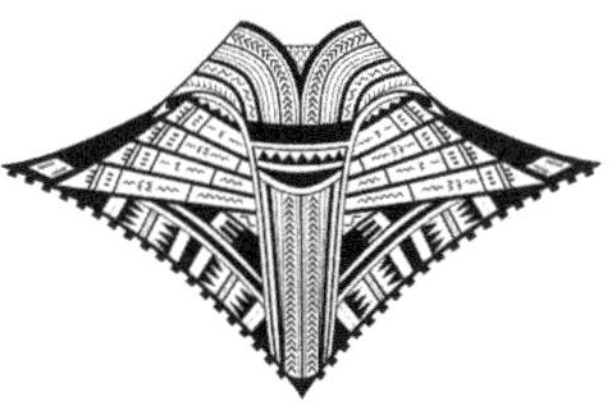

SAMOAN

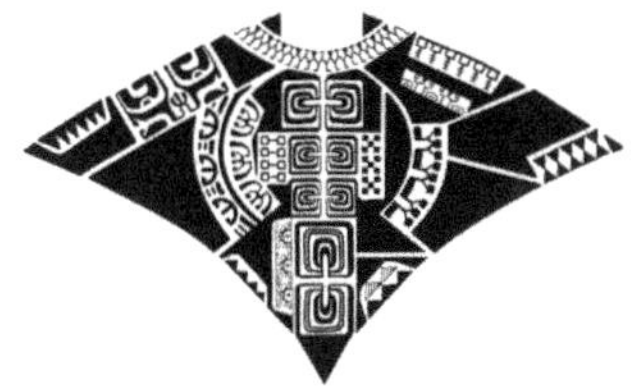

MARQUESAN

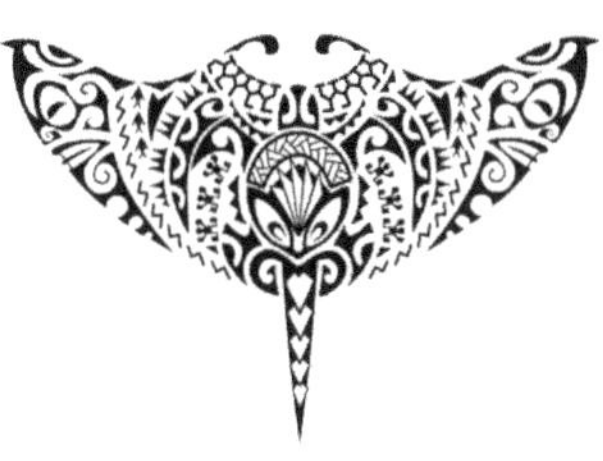

TAHITIAN

HAWAIIAN

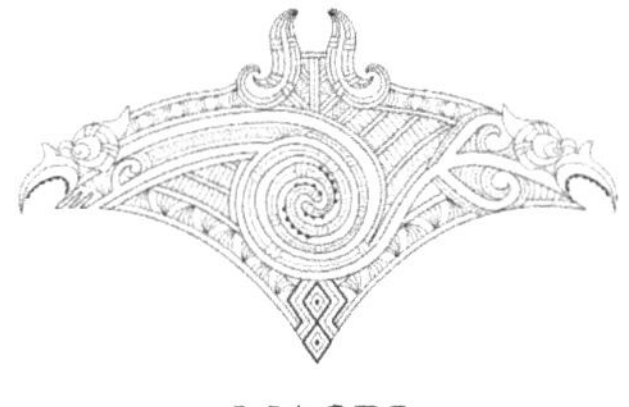

MAORI

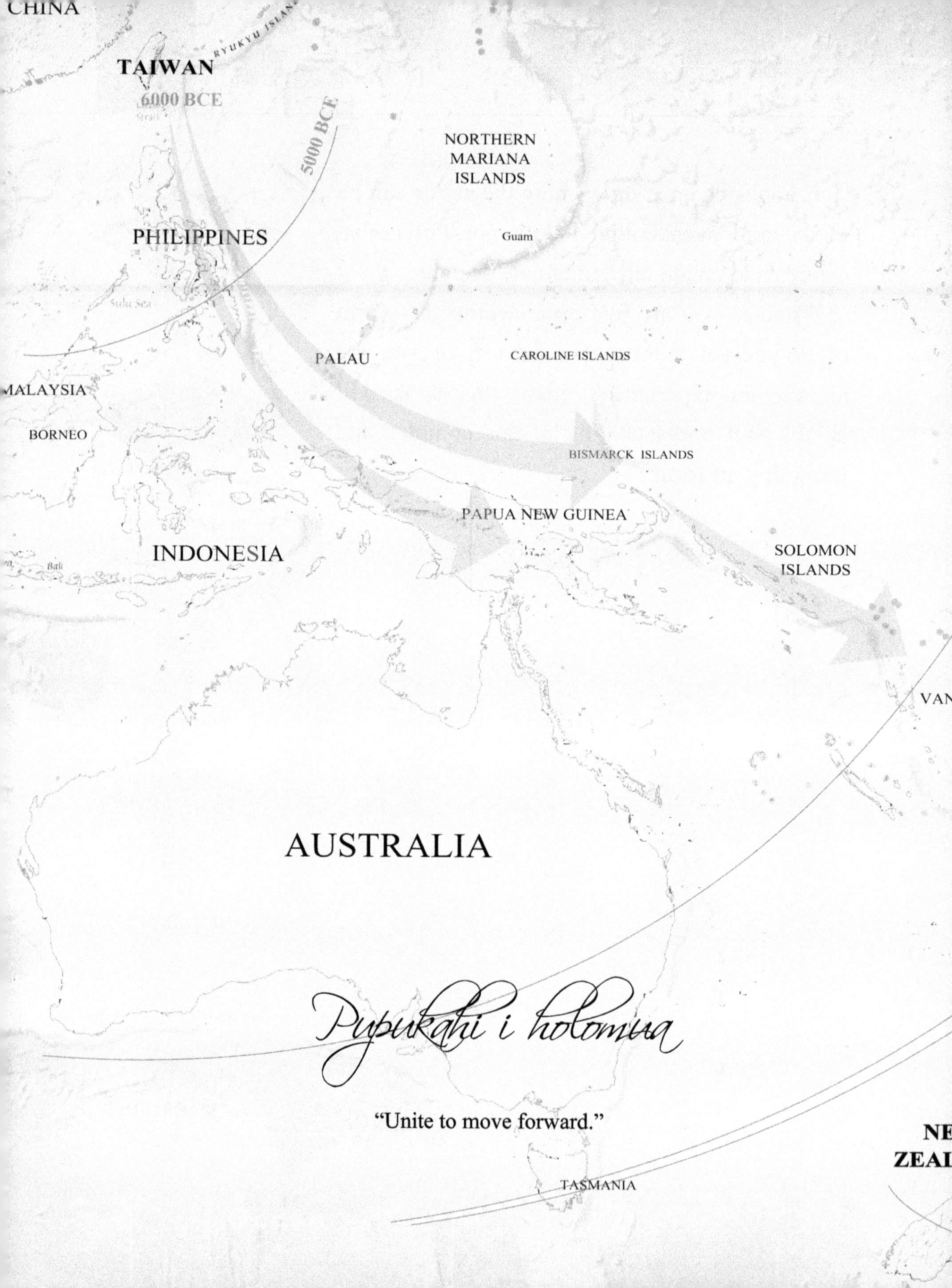

Pupukahi i holomua

"Unite to move forward."

2 A PEOPLE OF NAVIGATORS

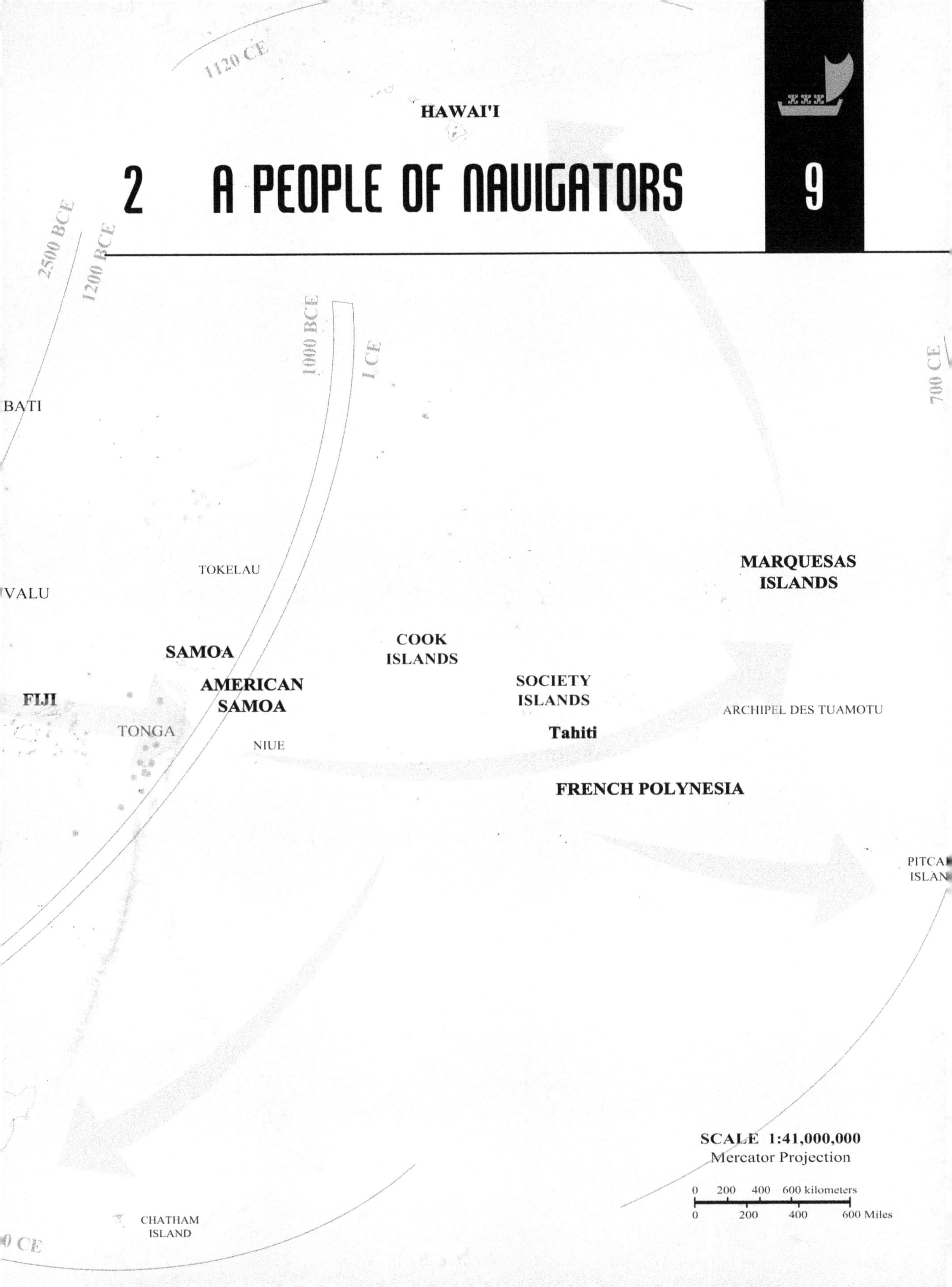

"Pupukahi i holomua."
—***Unite to move forward***:
We make progress by working together.

i. conquering the Pacific Ocean

Polynesia is a wide area that hosts several archipelagos, each with its own traditions, but it's not wrong to talk about a single Polynesian culture.

Linguistic, genetic, and archaeological evidence show how all of the cultures spread throughout the Pacific Ocean share a common origin. The study of Polynesian tattoos and of their styles provides us with further evidence, as tattoos shared similar traits and were applied using the same technique and tools from Micronesia to the most remote islands of Oceanic Polynesia. In all these areas, a wooden mallet was used to tap on a set of comb-like instruments made of shells, bones, or thorns, with a variable number of sharp teeth that punctured the skin, allowing ink to be inserted.

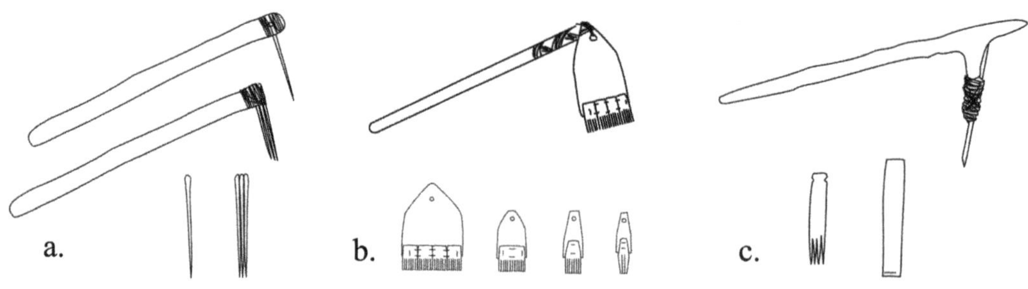

Fig. 2.1: (a) Filipino kisi, (b) Samoan 'au, and (c) Maori uhi.

While Melanesia, Australia, and part of nearest Polynesia had already been inhabited by people from the Indian peninsula crossing on land bridges thanks to the much lower sea level during glacial periods, the real colonization of the Pacific is much more recent, and it started from the area of present-day China, moving south to the islands of Micronesia from Taiwan around 6000 BCE. The Austronesian people, ancestors of modern Polynesians, continued their expansion south through Micronesia and Melanesia over a span of about 3,500 years. By that time they had developed rudimentary pirogues that allowed them to easily move from island to island over short distances, as shown by signs of frequent trade between different areas. This first expansion is shown in figure 2.2.

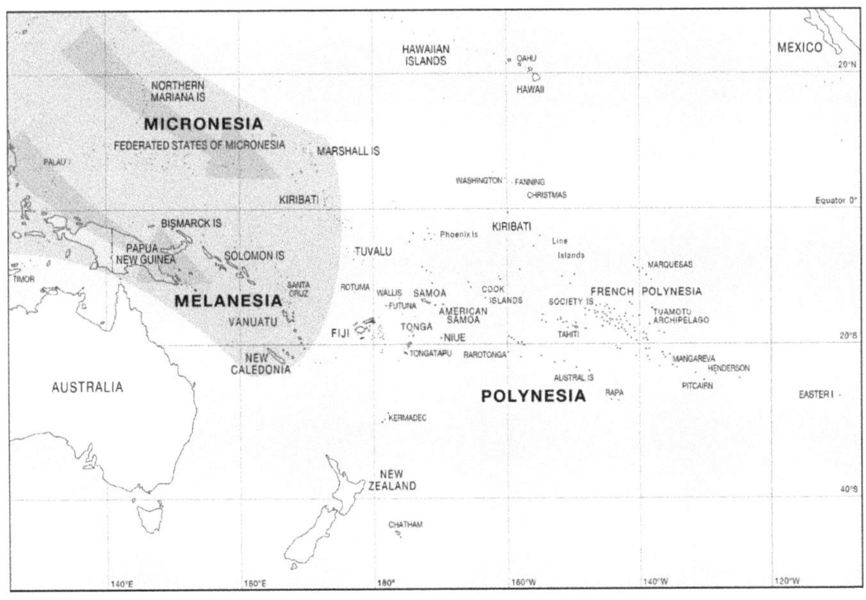

Fig. 2.2: The first wave of expansion stopped at the edge of Polynesia around 2500 BCE.

In particular, the archipelago of the Bismarcks became a thriving center for cultural and commercial exchanges, and the probable origin of the Lapita culture that is considered the origin of Polynesian arts and tattooing, around 3500 BCE. Pottery from this period shows the characteristic geometrical patterns that are now universally known from tattoos.

During this period, this proto-Polynesian society consolidated its settlements and improved its set of skills, setting the basis for the next stage of the colonization. While early canoes were built to cross short distances, technical innovations like the outriggers granted them more stability, allowing navigators to go further, settling on new islands that had remained out of reach until then (fig. 2.3).

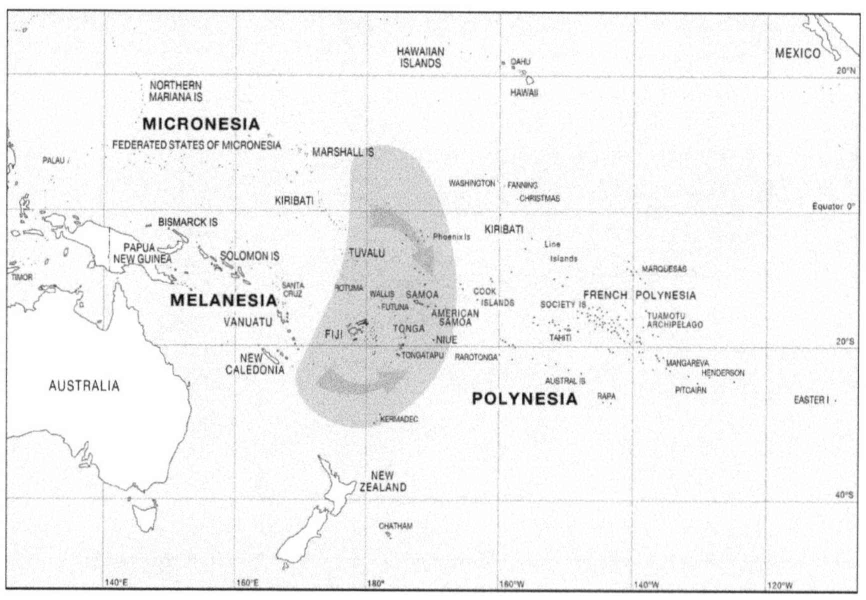

Fig. 2.3: Continental Oceania, from about 1200 to 1000 BCE.

This new area is known as Continental Oceania, as its islands are still relatively close to each other and to the continental lands, and this second wave of expansion stopped for about one thousand years at the edge of the open ocean, where new islands were more dispersed and could not be reached, or found, without embarking on long voyages that could last for months. The observation of recurrent migratory routes of certain birds suggested the existence of new lands to the east, but it was not until double-hulled voyaging canoes were built that they could be reached. Such vessels had wide bridges that joined the hulls, where small constructions were built to shelter entire families together with animals, food, and supplies for such long voyages. In about two hundred years this third wave of expansion reached every corner of central Polynesia, as shown in figure 2.4.

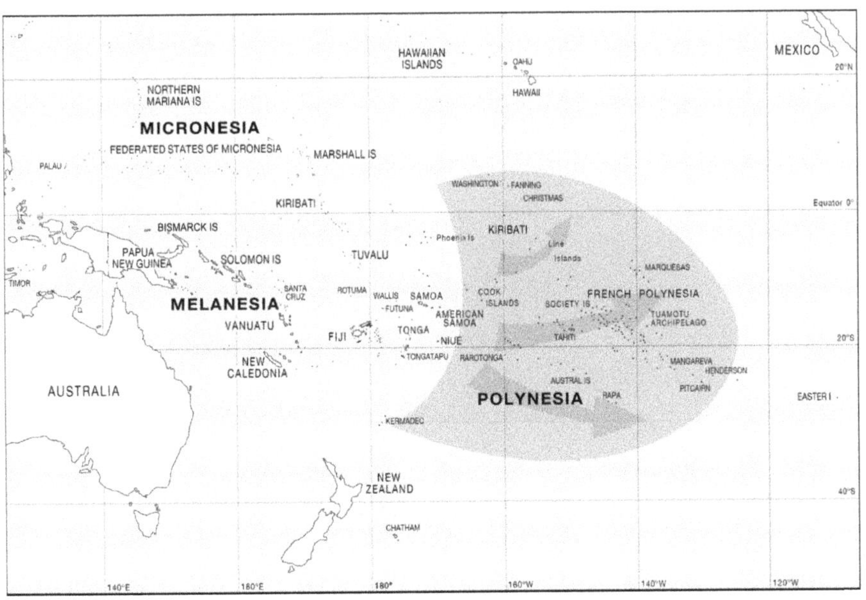

Fig. 2.4: The expansion through central Polynesia between 1 and 200 CE.

Central Polynesia offered optimal conditions, with islands and sea rich with food, mild climate, and a protective reef around most of the islands that granted easy access to the resources of the ocean.

Voyages to and through this preferential corridor joining central Polynesia to Micronesia trained the Polynesian navigators who, observing patterns in the ocean streams, winds, swells, and clouds, could devise a way of finding the route over longer distances. Migratory routes of birds and whales were then followed to the north toward Hawai'i, to the south toward New Zealand, and to the east to the coast of America.

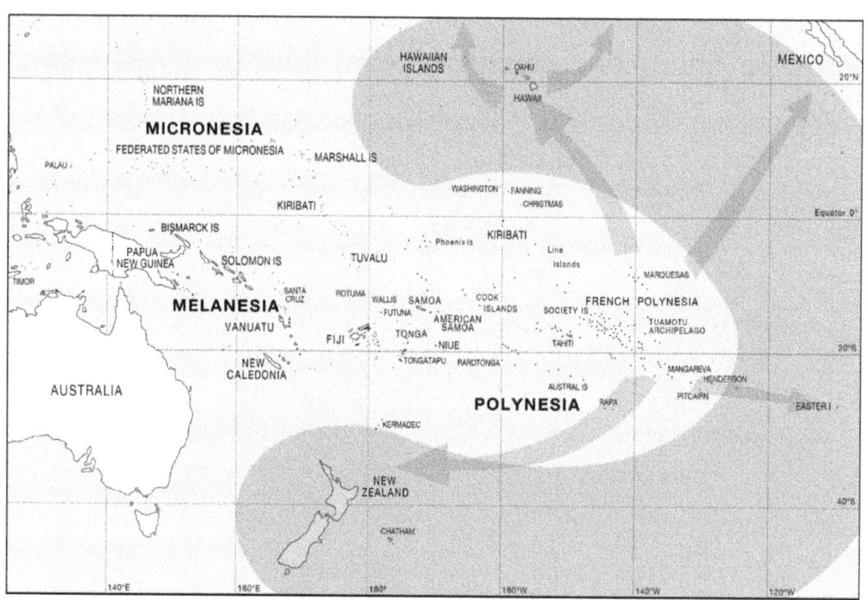

Fig. 2.5: Completing the exploration of the Pacific Ocean by 1280 CE.

Polynesian navigators even sailed westward into the Indian Ocean, reaching as far as the coast of Madagascar.

A linguistic approach shows how all Polynesian languages are like dialects of a single original mother tongue, with Hawaiian being the most simplified over time and Maori being the most entire in its forms. Fijian includes several Malay words that imply a later influence from the East Indies, while the Central and Western Polynesian dialects like Marquesan, Tahitian, and Hawaiian form a closely related group. This is also reflected in tattooing. For example, Samoa and Fiji share patterns with Melanesia and Micronesia. Hawai'i, probably due to a higher level of isolation, remained truer to the original style, even simplifying it over time despite elaborating new patterns from the most basic elements like shark teeth. The Marquesas and Tahiti being closer, maintained a higher similarity, with influences from contacts with the Americas (also testified by words from the Aymara language used by the Inca empire in Cuzco found in central Polynesian dialects). Maoris have an elaborate style of tattooing that matches the richness of their language.

ii. tattooing: symbolism and purpose

Tattoo art always adapted to the environment and to new situations to remain a faithful representation of the life of their bearers. This is a key concept in understanding the origin and purpose of this art form. Tattoos were initially a way to establish a contact with Nature and its forces, which seemed to be ruled by invisible powers that humans tried to appease by means of offers and rituals, including the shedding of the blood that comes with the tattooing process. Ink, originally obtained from ash or soot from burnt wood and nuts, was inserted below the skin and served to create a bond between humans and Nature and its spirits. It is not by chance that the Samoan words *'ele'ele* and *palapala* indicate both "soil, earth" and "blood". Several other examples testify to the importance of tattoos throughout Polynesia. The Samoan word *tatau* has the double meaning of "to strike till completed", and of "proper, necessary", for example. The Maori hero who brought permanent face tattoos to humanity was named Mataora, which literally means "living face". The word *mata* alone means "face", but also "raw, immature". Only after the tattoo is applied to the face does it become complete, "living". According to Mataora's legend, although humans are doomed to die, they become similar to the gods by receiving their tattoos, thus earning some kind of immortality.

Tattoos have a social function in Polynesia: they show ties to a community and represent a connection with the ancestors in a similar way as the meeting houses, the long houses where the community met and which had decorations and carvings representing ancestors. They both serve the double purpose of keeping the community bonds strong and of showing the lineage and ancestry of the chiefs. The parallel between tattooing and community houses is also evident from the names of some parts of the tattoos, which refer to rafters, beams, and other construction elements. This is particularly true in Samoan and Marquesan tattoos, where even the disposition of some elements recalls the structure of the houses, as we will show in the following chapters.

In order to better understand the nature of Polynesian tattoos though, it is necessary to introduce the dualism at the base of the cultures to which they belong: everything stems from the interaction between *pō* and *ao*, darkness and light, the world of the spirits, from where all knowledge comes, and the world of the living. The world of the spirits is sacred, and the world of the living is its secular counterpart. Where the *pō* enters into the *ao*, it imbues it with power and sacredness, making it forbidden to be approached without protection. Tattoos play on the alternance of black elements and empty parts. They are visible on the outside of the body but cause the sheddding of blood from the darkness within it when they are applied. They embody aspects from both worlds and can therefore represent a bridge between them.

The concepts of power and sacredness are fundamental in every aspect of Polynesian life, and they are called *mana* and *tapu*. *Mana* literally translates as "power, effectiveness, and authority", and it is a spiritual force with supernatural origin that imbues every living being as well as all inanimate objects. *Tapu*, or "sacredness", represents a quality related to this force: anything possessing a very high *mana* is sacred and therefore cannot be approached without adequate protection. Tattoos, on account of their dual nature, can give such protection. They form a barrier that protects from the *tapu* outside and prevents the *mana* inside from flowing out.

The inclusion of elements in the tattoo related to ancestors also helps collect and preserve their *mana*, fixing it into the tattoo and passing it on to their descendants. (The *ipu*, or “gourd, container”, is one of such elements used in Marquesan tattoos.)

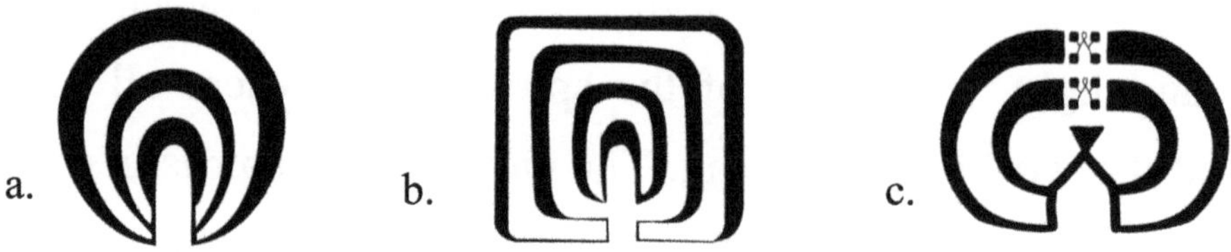

Fig. 2.6: The ipu is often considered as a schematic representation of the universe, but its shape and function (collecting ancestors' mana and representing genealogy) suggest instead that it is probably a stylized representation of a deified ancestor, as shown in (c), where an etua (“god”) is presented holding two people.

Finally, Polynesian tattoos do have a cosmetic function: they adorn the body to make it more appealing, and in some cultures they were used to contrast and disguise the wrinkles of age.

Polynesian tattoos also have a strong connection with sexuality and fertility, and the first tattoo marked the passage of both boys and girls from childhood to maturity.

iii. basic elements

The symbols used in Polynesian tattoos are strongly related to the surrounding environment and often come from everyday experience. The foundational elements include fish, birds, plants, people, and all sorts of designs derived from the observation of nature. Almost identical patterns can be found throughout the entire Austronesian area, sometimes associated with different meanings depending on the environment and daily lives of the people. Similar motifs can therefore represent a snake's skin in the mountains of the Philippines while being associated with the scales of the parrot fish on the Hawaiian islands.

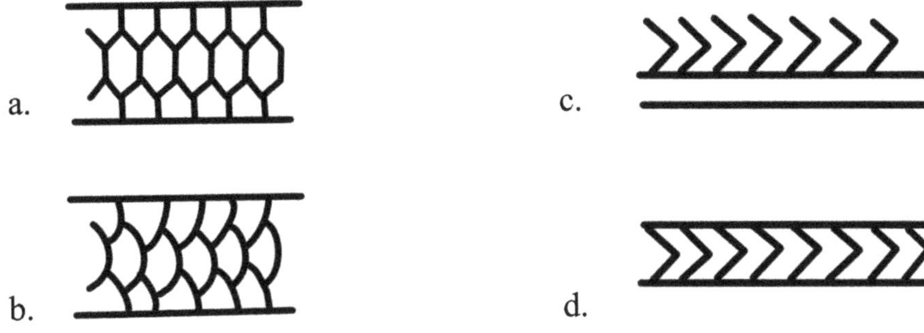

Fig. 2.7: (a) Tinulipao: snake's skin from Kalinga batok tattoos (Philippines), and (b) uhu: parrot fish scales motif (Hawai'i). (c) Tinikriku: centipede's legs (Kalinga) and (d) ivi puhi: eel's crest (Marquesan). They all share similar meanings, representing protection and a warrior spirit.

The western part of Polynesia closest to Melanesia shows clear influences from the latter, with common motifs and similar patterns. Central Polynesia, on the other hand, shows visual influences from the Inca and Aztec cultures of South and Central America. The *tiki* itself may be inspired by the stone statues of these areas, and there is a striking resemblance between the central part of the Aztec solar calendar and a

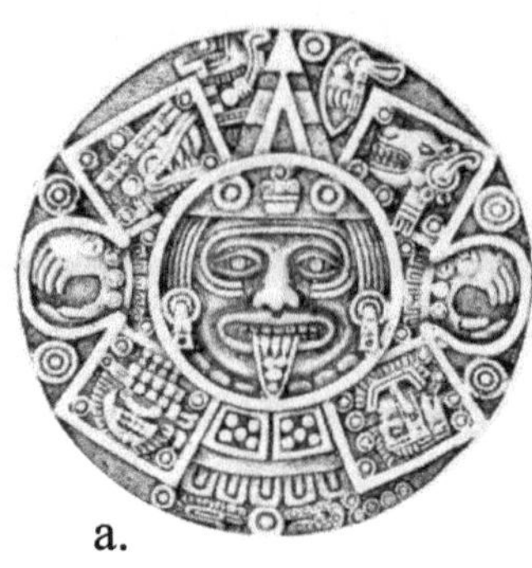
a.

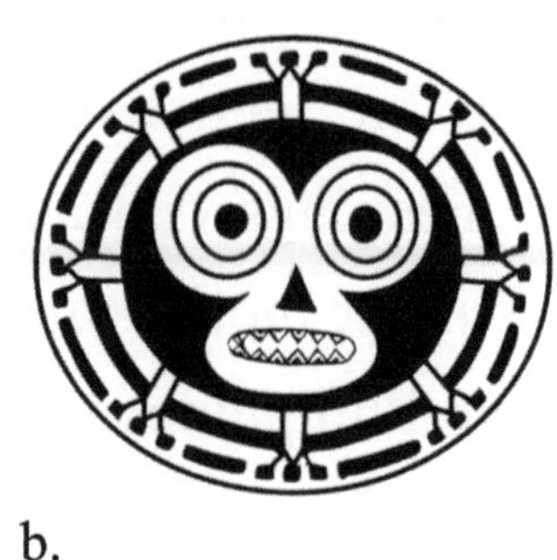
b.

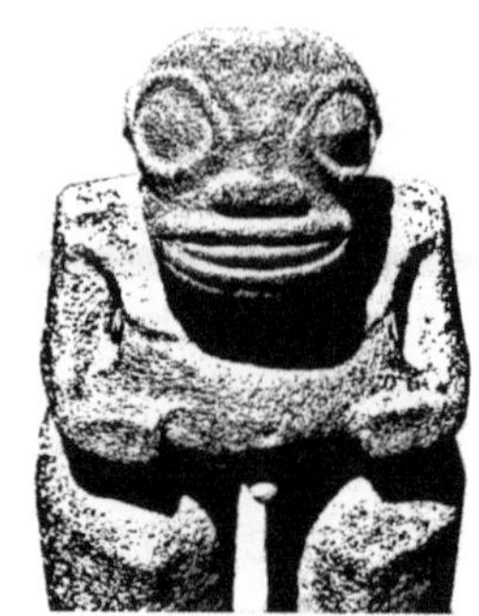
c.

Fig. 2.8: (a) Aztec solar calendar, (b) mata komoe, and (c) tiki statue. Notably, the human figure from the Aztec calendar has its tongue outstretched, a feature that will become prominent in Maori traditions.

Marquesan tattoo symbol known as *mata komoe*, as noted by Edgar Tetahiotupa in his book *Parlons Marquisien*, where he also remarks on linguistic similarities as well as related meanings among the terms.

Maori tattoos, with their extensive use of spirals, seem to have undergone the influence of contacts with South Asia (the prows of Maori war canoes share many similarities with carved doors and lintels from the Indonesian archipelago), and the images of some Indonesian demon figures closely resemble the *ruru* ("owl") figure of Maori carving, with its characteristic "split tongue" that looks graphically identical to the fangs of such demons.

The repeated contacts and cultural exchanges that occurred between the Pacific peoples over the centuries shaped the style of their tattoos into several different variants, but they did not change the symbolism

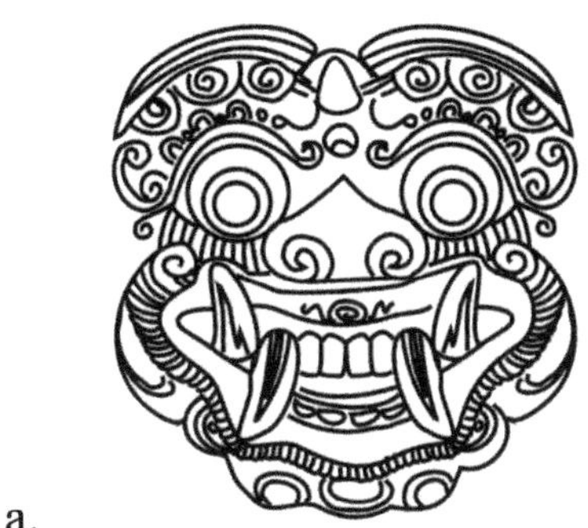

a.

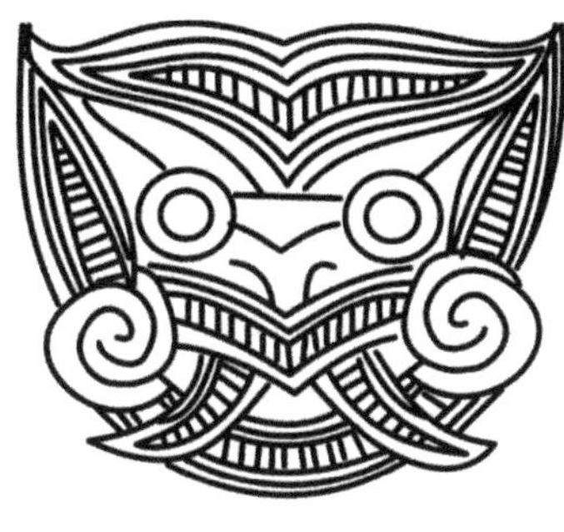

b.

Fig. 2.9: (a) Hindu statue from Ubud temple (Bali), and (b) ruru carving from Maori long house.

connected to their essence: showing community identity and belonging, honoring lineage and ancestry, giving protection, marking important events of life, and embellishing the body.

One last consideration about the basic elements before going through them: the individual symbols can have a *tapu* or *noa* quality to them. *Tapu* refers to symbols that belong to a specific lineage or family, which are therefore sacred and forbidden to anyone other than those belonging to that family, while *noa* means "common, free from *tapu*". *Noa* symbols make up the greatest part of the elements used in Polynesian tattoos, and they are the subject of this book. The following chapters will delve into the origins, symbols, and meanings of Samoan, Marquesan, Tahitian, Hawaiian, and Maori tattoos, giving valuable insight into their features, symbolism, and constructing elements, thus representing an essential aid in the creation of meaningful and respectful Polynesian designs.

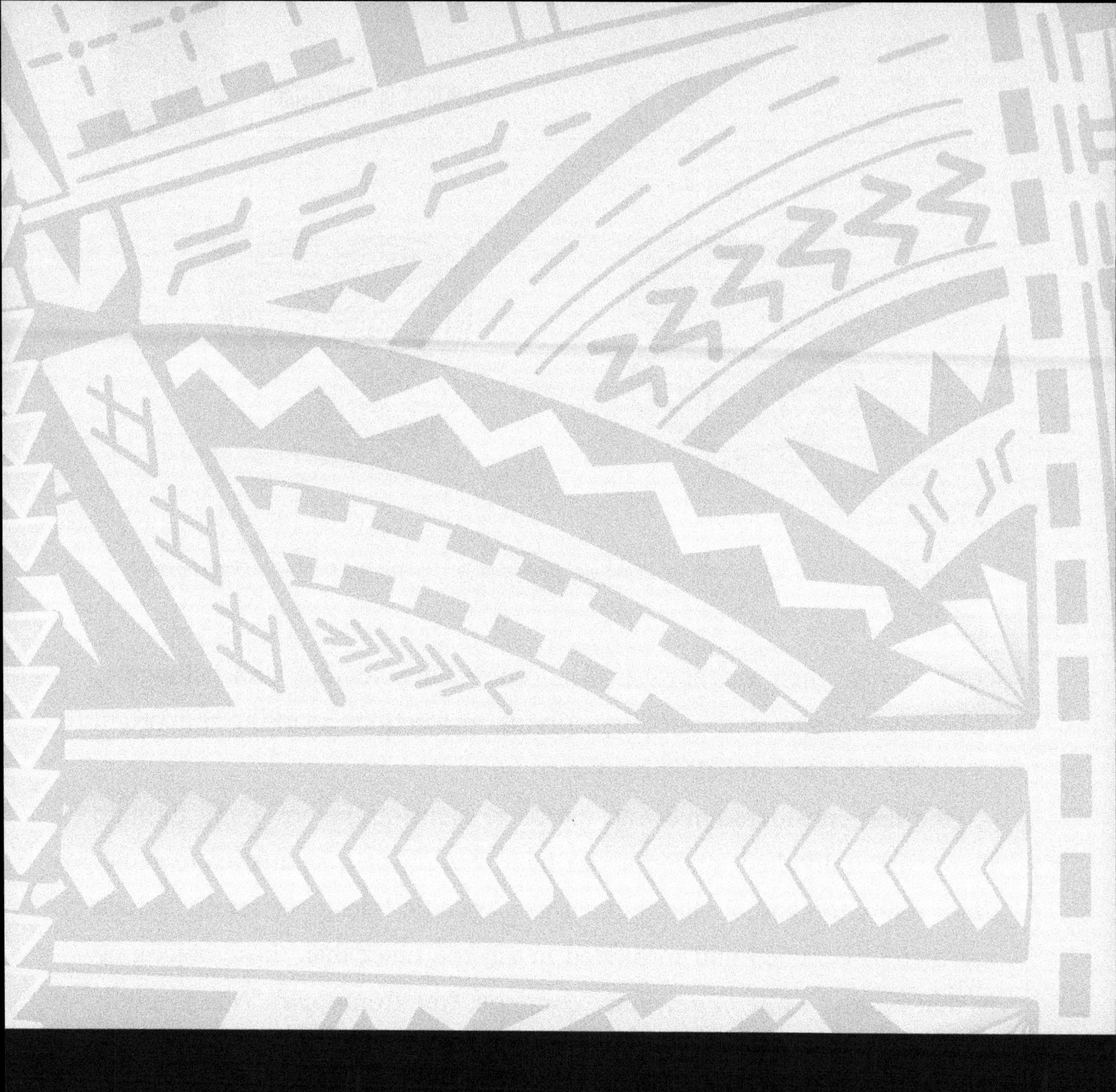

O le upega tautau, 'ae fagota

"Throw the net again and again, until it has fish."

3 SAMOAN

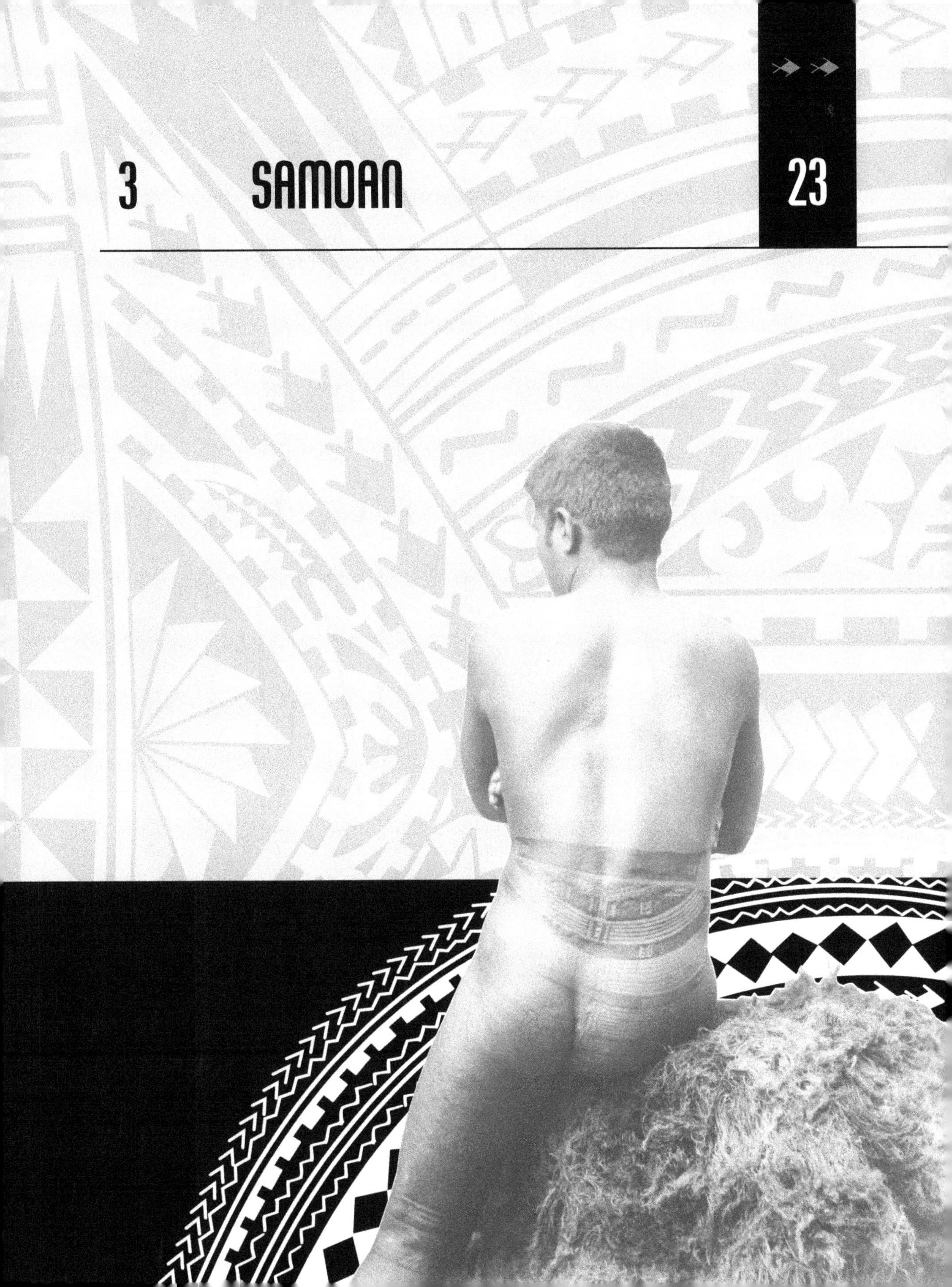

"O le upega tautau, 'ae fagota."
—***Throw the net again and again, until it has fish****:*
Never give up.

Features: rectilinear, geometrical, repetitive. Highly symmetrical body sides.
Purpose: to celebrate ancestors, to show worthiness, to give protection.

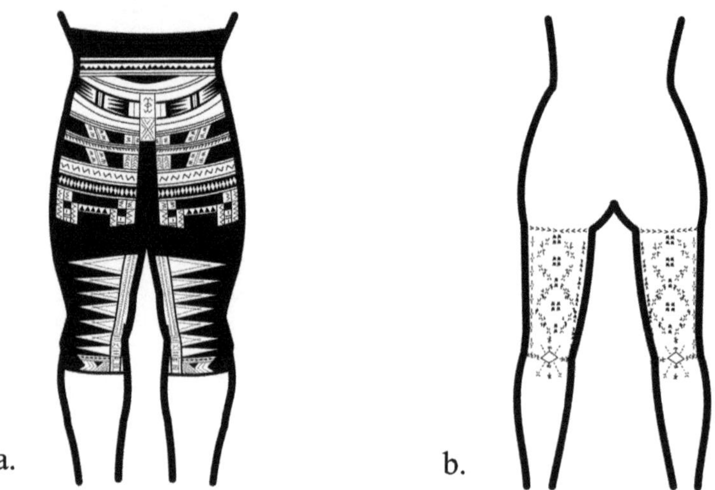

Fig. 3.1: (a) Male and (b) female traditional tattoos, back view. Drawings after K. v. d. Steinen.

i. about the style

Samoan tattoos are easily recognizable for their geometric style that follows and often enhances the lines of the muscles to create beautiful pieces.

The traditional male tattoo, called *pe'a* ("flying fox", the largest Polynesian bat), covers the body from above the hips down to just below the knees, alternating wider black parts and smaller geometric elements that create traditional motifs and patterns by repetition. The traditional female tattoo, called *malu* ("to shelter"), covers the thighs down to right below the knees.

The *pe'a* and the *malu* are visually different but they both have similar significance: to prove that an individual is worthy to become a valuable member of society. Society and service are core concepts in Polynesian cultures, embodied in Samoa by the two important words *alofa* ("compassion and sharing") and *fa'aaloalo* ("respect and service").

The importance of tattoos was so strong in this sense that contrary to what happened to the greatest part of the Polynesian islands, the practice of tattooing never ceased in Samoa following European colonization. (The word *tatau*, from which derives the term *tattoo*, has actually a dual meaning: its translation is "to strike until completed", in reference to how the tattoo was applied, but it also means "proper, necessary".) When missionaries followed the first navigators and forbid tattoo practices on the islands, owing to biblical prohibitions related to cutting or marking the body, alliances with converted monarchs granted them success on most of the islands, with few exceptions like Samoa.

Samoan tattooing traditions are among the oldest in Polynesia, reportedly inherited from Fiji, which actually shares many symbols and patterns with Samoa and Tonga.

Therefore we can safely say that Samoan tattoo art has continued uninterruptedly for over one thousand years, and it has been the inspiration of the renaissance of Polynesian traditional tattooing in the whole Pacific area during the final decades of the twentieth century. This can be attributed to traditional artists like Su'a Sulu'ape Paulo II, his brother Petelo, and their family.

While other styles changed after contact with Westerners, traditions were again stronger than fashion in the Samoan archipelago. Here tattooing not only retained the symbols but also the general structure, inherent philosophy, and original motivations of the ancient practice.

We can study the male traditional tattoo, the *pe'a*, to understand this better.

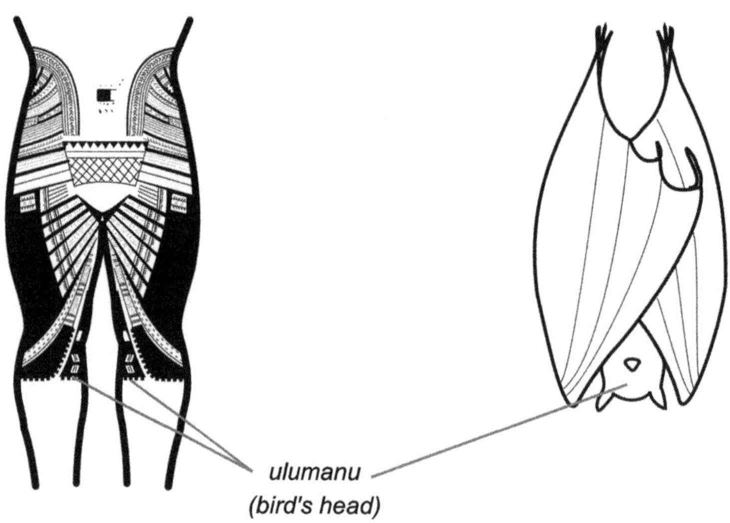

Fig. 3.2: The pe'a looks like a hanging flying fox in its frontal view. Ulumanu, meaning "bird's head", is the Samoan word for the part of the tattoo corresponding to the position of the bird's head.

The flying fox, which gives the tattoo its name and general shape, as shown in figure 3.2, is a social animal living in large colonies, who protects its young ones by surrounding them with its wings. This parallels the significance of the tattoo as a sign that the young man is now ready to provide for his family and to protect the youngest ones.

The elements that compose the *pe'a* are also a representation of the Samoan traditional meeting house, the *fale tele* ("big house").

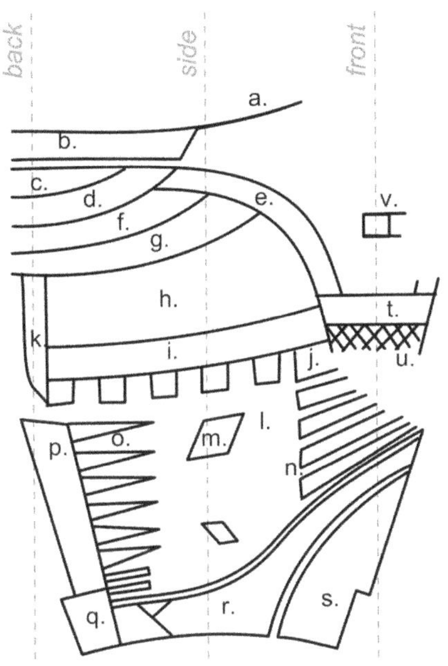

a. fa'aulutao
b. va'a
c. pe'a / pulatama
d. fa'alava
e. 'aso fa'aifo
f. 'aso laitiiti
g. pulatele
h. saemutu
i. 'aso talitu
j. selu
k. tafani tapulu
l. flausae
m. fa'aila
n. fa'avala
o. fa'amuli'ali'ao
p. atigivae
q. 'aso o le fusi
r. fusi
s. ulumanu
t. punialo
u. fa'aupega
v. pute

Fig. 3.3: After a drawing by Jack W. Groves.
General structure of a pe'a in order of application: (a) fa'aulutao: like spear heads, (b) va'a: canoe, (c) pe'a: flying fox / pulatama: little taro, (d) fa'alava: like a mantle, (e) 'aso fa'aifo: bent rafters, (f) 'aso laitiiti: small rafters, (g) pulatele: great taro, (h) saemutu: newly cut rafters, (i) 'aso talitu: supporting rafter, (j) selu: comb, (k) tafani tapulu: etched black parts, (l) lausae: new leaves (of a house), (m) fa'aila: marks in the skin, (n) fa'avala: well spaced, (o) fa'amuli'ali'ao: line of trochus shells, (p) atigivae: crab shell, (q) 'aso o le fusi: tie line, (r) fusi: tie, (s) ulumanu: bird's head, (t) punialo: pubis, (u) fa'aupega: fish net, (v) pute: navel.

The single, thin lines appearing in the tattoo are called *'aso*, which is also the word used to name the wooden rods that support the roof of such houses. The group of curved parallel lines that go from the back to the front of the hips, bowing down, is called *'asofa'aifo*, which literally translates as "bow-shaped rods", resembling the rods connected to the main rafter of the chief's house on the opposite rounded ends.

The *pe'a* serves the same purpose as the house, which is a meeting place, a connection between the past, present, and future of the community, helping perpetuate the traditions. There is a traditional sequence that must be respected in giving the traditional *pe'a* to someone, with each section being added in a very strict order: the first part to be inked is the line on the back of the ribs and waist ending on the sides of the ribs (the back is usually related to the past). (See fig. 3.3.a.) It gives the starting height of the tattoo, and it ends with spear heads to represent a warrior. This line is the starting point of the black stripe called *va'a* (canoe), the first element to be inked (fig. 3.3.b). It represents the canoe used by ancestors to get to Samoa, and it symbolizes the connection to the origins and to the ocean. The *pe'a* below is also referred to as *pulatama*, or "little taro". This symbolizes the immediate family, as does the taro plant, while the *pulatele* that surrounds it, or "big taro", represents the extended family embracing and supporting it.

The waist, buttocks, and thighs are then inked in that order to below the knee with elements relating to the present and to the life and story of the man being tattooed and of his family. This is similar to a meeting house where decorated panels display the genealogy and history of family groups and are used like textbooks by the new generations to learn about their ancestors.

The last part to be tattooed is the groin (the front relates to the future), where the *punialo* ("belly closure") is symbolic of procreation and fertility, thus ending a voyage that joins the roots to the offspring of the community, the ancestors to the descendants, and the past to the future. A square on the navel, called *pute* (fig. 3.3.v), is the final seal to be added, to symbolically represent the cutting of the umbilical cord, and therefore the new birth to adulthood. Symmetry is highly valued in each tattoo, and it is considered a proof of the master tattooist's skills.

As its name states, once started a *tatau* must be completed. An unfinished tattoo is not "proper"— it is not considered a tattoo at all, or even worse, it is a testimony that the trial failed. By undergoing the process of receiving a complete traditional tattoo, each individual accepts and upholds the honor of the family, proving to deserve the trust of the community and to be entitled to guide and protect the family.

In the words of Sulu'ape Petelo, "The person wearing the *tatau* must know that these are the stories made from their patterns that they wear and carry with them. Whenever they look down and see their *tatau*, they are reminded, this is my story and this is how I should live".

Both Samoan men and women could also wear tattoos on their hands. These are called *tapulima*, often incorporating stars and measure marks along the fingers, and fish around the wrist. They are most likely a reminiscence of the wayfaring techniques that led Polynesian people to cross the distances between islands on their explorations of the whole Pacific Ocean. By aligning the fish and the open thumb with the horizon and keeping the fingers perpendicular they could be used to measure distances, aligning the personal tattoo with stars in the night sky.

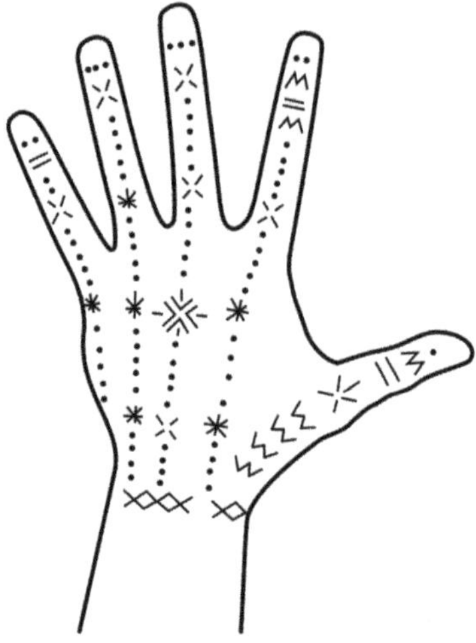

Fig. 3.4: An example of a woman's tapulima tattoo.

Different motifs in the female *tapulima* were required for women to be able to prepare and serve certain foods or beverages that were believed to be highly *tapu*, and reserved for the gods and for chieftains. In this case the tattoo served the dual purpose of protecting from the power of *tapu* and as a way not to compromise its sacredness with a profane touch.

One difficulty with Samoan traditional tattoos like the *pe'a* and the *malu* is that they require much time to be completed—weeks or months in some cases—and this does not fit in with the rhythms of present times. Tattoos have therefore naturally evolved to meet the needs of modern life, and this has eventually made them easier to be approached by non-Samoans too.

While traditional pieces tapped with stick and mallet are still usually restricted to those of Samoan descent, new renditions and reduced size allow foreign admirers of this fascinating culture to show their appreciation by receiving tattoos prepared in a large variety of different shapes and positions, designed using the traditional symbols and meanings. Some examples of such designs are shown and thoroughly explained in the last part of this chapter.

ii. elements

Samoan tattoos are mainly rectilinear and symmetrical, often based on the repetition of basic elements. Tradition says that the art of tattooing was brought to Samoa from Fiji by two Siamese sisters, Tilafaina and Taema. This is consistent with the route followed by proto-Polynesians during the exploration of the Pacific Ocean, moving from Fiji to Tonga and Samoa in a short span of time. Contacts also remained constant among these archipelagos, allowing the style of tattooing to remain almost unchanged on all three of them.

It is also the closest style to what is considered the origin of Polynesian art, the so-called Lapita motifs, and retains several similarities with traditional styles from Melanesia and Micronesia as well. All these tattoos are based on the repetition, usually in rows, of a series of basic symbols, a list of which is the subject of this section.

Samoan tattoos relate to family, community, genealogy, and sacred animals (each family revered an animal as the personification of an *atua*, or god). The following list shows many of the basic symbols together with their name and meaning.

Symbol	Name and Meanings	Variants
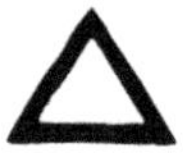	**'ali'ao = trochus shell** *meaning: prosperity, status* Shells were a source of food and were used as ornaments and utensils. Polished shells were carved, decorated, and used as exchange goods.	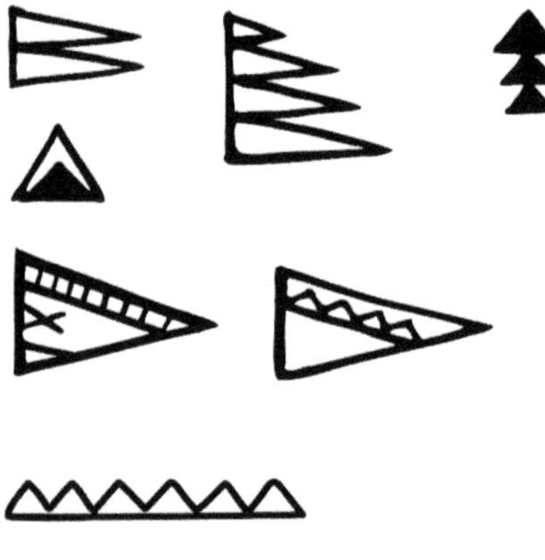
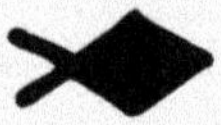	**i'a = fish** *meaning: abundance, prosperity*	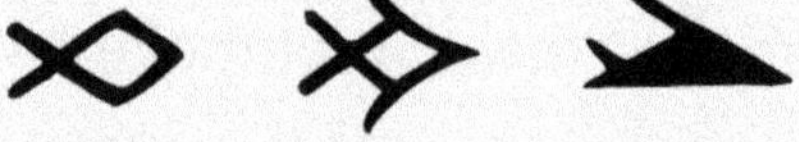

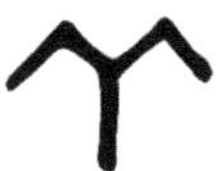

fa'agogo = tern

meaning: safe return

Arctic terns cross the ocean from pole to pole and back safely without ever loosing their path. Furthermore, the tern never passes the night at sea. If navigators followed terns, they were sure they would spend the night on land.

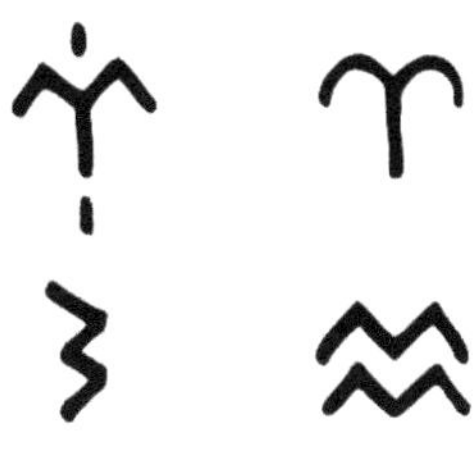

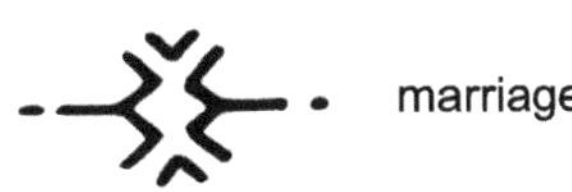

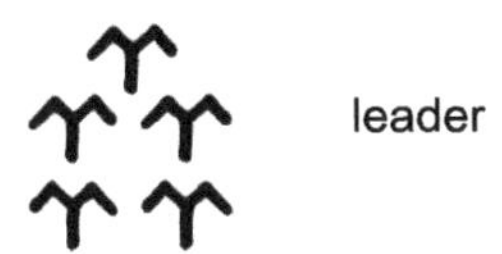

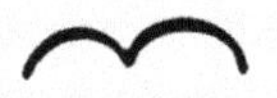

fa'atuli = plover

meaning: divine connection, voyage

The golden plover, or *tuli*, was the bird involved in the creation of humankind and it is still regarded as a messenger from the gods.

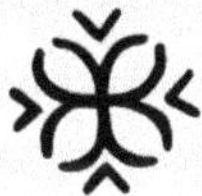  

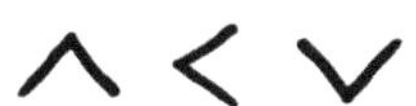

fa'avaetuli = plover legs

meaning: ancestors, gods

Tuli also translates as "knee" and this motif is sometimes called "bent knee".

  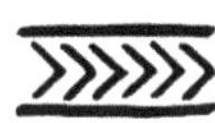

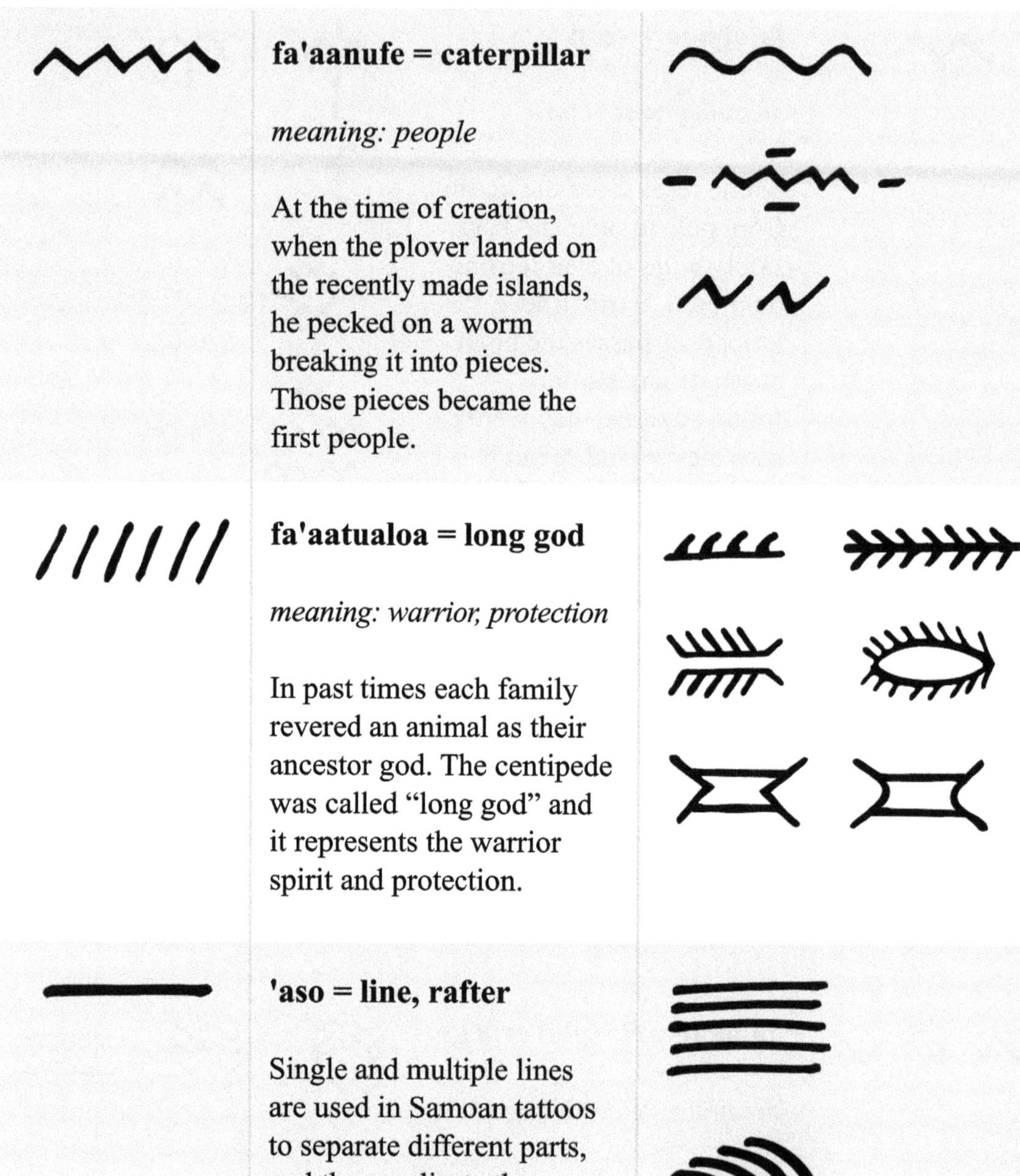

fa'aanufe = caterpillar

meaning: people

At the time of creation, when the plover landed on the recently made islands, he pecked on a worm breaking it into pieces. Those pieces became the first people.

fa'aatualoa = long god

meaning: warrior, protection

In past times each family revered an animal as their ancestor god. The centipede was called "long god" and it represents the warrior spirit and protection.

'aso = line, rafter

Single and multiple lines are used in Samoan tattoos to separate different parts, and they replicate the rafters of the *fale tele*, the long community house.

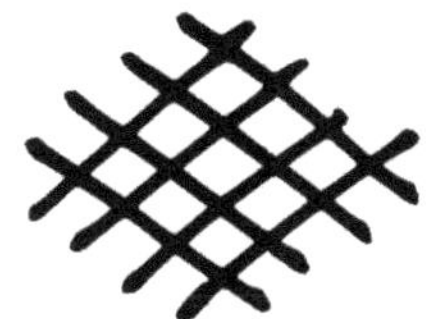

fa'aupega = net

meaning: ability to provide

The net is a symbol of prosperity, but its woven cords also symbolize cooperation, responsibility, and protection.

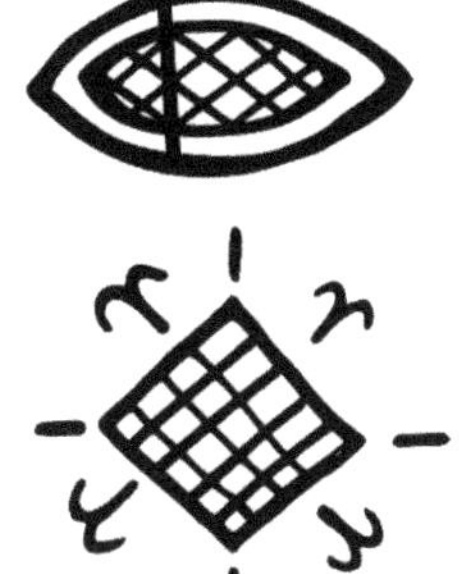

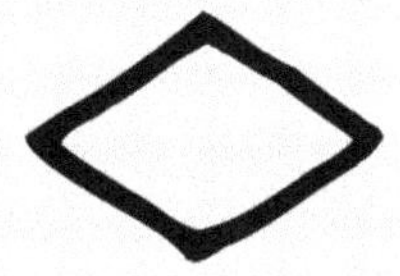

malu = protection, shelter

Similar to the fish net in shape and meaning, it represents protection.

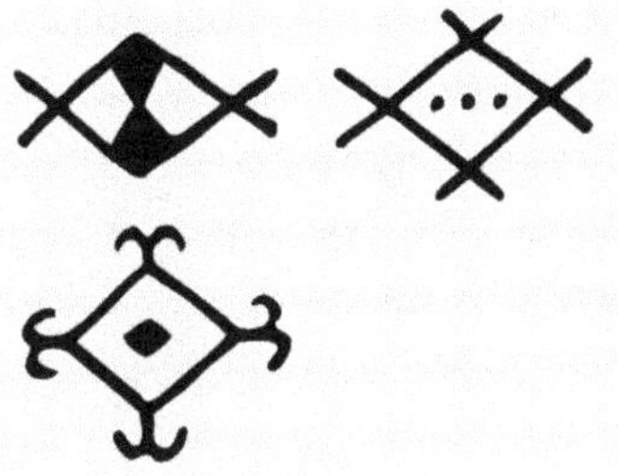

fa'asigano = pandanus male flower

meaning: ancestors, prosperity

Pandanus and taro appear in many legends where their origins are strongly connected with the origins of humans. On this account their flowers and leaves symbolize ancestors, union with nature, and prosperity.

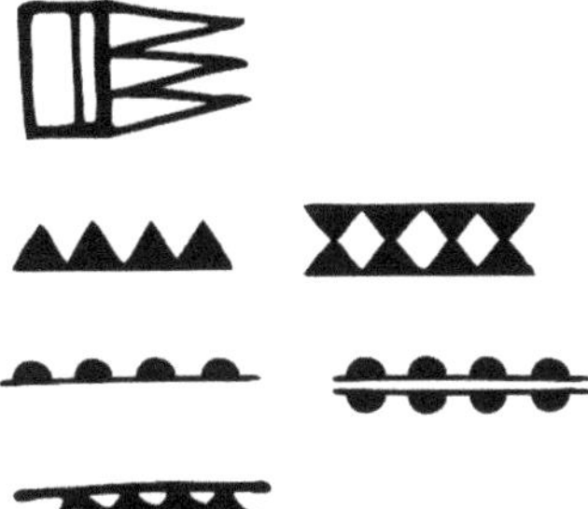

fa'alaupaogo = pandanus leaves

mainly used in *siapo* (bark clothes):

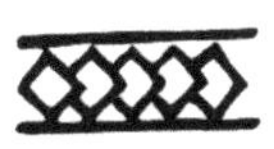

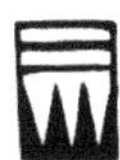

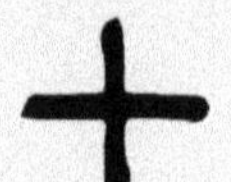

fetu = star

meaning: direction, origin

Stars helped Polynesian navigators follow their path on the ocean, and they symbolize direction and importance, as well as origins.

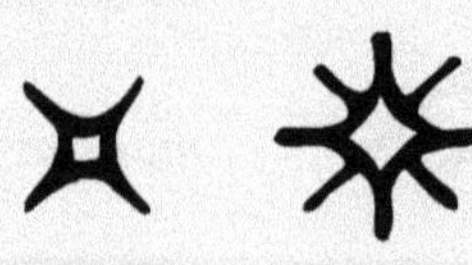

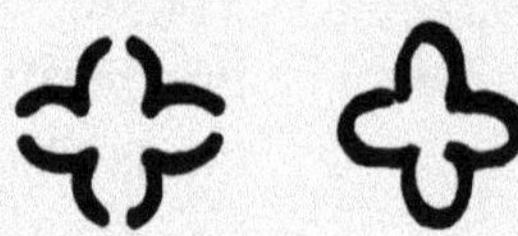

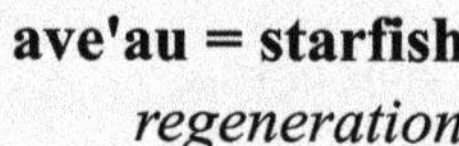

ave'au = starfish
regeneration

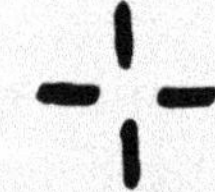

'alu'alu = jellyfish
patience

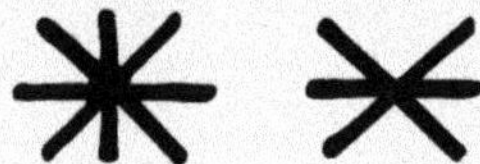

togitogi = measure marks

meaning: steps, goals

They represented distances on seafaring voyages.

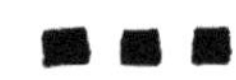

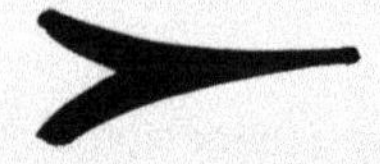

fa'aulutao = spearheads

Spearheads represent the warrior, the hunter, and they are symbolic of skills, too.

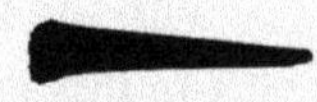

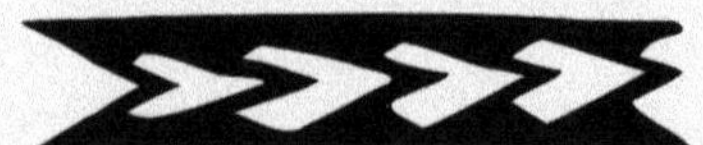

mainly used in *siapo*

va'a = canoe

meaning: voyage, ancestors, ocean knowledge

From the canoes used by ancestors to reach Samoa.

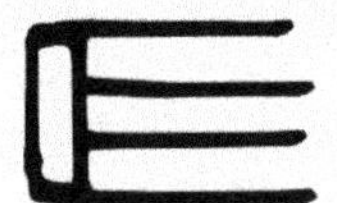

selu = comb

meaning: beauty, status

vaeali = headrest

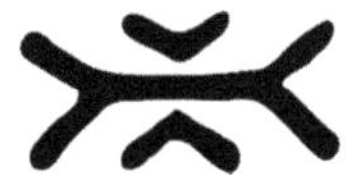

meaning: status

Vaeali translates as “legs of the bamboo pillow”, and it represents a low stool on which chiefs rested their heads. Like the comb and the shells, it’s a symbol of status.

fusi = tie, ligature

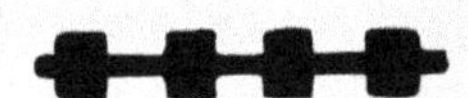

This element visually represents the tentacle of the octopus and it symbolizes a tie or bond.

fa'atala = thorns, spikes

meaning: challenges, trials

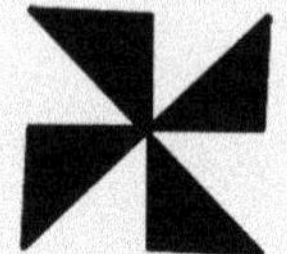

manulua = two birds

meaning: blessing, prosperity, protection

This design symbolizes bringing two families together.

fa'afualeva = fruits of the sea mango

meaning: tradition, knowledge

Fualeva has a double translation: “berries of the sea mango” and “long time ago”. Its sap and fruits are highly poisonous and were used for hunting.

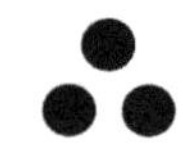

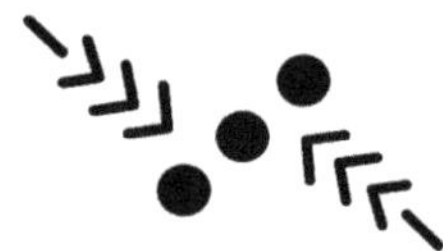

tafani = dark band

meaning: pō, origin

Dark bands balance the lighter parts of the tattoos, and they represent the world of the spirits and of the gods.

iii. tattoo examples walkthrough

This section goes through some examples of Samoan-styled designs, deconstructing them to show their building elements and meanings.

Only the *pe'a*, the *malu*, and the *tapulima* are strictly traditional, while the tattoos presented in this section, like most of the tattoos prepared nowadays, are modern renditions created using the traditional symbols.

We decided to respect the general structure and characteristics of the traditional tattoos, adapting them to fit the new shapes that we chose: a manta for the upper back, a half sleeve, and a band for the wrist or ankle.

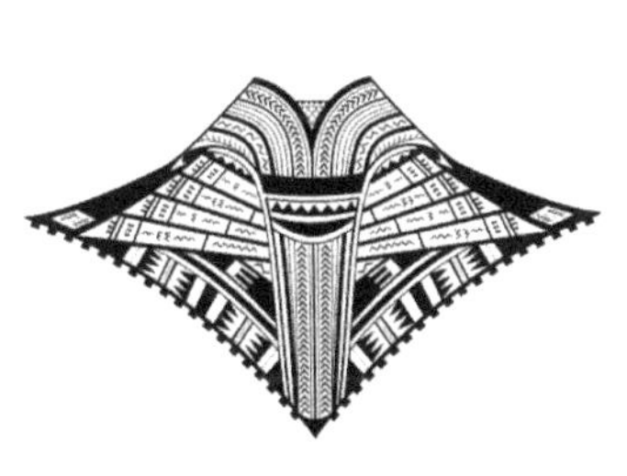

Upper back manta, man

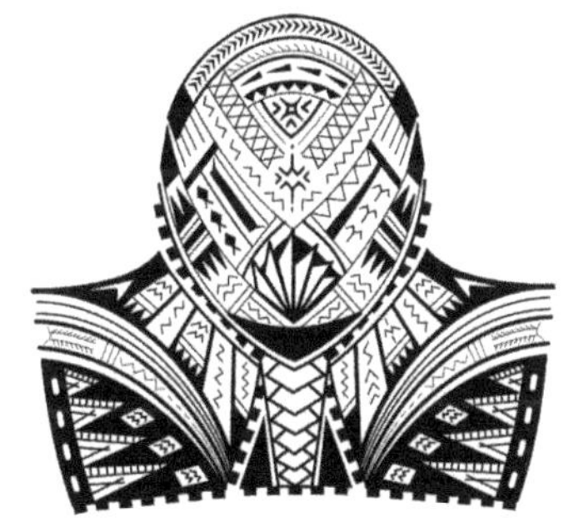

Half sleeve, man

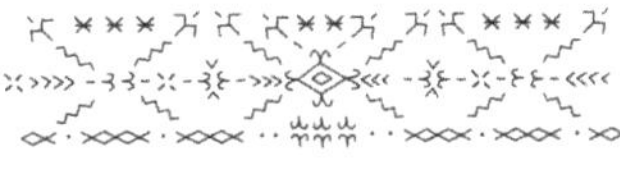

Band, woman

Upper back manta

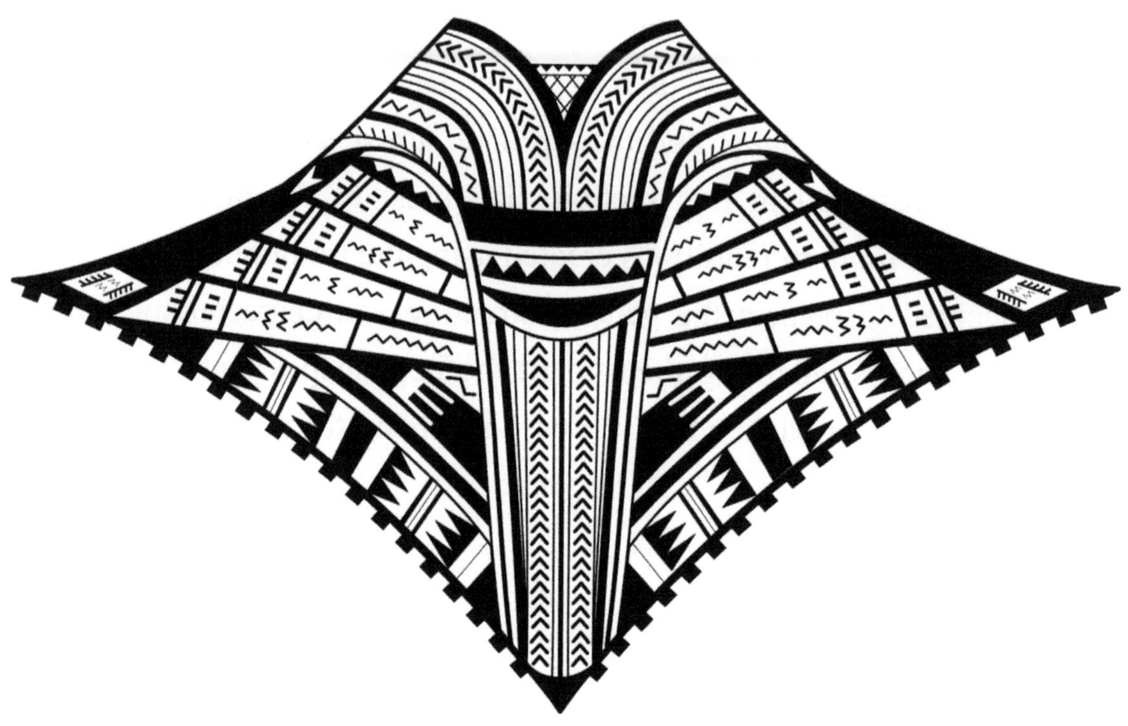

Request: *a manta for the upper back representing the centrality of family and traditions, and protection to the family.*

The requested meanings combine well with the purpose of male Samoan tattoos, and this allowed us to prepare this design mostly following the structure of the *pe'a* while adapting it to the requested shape. Here's a detailed breakdown of the main elements.

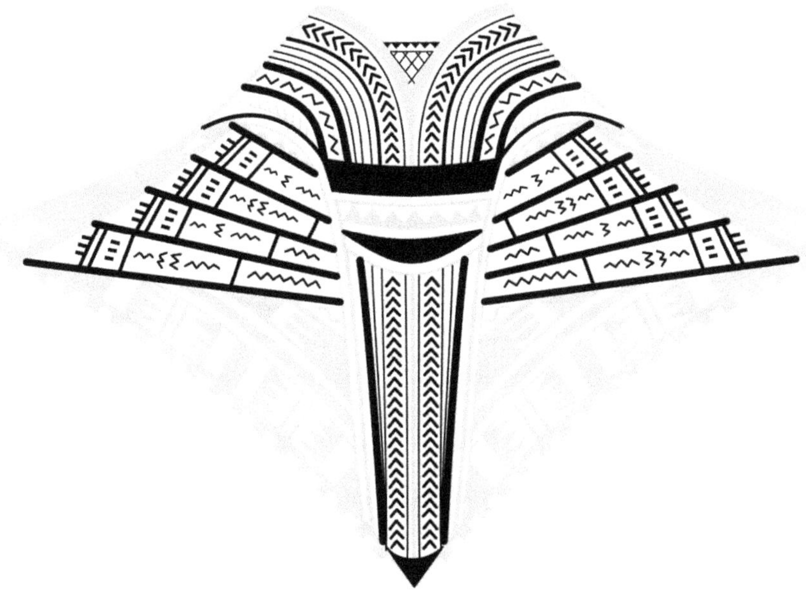

Fig. 3.5: Family-related elements.

The first meaning is family, therefore the related elements have been positioned centrally to symbolize its importance. This part is made up of two interwoven layers: structural elements and storytelling.

Structural elements are similar to the posts and rafters of the community house; they build up the tattoo and support the other elements, as shown in figure 3.6. The storytelling portion deals with relatives and ancestors, as shown in figure 3.7 where each rafter includes elements for a different family.

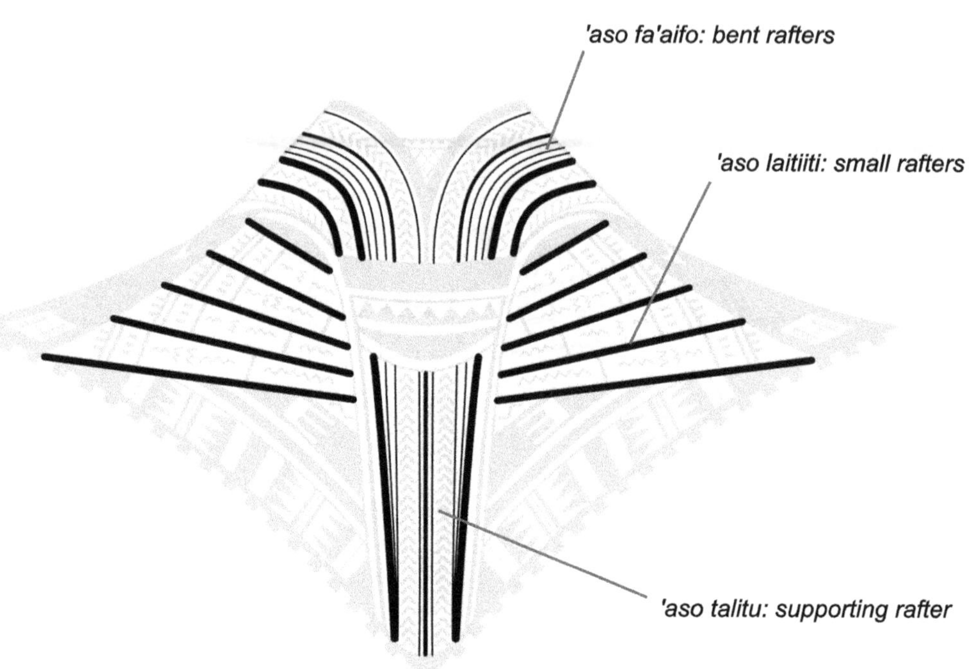

Fig. 3.6: Community house rafters.

The central row of elements symbolizes the main posts and rafter, the back bone of the community house, with other elements radiating from it like the side rafters that sustain the roof of such houses. These structural parts are "decorated" similar to how the real houses were decorated: the central main post includes the *fa'avaetuli* motif, which represents the ancestors, as they are the foundation of the family, going from the base of the tattoo to the top of it throughout the whole extension of the manta, thus symbolizing the continuity of lineage and tradition in the family.

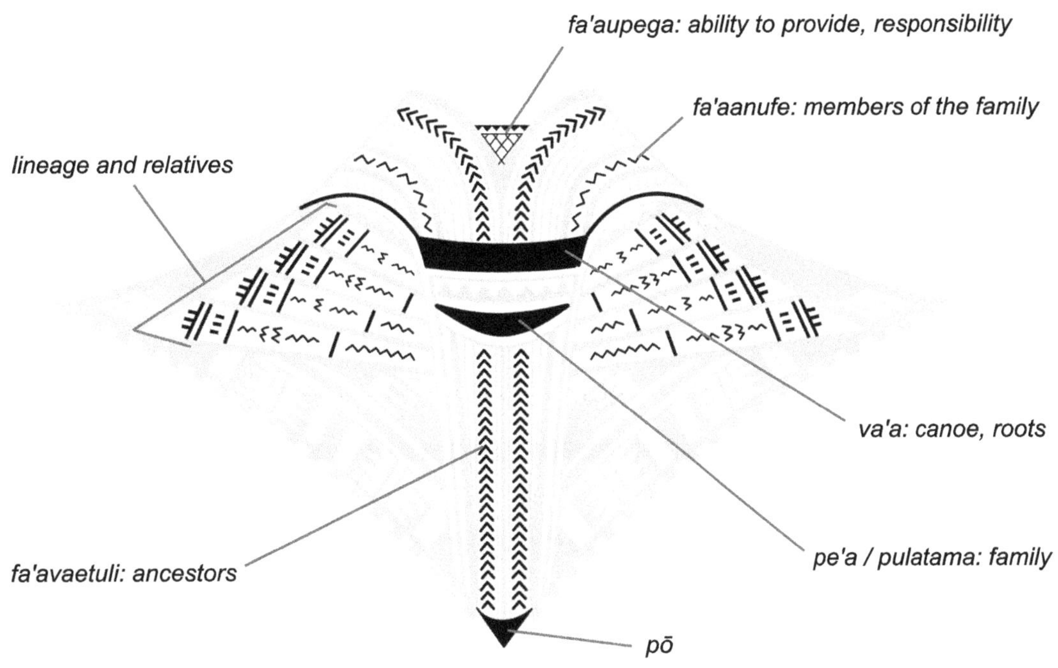

Fig. 3.7: Family-related elements (detail).

The black triangle at the base symbolizes the origin of everything, the *pō,* where the spirits of the ancestors reside with the gods. There are two lines of ancestors symbolizing the two lineages that joined to form the new family represented by the *pe'a*. The *va'a* represents the continuity of the family, the single story that connects all its members through the ages, from past to present and future. The *fa'aanufe* motifs above the *va'a* were used to represent the members of the family, one element for each of them.

Similarly, the designs used on the side rafters represent relatives. Birds, zigzags, and mark signs can all be used to symbolize them. Symmetry is very important, and these may be the only parts that are different from left to right, as they depend on the composition of the family.

The fish net on top shows that the person wearing the tattoo can provide for his family and is ready to guide it. It symbolizes responsibility. The rest of the design incorporates some elements representing the characteristics of the person wearing the tattoo. They have been positioned on the sides to keep the elements related to family surrounded and protected in the center, and they symbolize a warrior, protection, and prosperity.

Fig. 3.8: Personal characteristics.

Figure 3.9 shows which elements are representative of the warrior. They shape the outer border of the manta as a protective shield, and they include *fa'aatualoa* motifs for the centipede representing a fighting spirit, two spearheads at the ends of the *va'a* for the warrior, and octopus tentacles closing the lower edges for tenacity and adaptability.

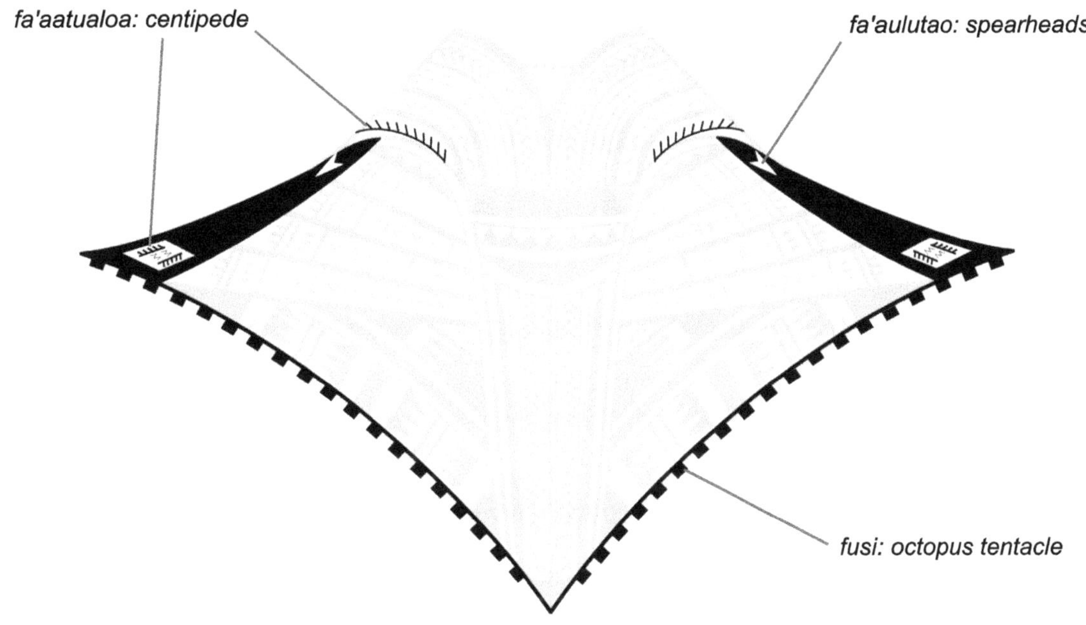

Fig. 3.9: Warrior-related elements.

The other elements incorporated, as shown in figure 3.10, include the motifs of the leaves and male flowers of the pandanus for prosperity and connection to traditions, while the two combs are symbolic of beauty and status.

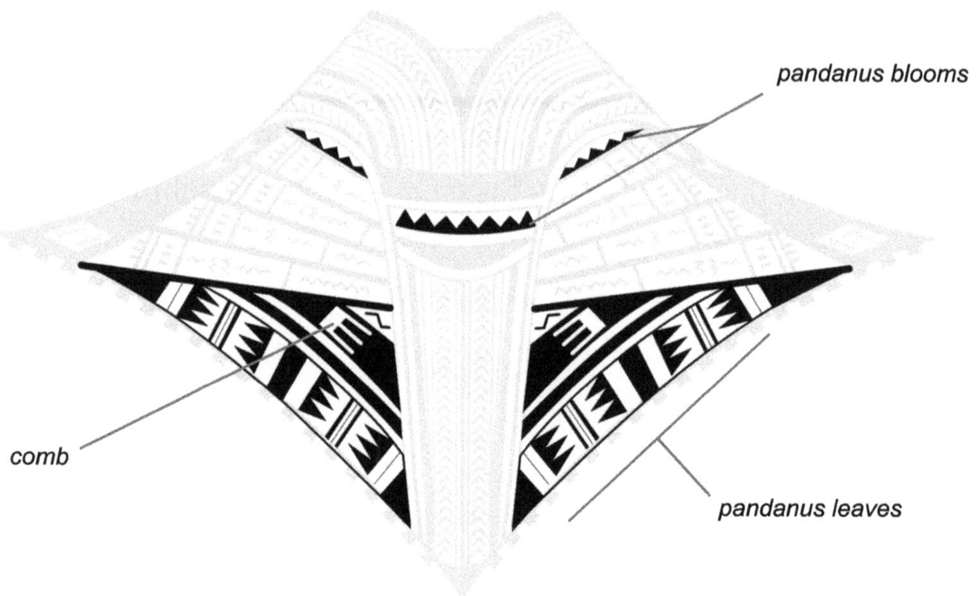

Fig. 3.10: Personal qualities.

All of the elements are woven together into a flowing design that follows and enhances the lines of the muscles, as one purpose of Samoan tattoos is to beautify the body and decorate it through the use of small elements and symmetry. The balance between light and dark areas is representative of the alternation of day and night, light and darkness, *ao* and *pō*, and it is constant throughout the tattoo.

Half sleeve

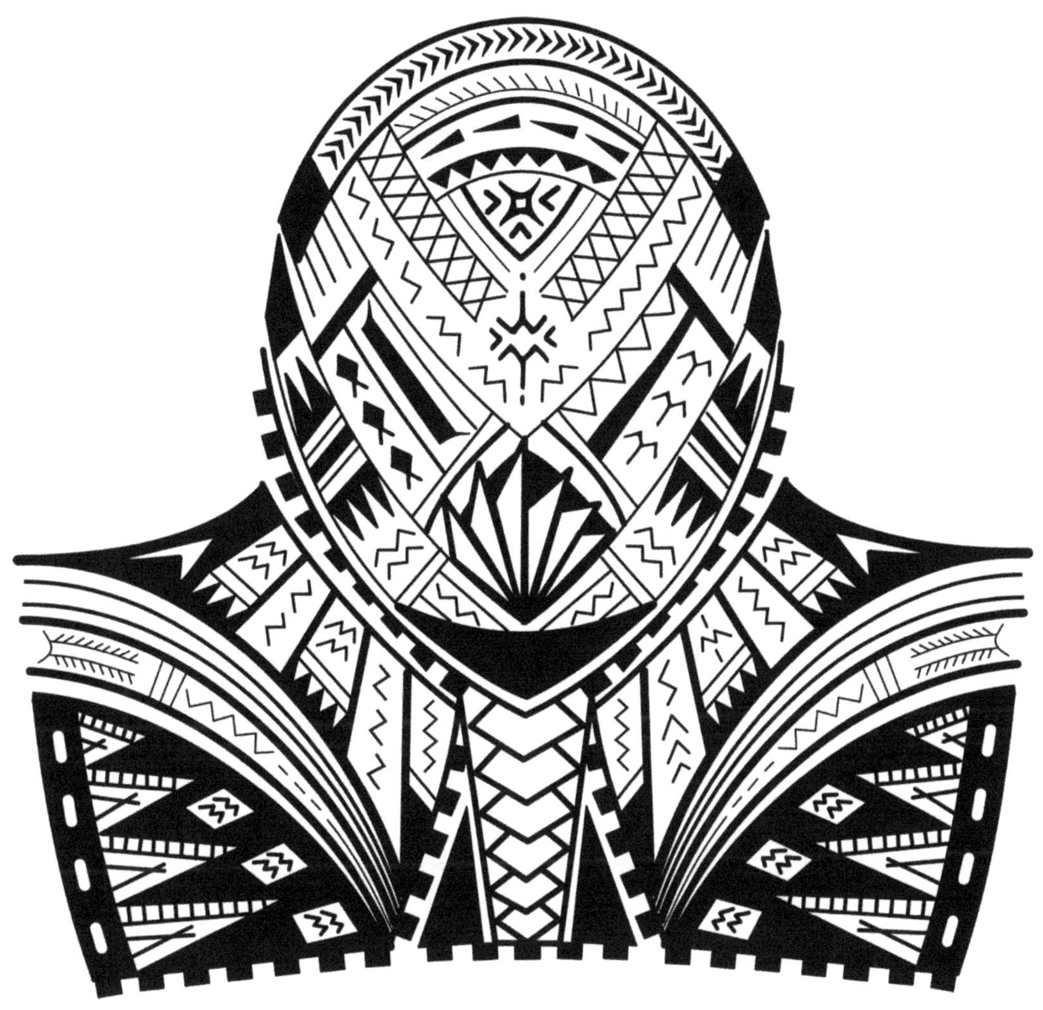

Request: *a half sleeve representing a family that left in search of fortune and is now going back to the island of the ancestors.*

To understand the composition and meanings of this half sleeve, we are going to analyze its parts separately, starting from family–related elements as shown in figure 3.11.

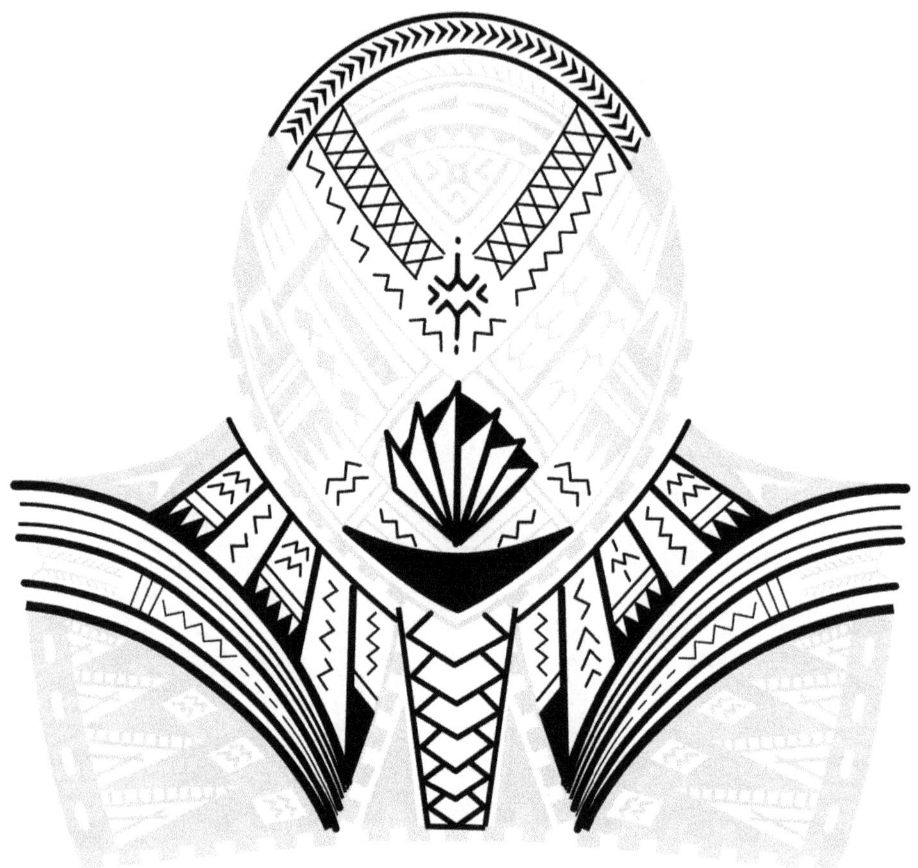

Fig. 3.11: Family-related elements.

To maintain the similarity with the community house, we designed the bent rafters on the two sides, with small side rafters joining them to the central main post. The exact structure is shown below. The bent rafters join on the back of the arm and they outline and highlight the biceps and triceps muscles. Again, the structure of the house shapes the tattoo, which develops along the lines of the rafters adapting to the body.

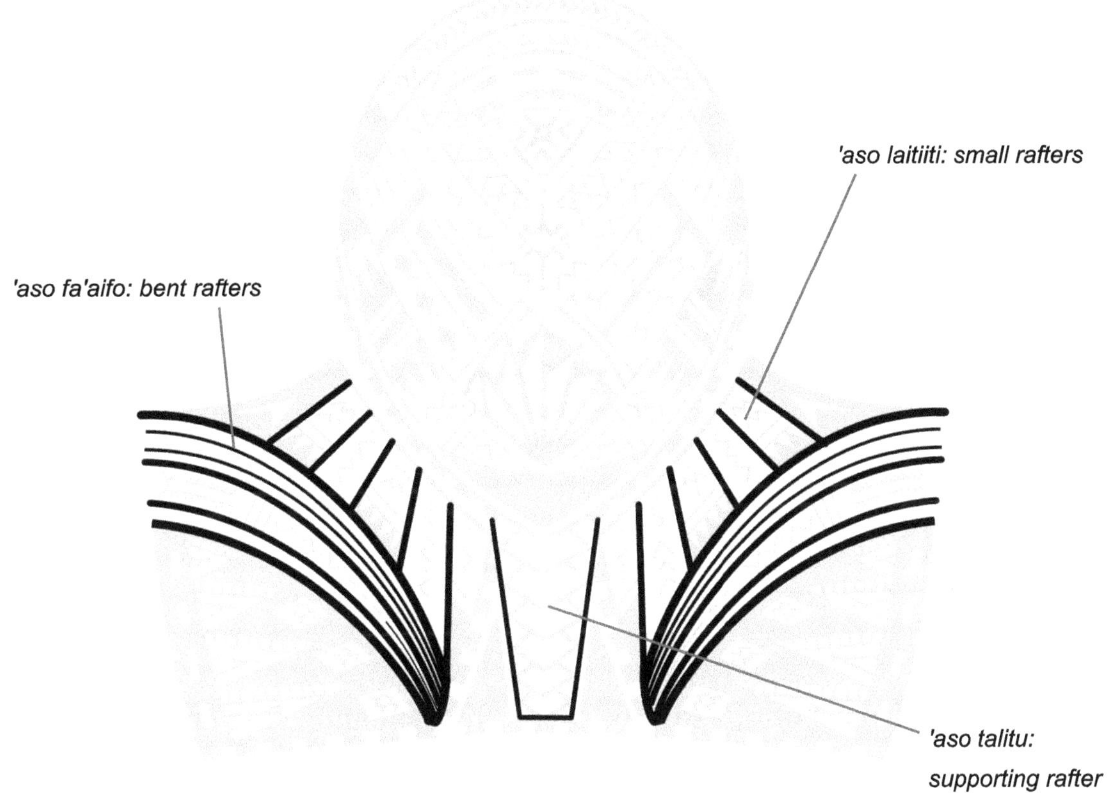

Fig. 3.12: Rafters structure.

The central space on the shoulder is reserved for family and for the elements that represent their voyage, as shown in the following images.

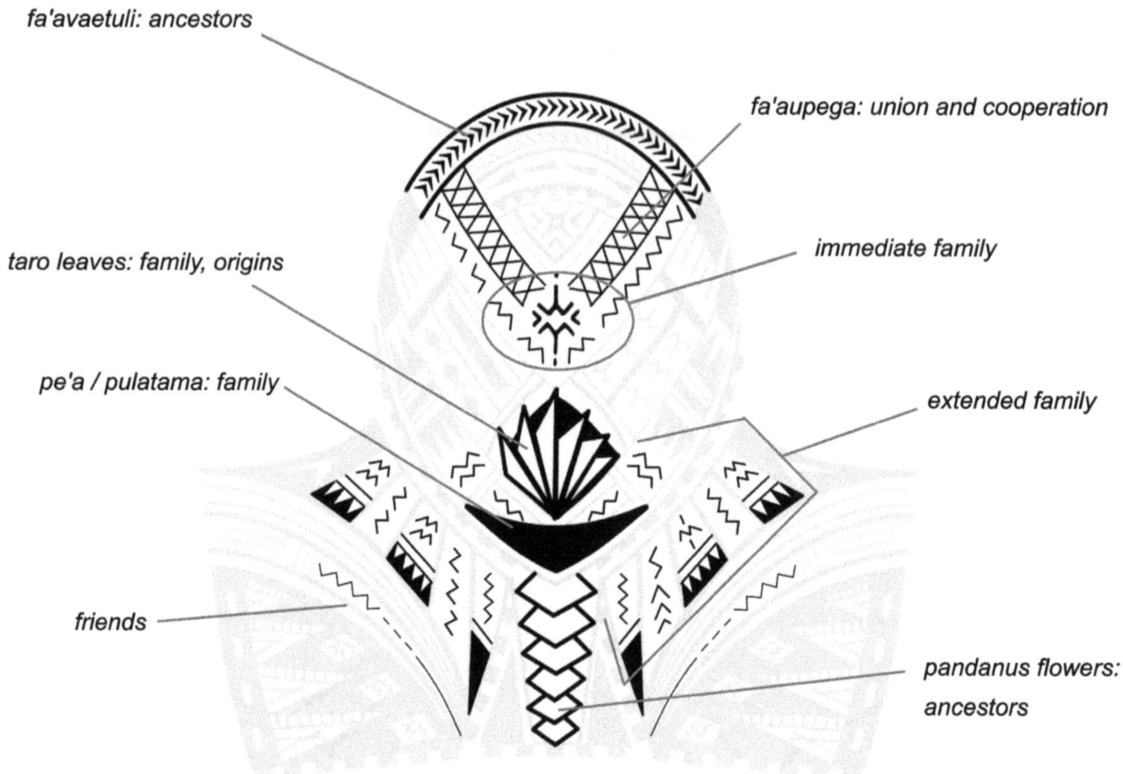

Fig. 3.13: Family-related elements (detail).

Centrally, from bottom to top, there are pandanus flowers, a *pe'a*, and taro leaves representing family. The symbols above the taro leaves represent the members of the immediate family, with two facing birds in the center symbolizing the two parents and three more birds on their sides representing their children, as shown in figure 3.14. The fish net bands above them symbolize their union, and the *fa'aanufe* motifs on their side are for friends who have been like family while far from home.

The row of *fa'avaetuli* on top symbolizes ancestors guarding the family from above, and the small rafters and bent rafters include elements representing the extended family of relatives and close friends.

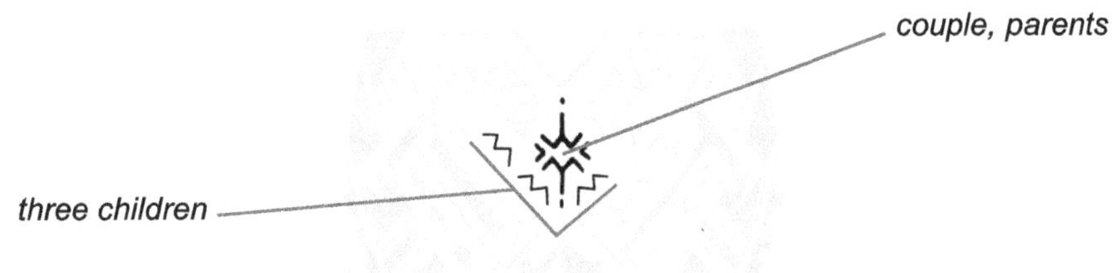

Fig. 3.14: Family members.

Around the immediate family we placed the symbols related to their voyage, as shown in figure 3.15: the canoe over the row of fish symbolizes their voyage in search of prosperity; the two rows of birds flying in opposite directions symbolize the voyages going away and then back. The star on top surrounded by plover footprints symbolizes the island of the ancestors, to which the family is returning.

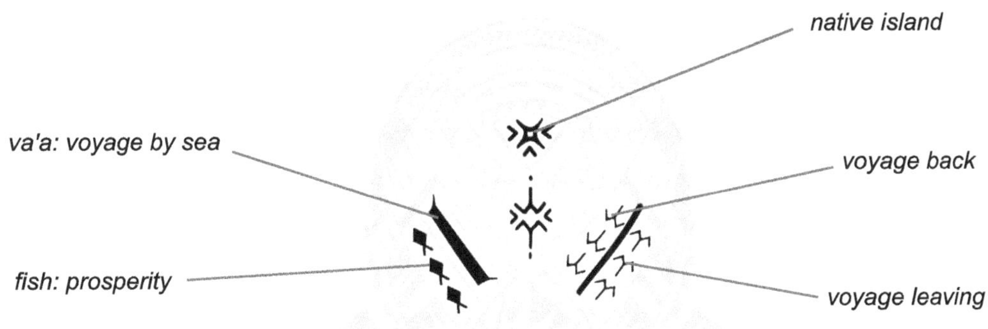

Fig. 3.15: Voyage theme.

Stars aided navigators on their voyages, showing the direction to be followed. They came to symbolize a fixed point, a goal, or islands.

The rest of the tattoo (fig. 3.16) represents prosperity, as it was the aim of the voyage, and the warrior spirit necessary to pursue it far from home.

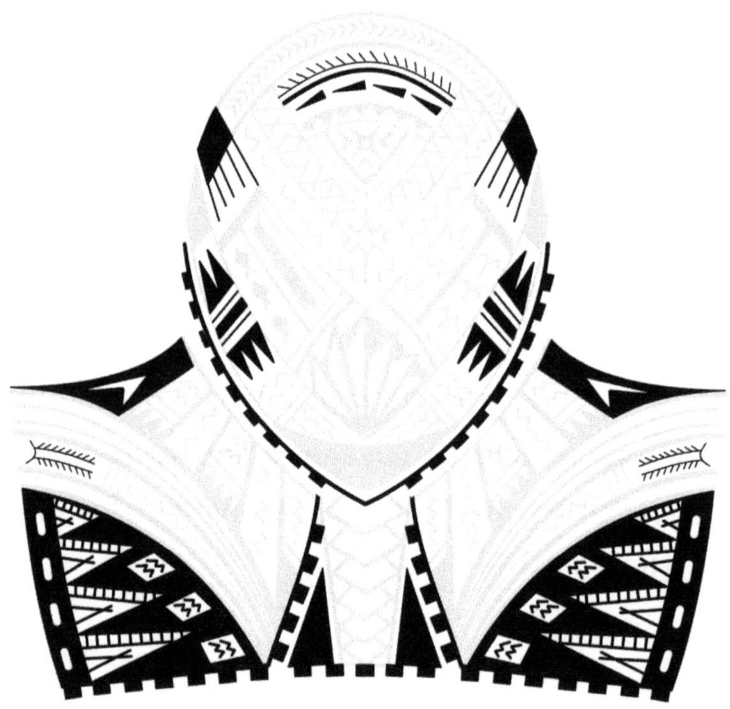

Fig. 3.16: Personal story.

The elements related to prosperity are the pandanus blooms, two combs, and several trochus shells positioned at the base (fig. 3.17). The number of shells in the *pe'a* indicated the rank of the person who wore them, and whether he was a chief, a talking chief, or a priest.

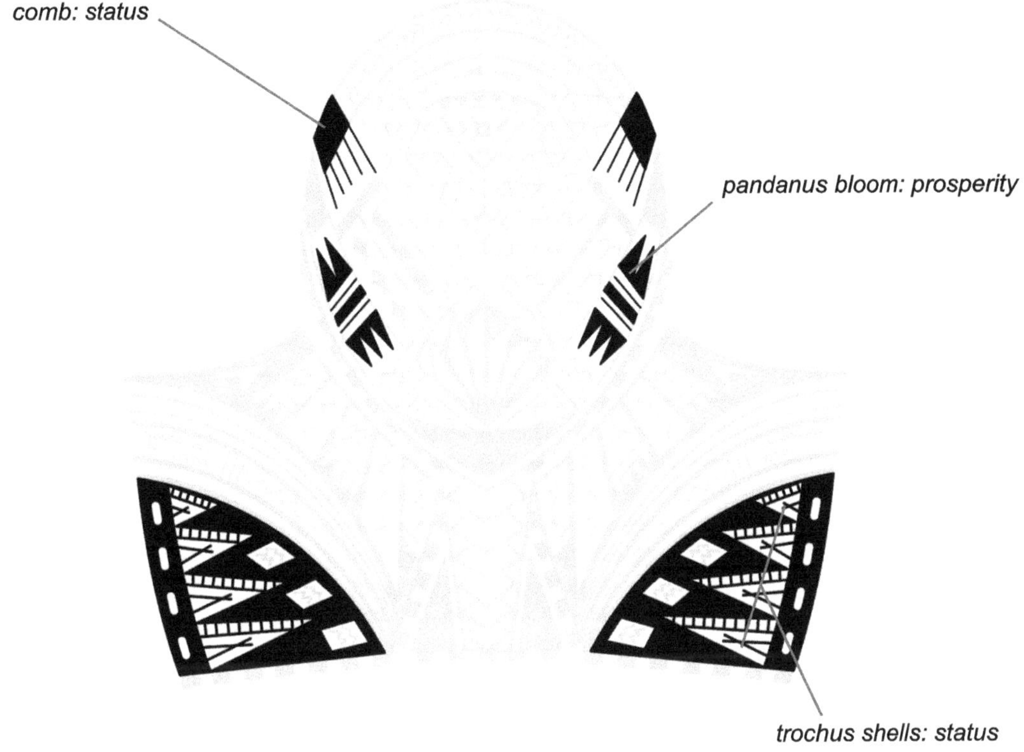

Fig. 3.17: Prosperity and status.

The remaining elements, shown in figure 3.18, represent the fighting spirit and courage needed to leave everything in search of a better life. There are centipede and spearheads motifs on top below the ancestors and on the sides, and octopus tentacles along the bottom for union and tenacity.

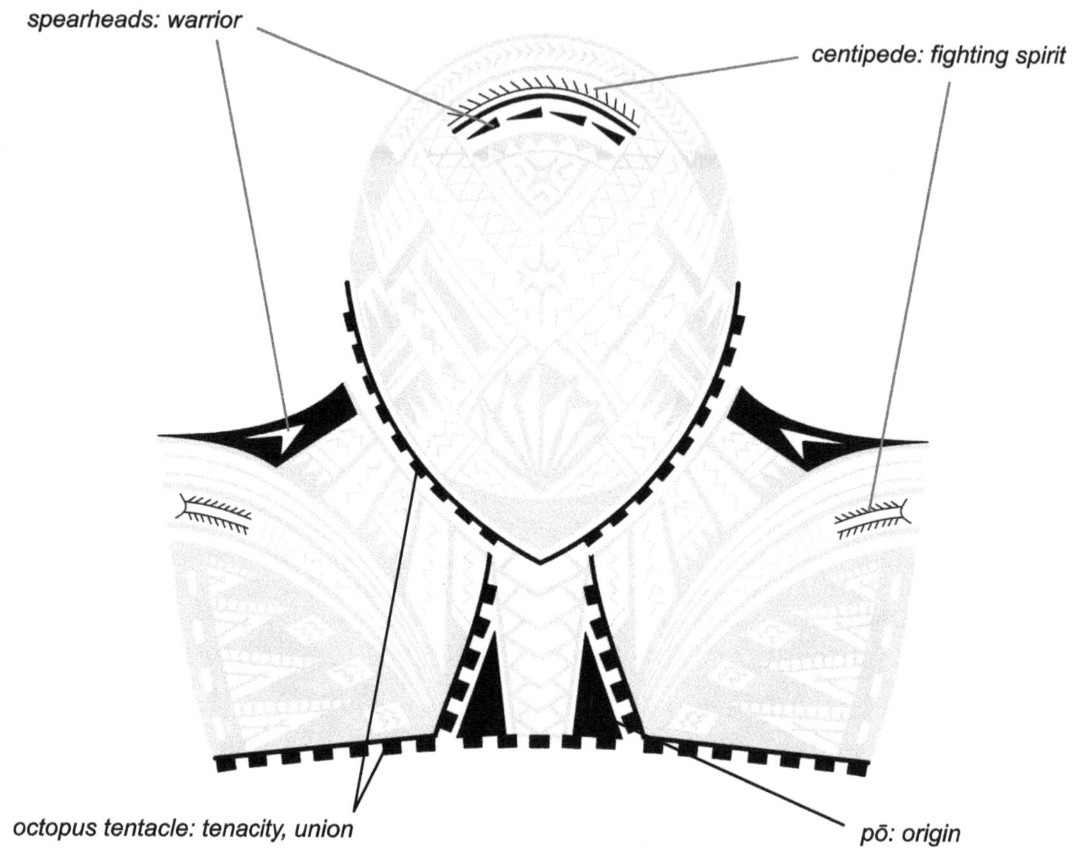

Fig. 3.18: Warrior elements.

The solid black triangles at the base recall the *ulumanu* element and were added to represent the *pō*, the origin of everything and a powerful source of *mana*.

Band

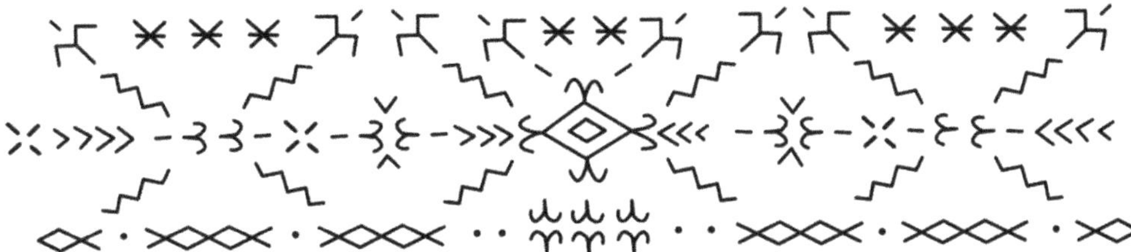

Request: *ankle band for a woman representing protection and tenacity to pursue and achieve every goal in life.*

The requested meanings led us to choose the Samoan style for this tattoo. Traditional female *malu* tattoos were designed to give protection, and we decided to keep their structure for this band.

The net in the center (see fig. 3.19), from the *malu*, is used to symbolize protection, union, and prosperity.

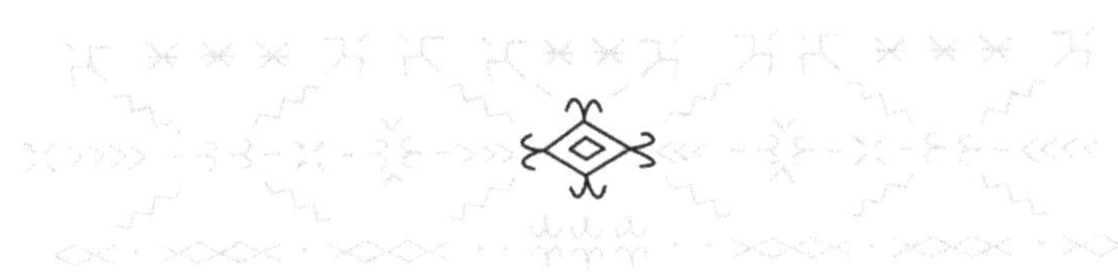

Fig. 3.19: Fa'aupega, the net.

Around the central *fa'aupega*, elements are disposed to form a bigger net, where family and friends are all interconnected in a single unique extended family.

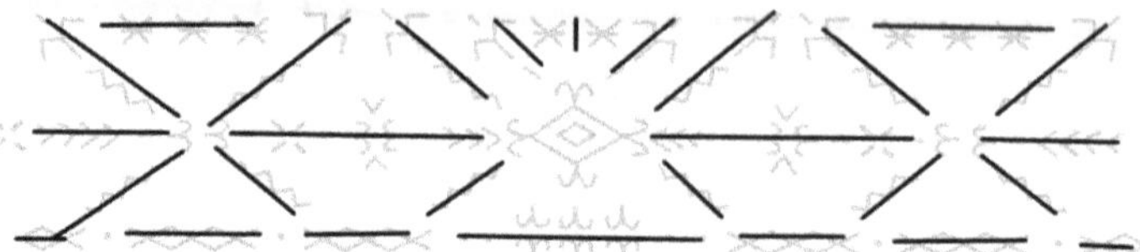

Fig. 3.20: Net-like structure of the band.

The same net also ties in the elements representing goals and environment, to symbolize that it's all interconnected.

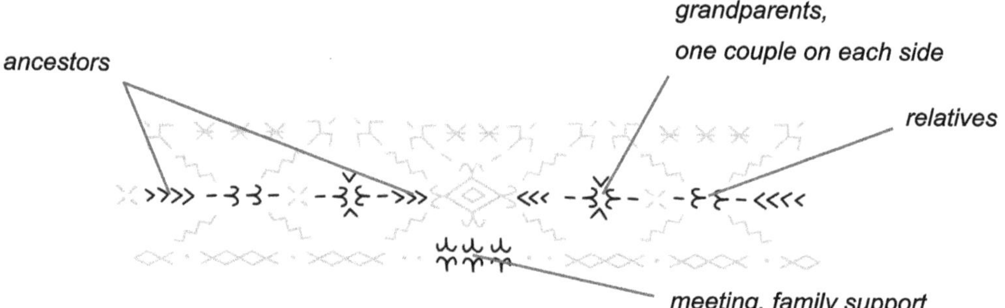

Fig. 3.21: Immediate family.

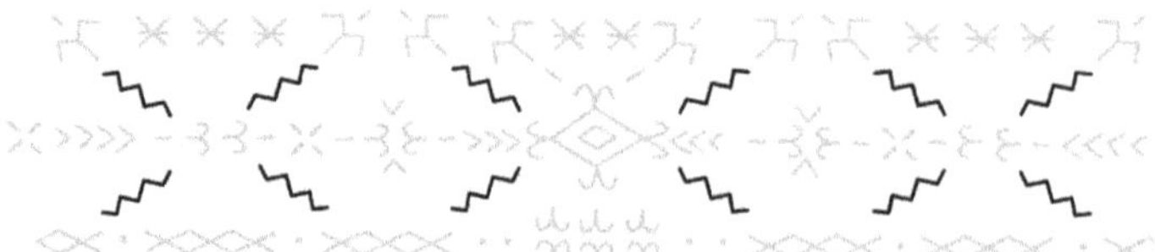

Fig. 3.22: Extended family, friends.

The row of fish intercalated by dots closing the bottom of the tattoo symbolizes material things and achievements, while the upper part includes stars and birds to represent the desired goals and the paths to reach them. The birds symbolize voyage, and each one will bring an achievement, represented by a star.

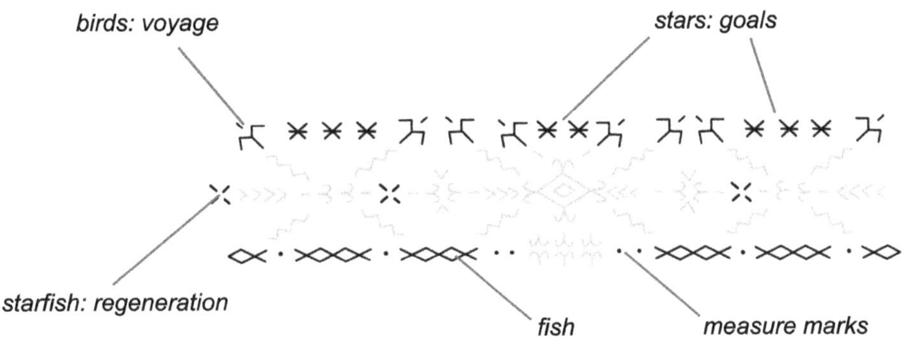

Fig. 3.23: Achievements and goals.

The starfish symbol is often used as a star, and we placed some within the central line to symbolize intermediate goals already reached, which helped persevere along the chosen path.

E mea tono te tino 'enata
e mea te e tono noa te kuhane 'enata

"The body of a person is heavy, the spirit of a person is not."

4

MARQUESAN

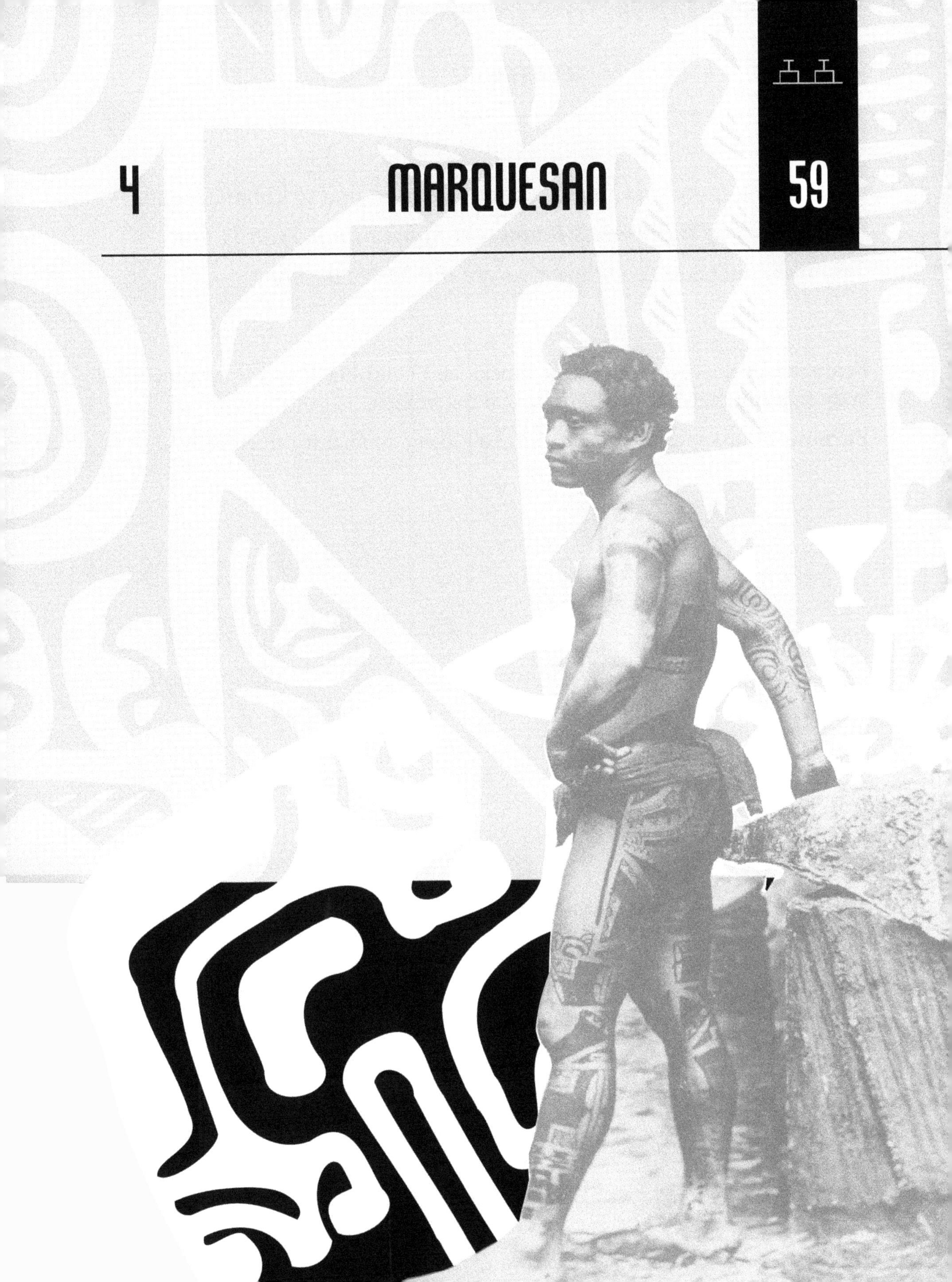

"E mea tono te tino 'enata, e mea te e tono noa te kuhane 'enata."
—***The body of a person is heavy, the spirit of a person is not:***
The spirit can reach even where the body can not.

Features: geometrical with large blocks and solid black areas. Asymmetrical body sides for men, mostly symmetrical for women.

Purpose: to strike terror into enemies, to protect, to identify, to embellish.

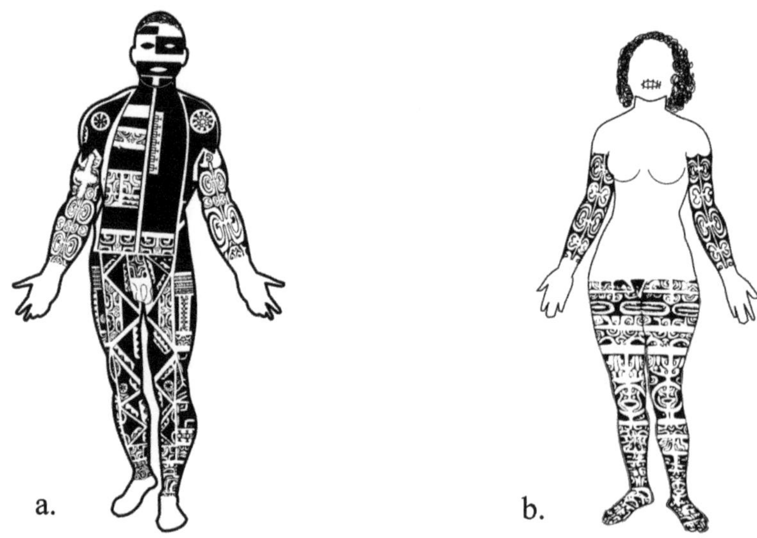

Fig. 4.1: (a) Male and (b) female Marquesan traditional tattoos. Drawings after K. v. d. Steinen.

i. about the style

The Marquesas Islands present substantial differences from the other archipelagos of Polynesia, both geographically and socially.

Most of Central Polynesian islands have sandy beaches and a protective reef surrounding them, making it safer and less perilous for the sailboats to go fishing, but the Marquesas generally have steep rocky coasts with fewer beaches and no protected access to the resources of the ocean. For this reason they suffered at times from scarceness of food and even famine, paving the way to a concept that is almost unique to the Marquesas in the life of ancient Polynesia: private land, with family groups trying to secure for their kin the lands that were most productive, as well as the best fishing grounds.

This deeply affected the way of living of the Marquesan people, leading to profound changes in all aspects of their life, from their social structure to the style and purpose of their tattoos. This eventually resulted in a divided society with separated castes, where the land was not commonly shared by the whole community. Chiefs were not chosen by divine right and had to maintain their position by proving that they could provide for their clan, by means of strength and alliances with other families.

The semi-constant state of warfare that was the consequence of these circumstances continues to be strongly reflected in the style of Marquesan tattoos: despite still retaining meanings and concepts similar to the other tattoo traditions from around the Pacific (like family and community bonds), their focus shifted more toward warrior-like qualities and values, and tattoos become distinctive of one's caste. The primary intention of this style, at least for men, was not to embellish and make the bodies appealing, but to strike fear into the enemies, to convey an idea of strength and fierceness, while giving protection by increasing a person's *mana*. This was achieved by tattooing the whole body, including the face, and by introducing asymmetry into the designs.

Extensive use of large black areas, and asymmetry, are key features to achieving this result: asymmetry can be disturbing at an unconscious level and was also believed to be a prerogative of the gods. This way asymmetrical tattoos made warriors resemble frightening spirits rather than humans, whereas symmetry and balance, having a soothing effect, were not apt for what the Marquesan warriors wanted to convey with their tattoos. In some cases the body would be completely colored in solid black to exaggerate the visual impact. The full body tattoo is called *pahu tiki*, which can be translated as "wrapped in images".

What is suggested by the looks of the tattoos becomes evident when we analyze their foundational elements: a common theme is the presence of symbols depicting mythical heroes like Kena and Pohu, two legendary warriors, joined by a host of other symbols related to them, their stories, their armies, and their possessions. Other ubiquitous elements are *tiki* ("figures", representing protectors), *etua* ("gods"), and the *ipu* (literally "gourd"). The last one is used to symbolize ancestors and to collect their *mana*, transferring it to a person by tapping it into the skin. These symbols are among the most recurrent ones, testifying the final purpose of these tattoos.

Extensive tattoos were equally popular among men and women, but they were different in style, with male tattoos being much darker and more geometrical. Female tattoos tended to be lighter, more figurative, and were usually limited to the legs and arms as they were not designed for war but for protection and embellishment.

Within the Marquesan tattoos we must acknowledge that there are two distinct styles, as the Marquesas are divided into two main groups: the southeastern (SE) group, with Hivaoa and Fatuiva being the biggest inhabited islands, and the northwestern (NW) group that has its center in the big island of Nukuhiva.

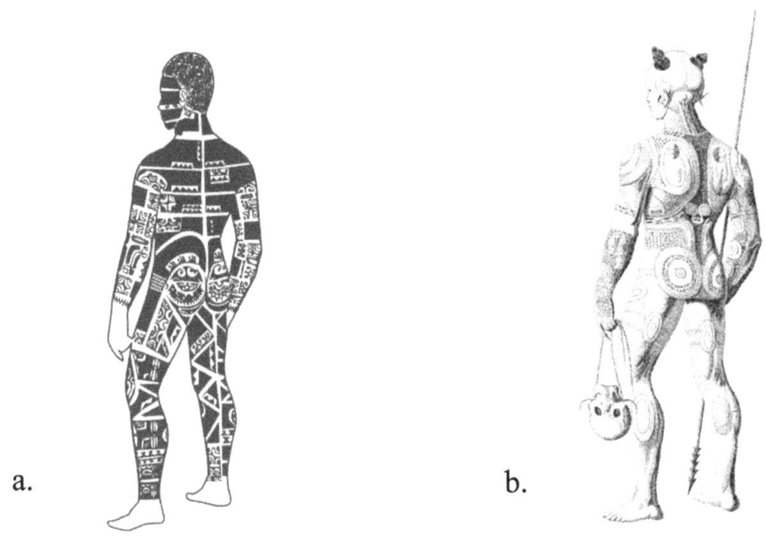

Fig. 4.2: Examples of Hivaoa and Nukuhiva male tattoos, (a) after a drawing by K. v. d. Steinen, and (b) from a drawing by Langsdorff.

While European contacts with the SE group were established as early as 1595, the NW group was explored only about two hundred years later.

This gap is possibly the reason why the two styles are applied differently, despite using mostly the same symbols. The SE style is darker and more pervasive, and the NW style is less cluttered, with more space between elements (fig. 4.2). The full armor of the European explorers may have inspired the pervasiveness of the full body tattoo in the SE group, as we have early drawings showing tattoos on fewer parts of the body, like the usual waist to knee area. This is not a definitive proof though, as initial contacts were limited and drawings may not be representative of the whole Marquesan society of the time.

The style we know more of is that of Hivaoa, in the SE group, which was extensively studied and described by Karl von den Steinen in his trilogy named *Die Marquesaner und ihre Kunst* ("The Marquesans and Their Art"), first published in 1928. It is based on his own experience, on the study of art pieces from several museum collections, and on drawings and accounts from earlier explorers and naturalists such as Quirós, Tilesius, Langsdorff, and Lafond, among others. All three volumes are equally important for those who want to approach Marquesan ancient society and culture.

Male tattoos usually comprise square patches on the upper body and torso, also incorporating smaller elements to bring movement and asymmetry to the tattoo. The legs are mainly covered in triangular shapes, each one composed of several smaller symbols.

An interesting feature of the full body tattoo is a design that goes from the side of the waist down onto the leg. It's called *kohe ta*, which is usually translated as “bamboo knife”. If we consider the idea that the name may have changed over time together with the purpose of the tattoo, we can note that *ka* can be translated as “beam”, or “in the way of the sun rays”, so the very similar term *kohe ka* could be translated as “bamboos placed radially”. This is reminiscent of the similar curved pattern that Samoan tattoos have in the exact same spot (*'aso fa'aifo*, “bent rafters”). You can refer to figure 4.3 below for comparison.

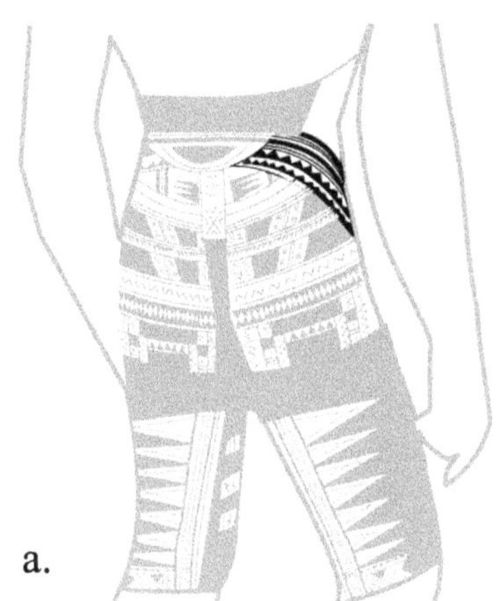
a.

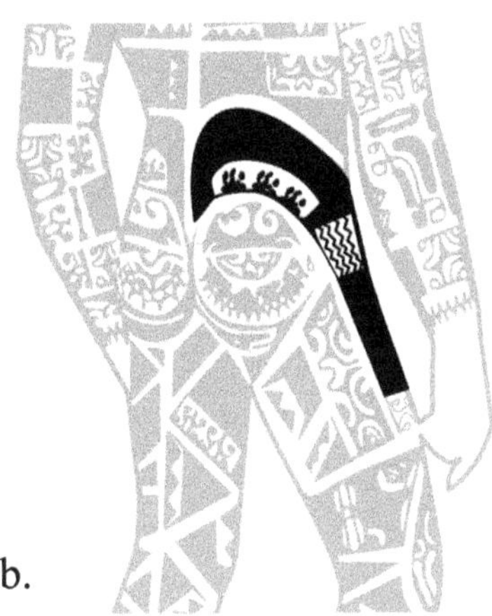
b.

Fig. 4.3: Samoan and Marquesan waist tattoo comparison, (a) Samoan 'aso fa'aifo, (b) Marquesan kohe ta.

Interestingly, female tattoos, not being designed for war, still retained a closer resemblance to their original purpose and style, being much lighter, with smaller elements, and often symmetrical on the right and left sides of the body.

We also have examples where some parts of the female hand tattoo (*tumu'ima*) still retain names derived from the community buildings as shown in figure 4.4, where the central line is called *ka'ava* ("ridge pole") and the round elements near the base of the fingers are called *paka'a* (wooden shoulder rest for the rafters). This hand tattoo seems to show an actual schematic representation of the community house.

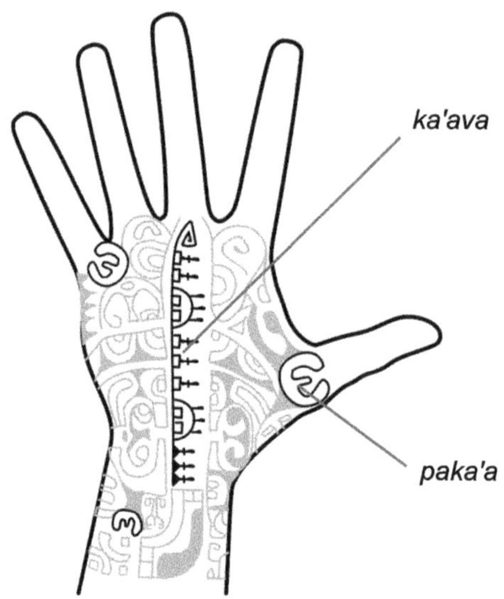

Fig. 4.4: Female hand tattoo with ka'ava and paka'a motifs.

Similarly, the triangular shapes on the legs of men recall Samoan tattoos, where the back of the legs was covered by the triangular motifs of the trochus shell.

All these could be proof that the purpose of Marquesan tattoos changed over time along with their aesthetics to adapt to the new model of society induced by the harder environmental conditions, evolving from the original style and changing the focus from family ties to warrior qualities.

ii. elements

Of all the Polynesian styles, Marquesan tattoos are the ones we know more of in terms of symbols: Karl von den Steinen collected and described almost two hundred symbols and elements accompanied by photos and considerations on their use. They were mostly geometrical, bold, and rich with large, solid black areas. Even if we don't know the meaning of all of the collected elements and symbols, they still represent a wealth of information for those interested in approaching this style of tattooing.

Few of the symbols, usually placed on the joints (shoulders, knees, hips), have rounded shapes, while the majority are straight-edged and include smaller elements inside, often as visual separations between black parts.

One characteristic that immediately becomes evident is the presence of many symbols representing human figures. While some relate to family, most of them deal with warfare and mythical heroes and legends.

The style is more pictorial than the Samoan one, and its elements are visually more recognizable and more detailed. We can better appreciate the difference in the example shown in figure 4.5, where the symbols representing ancestors are compared: Samoan tattoos symbolize ancestors using a V-shaped element, which represents the leg of the plover, the bird that created the first humans by pecking a worm into pieces; the Marquesan motif representing ancestors, called *'ani ata* ("cloudy sky"), is a stylized representation of a row of people with their joined hands lifted up, since divine ancestors separated the sky father Rangi from the earth mother Papa by pushing him up in order to let the light in for humans to live. This more heroic approach to the origins of humankind reflects the Marquesan approach to life in general, where warriors are the most highly appreciated, and valued for their courage and strength.

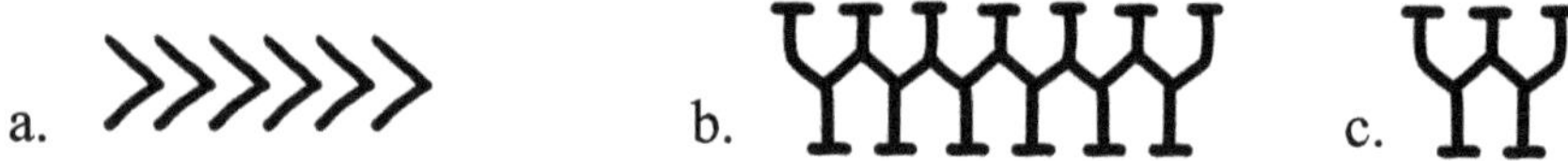

Fig. 4.5: Ancestors as (a) Samoan fa'avaetuli motif and (b) Marquesan 'ani ata. (c) The basic element used to create the 'ani ata pattern is a person with arms raised. It represents an ancestor pushing the sky upward.

The same motif is also sometimes known as *'ani a Tiu* ("sky of Tiu"), since Tiu is the northeastern wind bringer of cloudy skies and rain.

Symbol	Name and Meanings	Variants
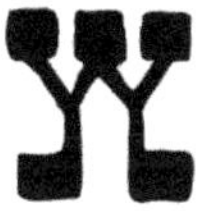	**'enata = person** *meaning: people* This symbol is one of the most ubiquitous, with several variants used to symbolize both common people and heroes, with a few small changes.	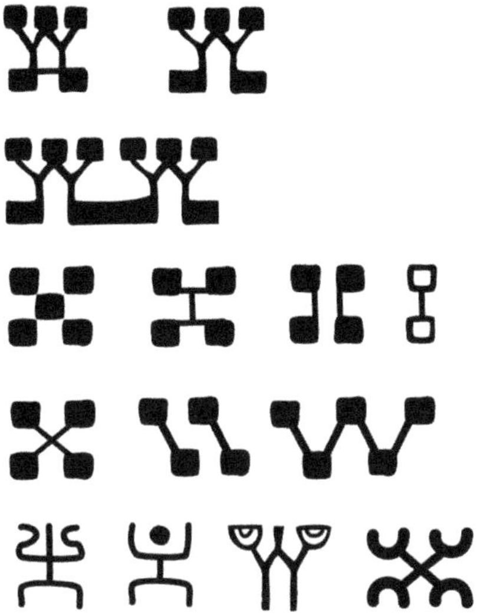
	Kena *meaning: warrior, strength* Kena was a legendary hero.	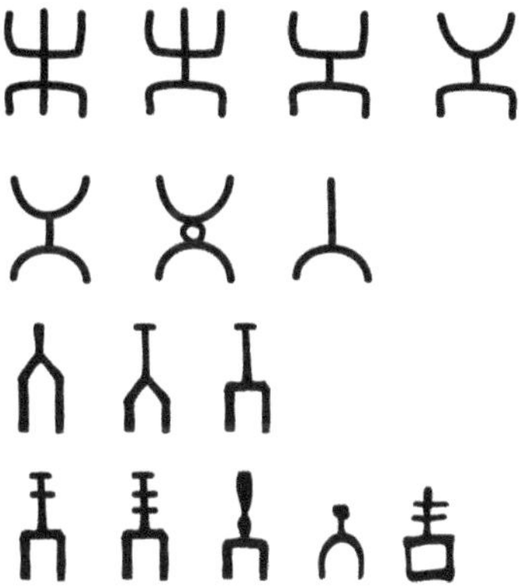
	Tefio *meaning: beauty, woman* She was the wife of Kena.	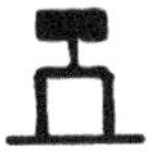
	fanaua Female spirits.	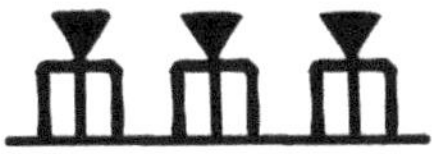

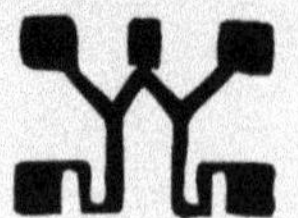

etua = god

meaning: protection

The *etua* symbolizes a divinity and is visually similar to a sitting *'enata* with bent legs.

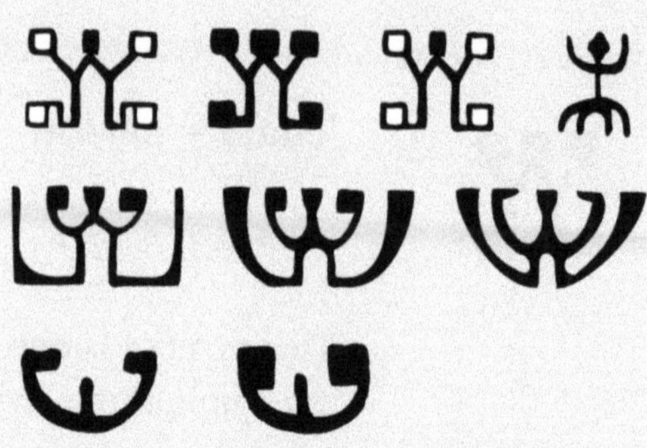

Pohu

meaning: warrior

Pohu was another legendary hero.

'ani ata / 'ani a Tiu = cloudy sky / sky of Tiu

meaning: ancestors

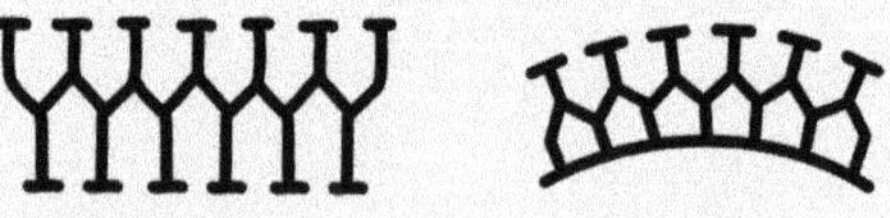

pi'i a Tiu = Tiu's army
(representing the clouds)

meaning: ancestors

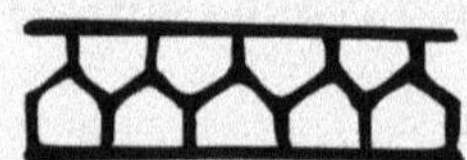

kea = turtle

meaning: protection, family, navigator

There are several symbols representing the turtle, including some created by joining two mirrored *etua*. The turtle was revered as an animal able to defend itself from dangers thanks to its protective shield in the form of its shell.

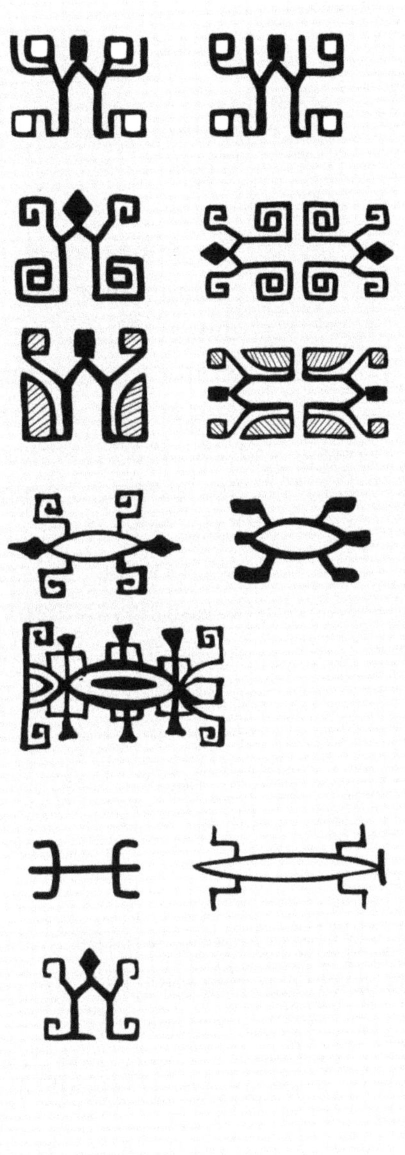

mo'o / moko = lizard

meaning: protection, messenger of the gods

The lizard was believed to be able to move between the worlds of humans and of spirits, and it was revered as a messenger of the gods.

pakiei = crab

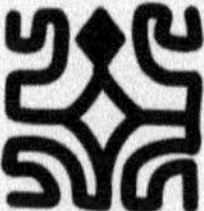

meaning: protection, warrior

The crab is another example of an armored animal. The claws and the protruding eyes that see danger from far away make it a perfect warrior. Some designs called *mata hoata* ("brilliant eyes"), described as stylized *tiki* faces, may actually be representations of the crab portrayed with its main physical characteristics.

Mata hoata:

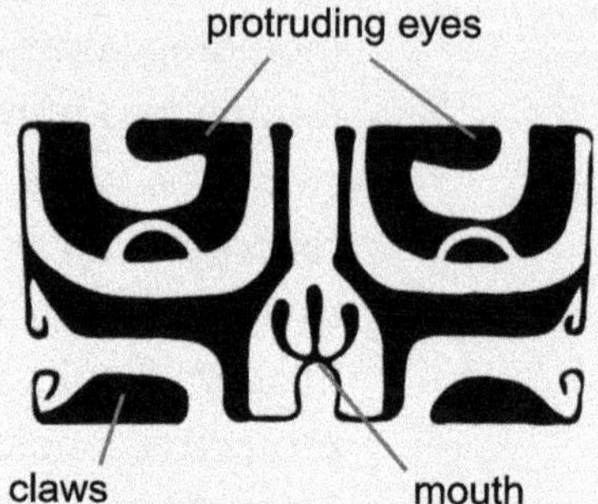

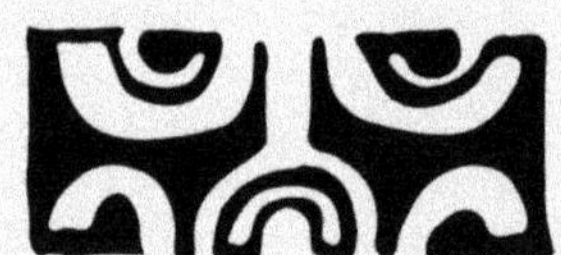

peka 'enana = cross of the people

meaning: feelings, harmony, balance

The Marquesan cross symbol is derived from the crab symbol without a head and with the four limbs symmetrically woven. Polynesians believed that the center of emotions was in the stomach. This is therefore to be considered a complete design in its own right.

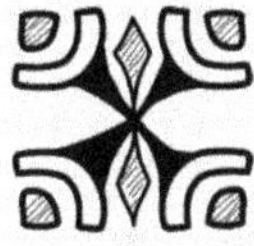

vai o Kena = Kena's bath

meaning: status

Some natural pools were considered sacred, and only the greatest chiefs could bathe in them.

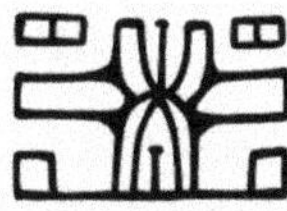

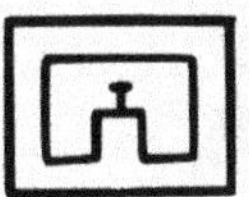

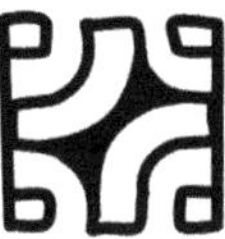

hope vehine = woman's back

meaning: ancestors, woman

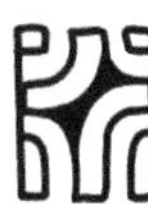

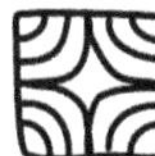

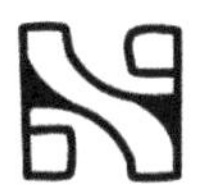

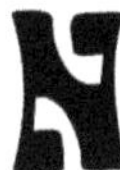

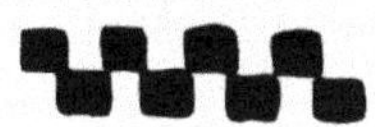

te vehine nalu = my little woman

meaning: love

This pattern is usually applied near the wrist or at the ankle, and it symbolizes love and commitment.

niho peata = shark teeth

meaning: fierceness, fighting spirit, tenacity

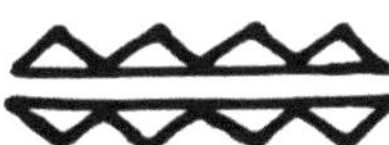

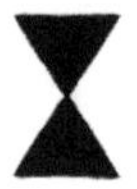

hiku atu = bonito tail

meaning: prosperity, focus, to provide

The bonito (a long-finned tuna) was considered akin to sharks and therefore its symbols are very similar to shark teeth.

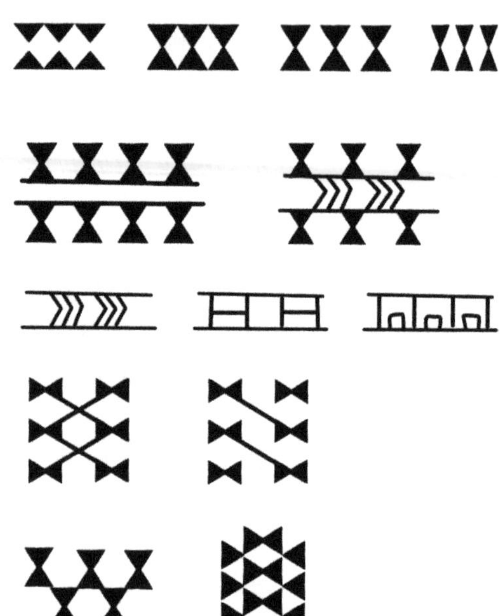

kofatie = bent

This simple symbol is at the base of many different elements, like the motifs of the fan, the eel, and the wind.

breeze / fan:

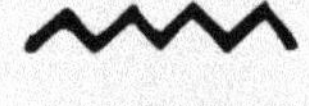

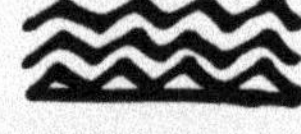

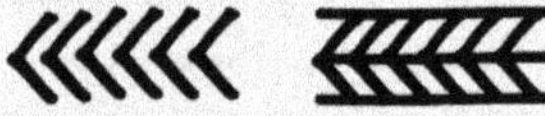

trade-winds (periodically reversing):

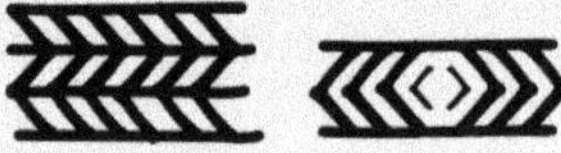

crest of the eel:

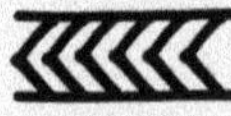

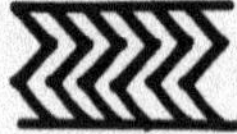

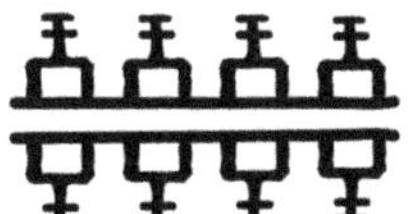

a'a tikau'e = row of flies

meaning: adversities, death

Swarms of flies always gather on dead bodies.

tahi'i = fan

meaning: status, protection from death

Only chiefs and priests could afford to have someone waving fans over their dead to keep flies away. Because of this, fans are symbolic of chiefs and of keeping death away.

puhi = sea eel

meaning: adversities, fierceness, protection

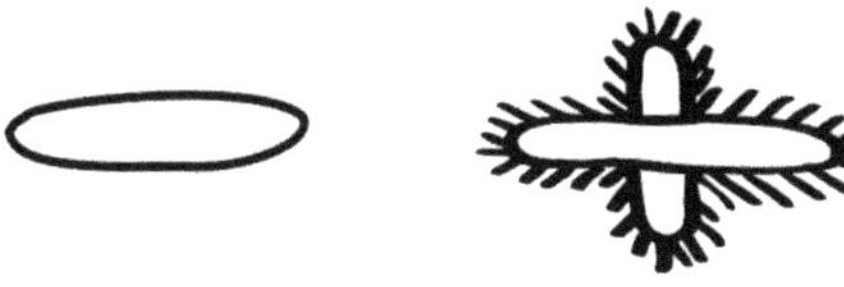

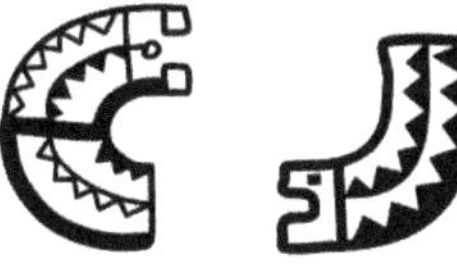

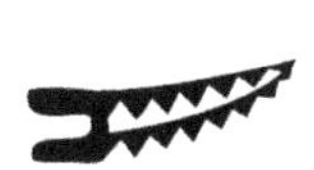

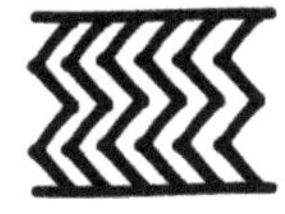

ivi puhi
eel crest

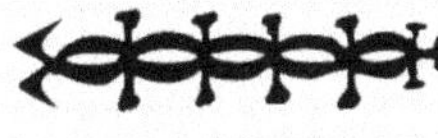

kiva puhi = centipede

meaning: fighting spirit, warrior, genealogy

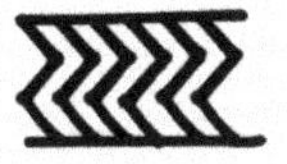

ivi 'einui
centipede legs

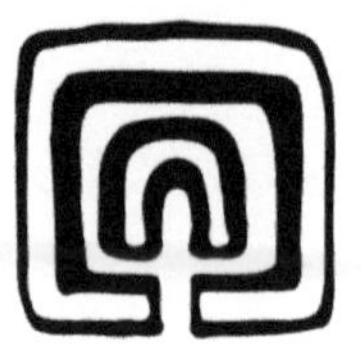

ipu = gourd

meaning: prosperity, genealogy, mana

The *ipu* depicts a gourd and it symbolizes a container of anything, from food to wind to *mana*, according to different legends. As a container of *mana* it is also used to represent ancestors.

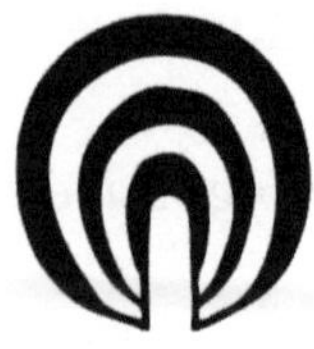

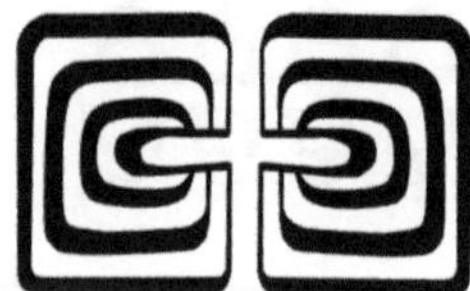

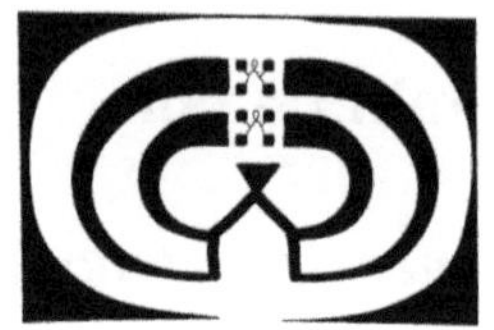

ouhoi = yam leaf

meaning: prosperity

The sweet potato was an appreciated source of food.

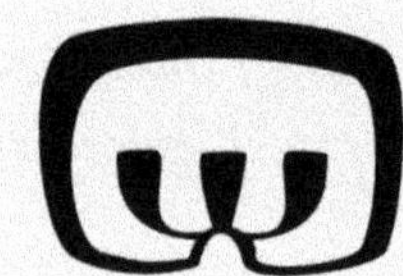

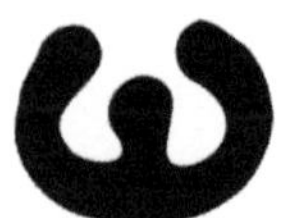

poka'a

Wooden shoulder rest / round hole where rafters sit.

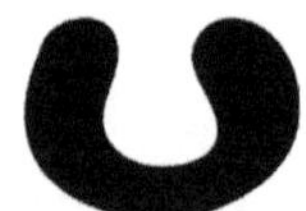

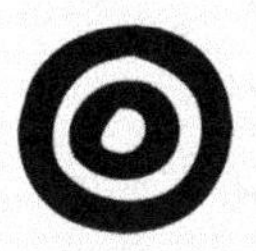

toata = swamp shells

meaning: food, prosperity

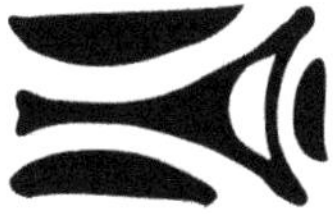

opea = bird

meaning: safe return, messengers

i'a = fish

meaning: prosperity

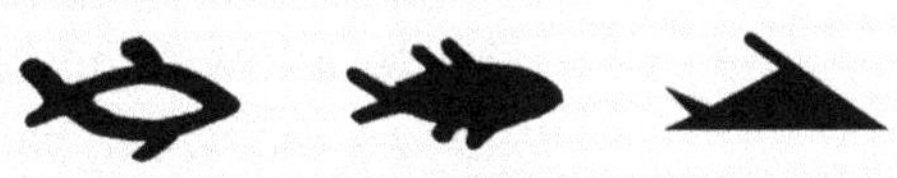

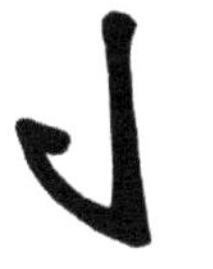

matau = fish hook

meaning: prosperity, knowledge

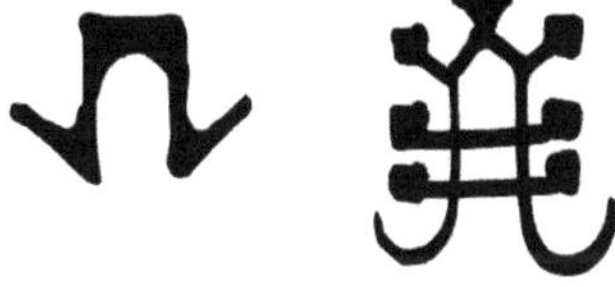

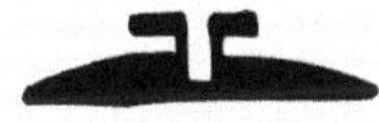

hai / fafa'ua = ray / white-spotted ray

meaning: wisdom, beauty

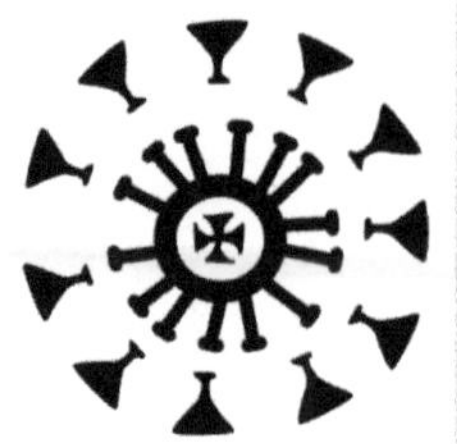

feo'o = compass

meaning: direction

The Polynesian compass was a system of references based on stars. That, together with the knowledge of currents, winds, and the observation of clouds and birds, allowed navigators to sail the ocean safely.

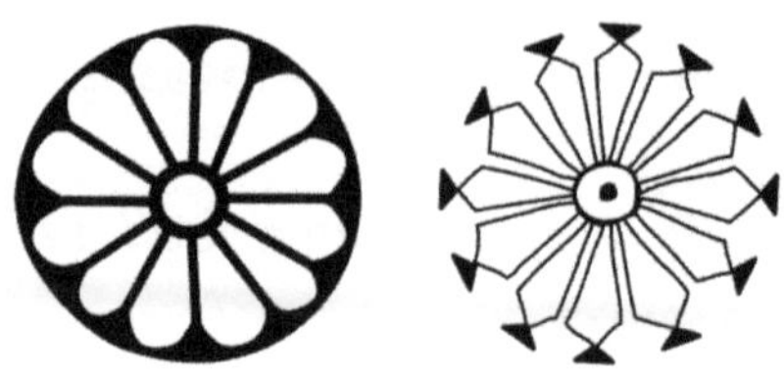

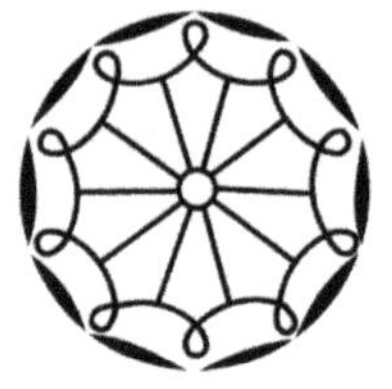

cucurbit flowers were sometimes used to represent compasses

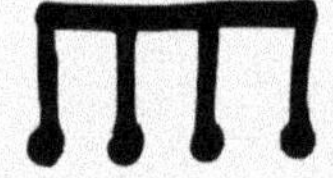

mana fa'a = pandanus branches

meaning: children, offspring

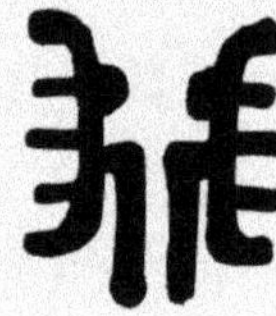

ponapona = union

meaning: knot together, alliances

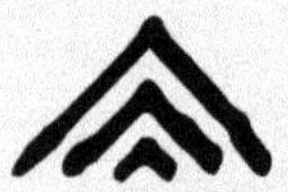

kaka fa'a = pandanus roots

meaning: origin, ancestors, roots

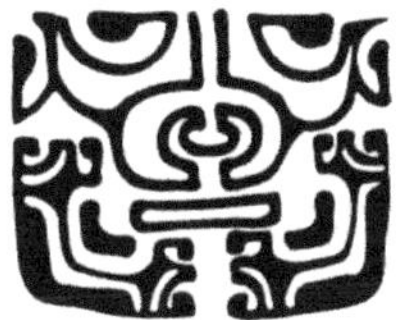

tiki / ti'i = figure

meaning: protection

According to some legends, Tiki was the first man to be created. The image is symbolic of ancestors and protection.

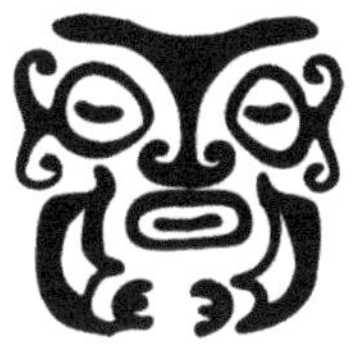

version derived from carving

mata hoata = brilliant eyes

Usually considered as a stylized version of a *tiki* face, it may actually be a simplified crab design.

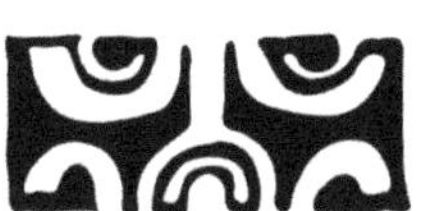

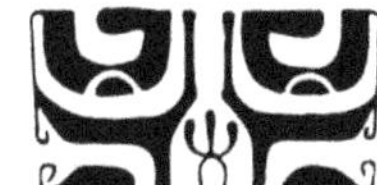

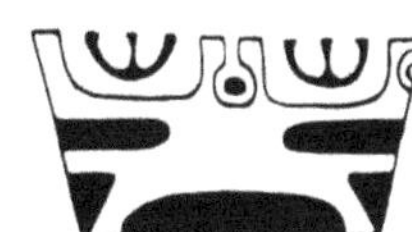

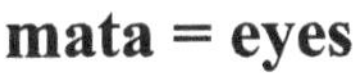

mata = eyes

Sometimes only parts of the *tiki* are incorporated into the tattoo.

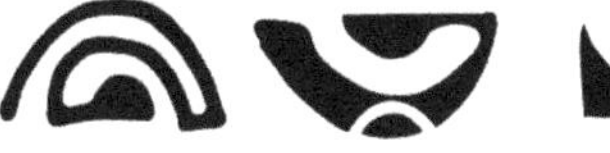

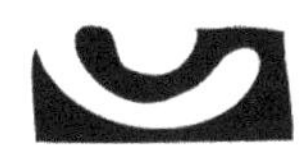

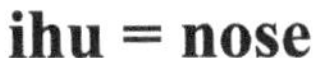

ihu = nose

The legend says that the *tiki* can smell danger even before seeing it.

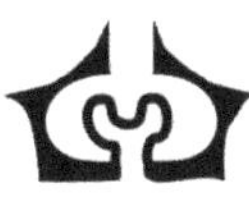

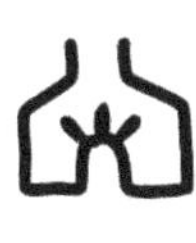

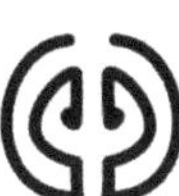

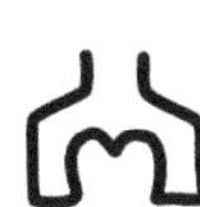

pua'ika = ear

tima = hands

kake = arm

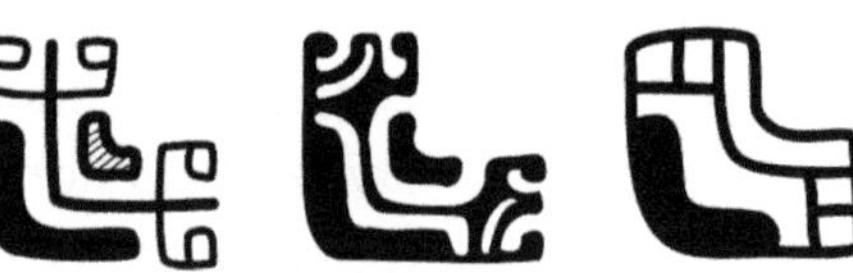

Arms represent strength, work, and skills. When lifted upward, they are representative of growth.

uma hoka = chest closure

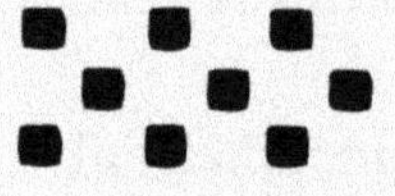

meaning: protection

hupeka = fishing net
protection, union

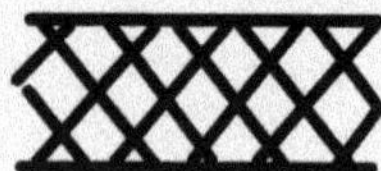

pepehipu = hammered

meaning: pō, origins

iii. tattoo examples walkthrough

The sample designs in this section follow the themes of the previous Samoan chapter to show how the same tattoos would be approached from the point of view of the Marquesan style. All of them will be similarly deconstructed to show their separate parts, building elements, and meanings.

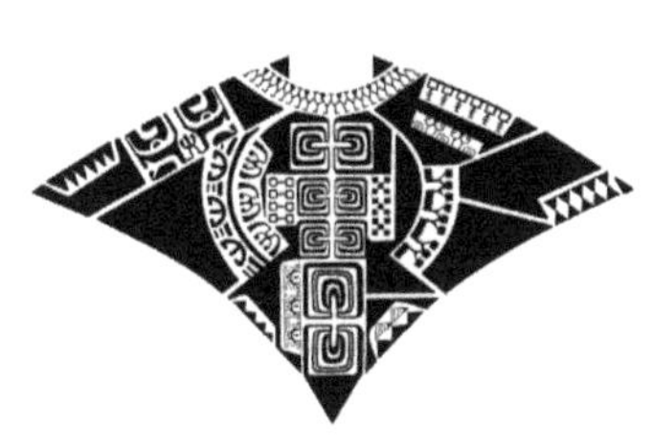

Upper back manta, man

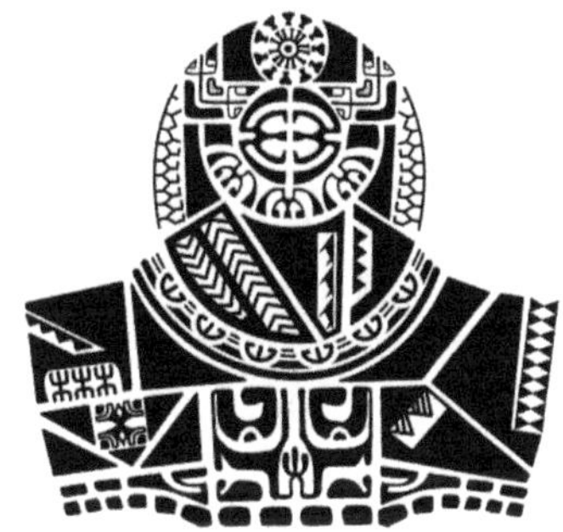

Half sleeve, man

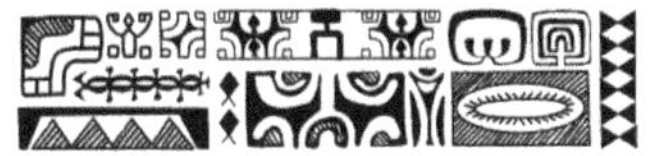

Band, woman

Upper back manta

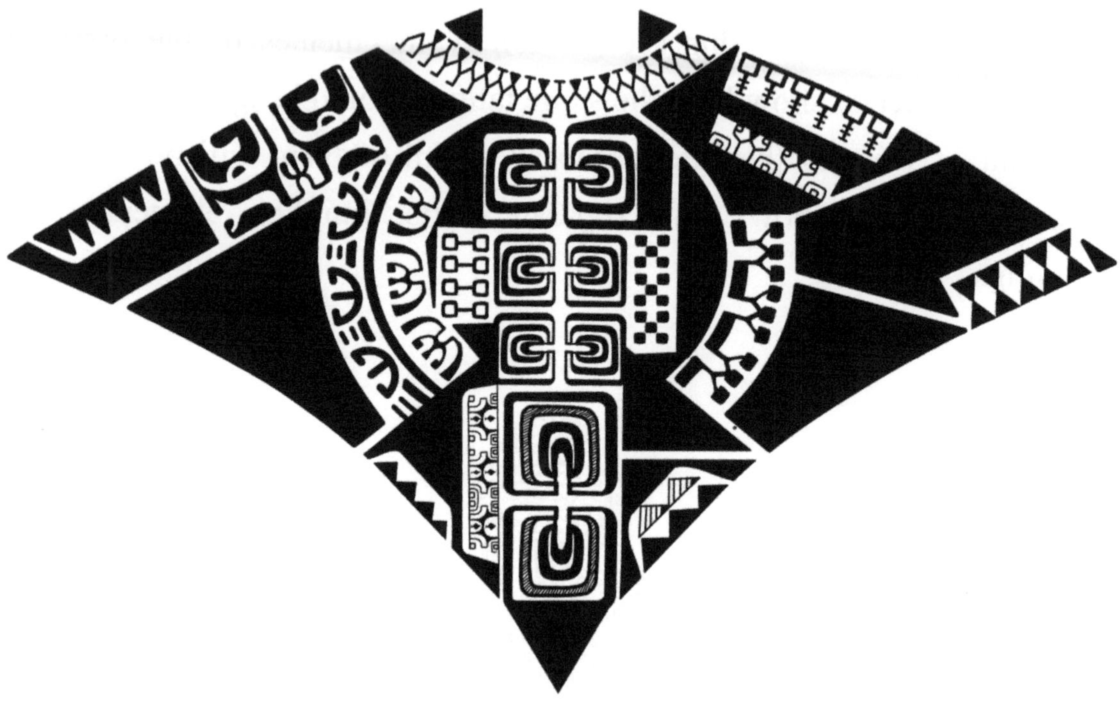

Request: *a manta for the upper back representing the centrality of family and traditions, and protection of the family.*

The style of this Marquesan tattoo is bold and quite dark, and family elements sit side by side with warrior symbols. Let's look in detail at the main parts that make it up.

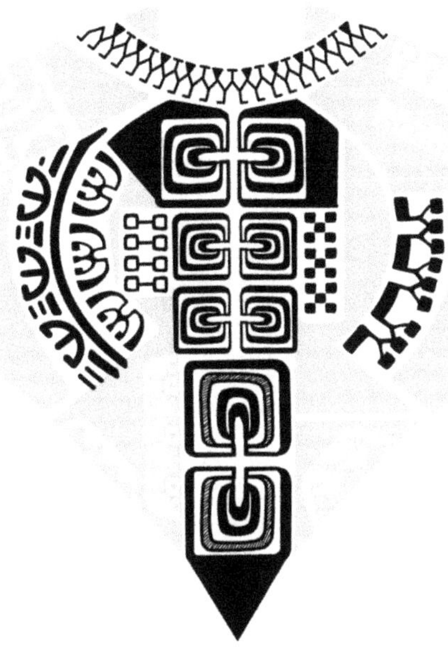

Fig. 4.6: Family-related elements.

The first elements that we are going to study are those related to family. These are positioned in the center and guarded by protective and warrior symbols placed around them. They represent both ancestors and the immediate family, with ancestors being the central pillar of the ideal house, and with the immediate family and relatives around them. Figure 4.7 shows ancestors, represented by the row of coupled *ipu*s and by the *'ani ata* motif on top. The *ipu* symbolizes a gourd, a container, and it is added in tattoos supposedly to collect and contain the *mana* of ancestors, thus adding it to the *mana* of the tattooed person. Each coupled *ipu* represents one couple of ancestors who had a great influence on the

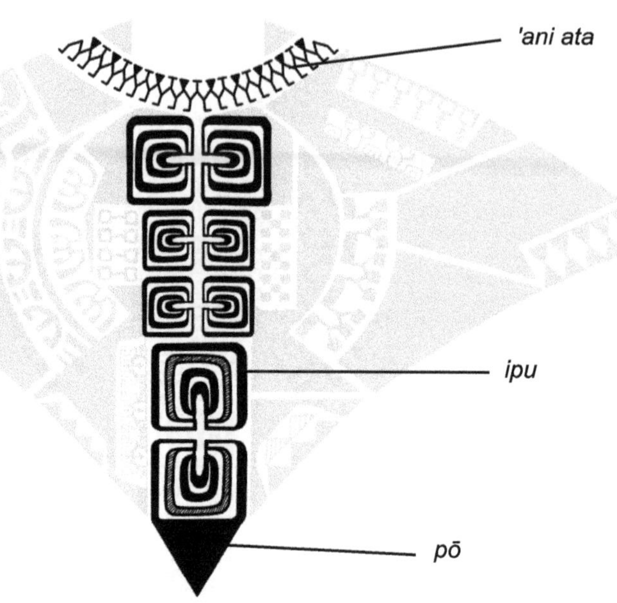

Fig. 4.7: Ancestors are the main pillar of the family.

family lineage. It all stems from the *pō* at the base of the manta, the origin of everything, with the *'ani ata* on top symbolizing all the ancestors guarding the family.

We can imagine the piled *ipu*s as the main post of the chief's house and the row of *'ani ata* on top as the main rafter resting on it. The elements around the main post, comprising of several types of *'enata*, represent family and relatives, and they help shape the tattoo in the same way as the rafters of a house help shape and strengthen its structure. We chose five different types of *'enata* to represent five different families, the closest ones, and the number of *'enata* used to represent them is related to the

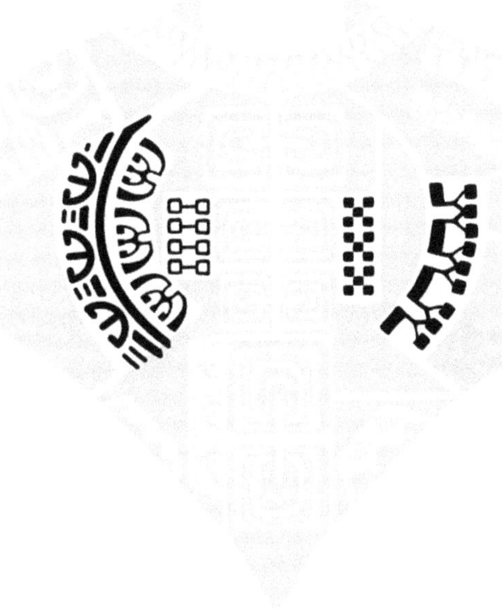

Fig. 4.8: Five types of 'enata representing five families.

number of the members in each family.

Adding small differences while designing the *'enata* is a way to identify specific members of the family. For example, the three *'enata* on the right of figure 4.8 all look very similar, but two of them are very close to each other and the third is slightly separated. We did this to symbolize that one of them remarried after splitting, and all three of them are important to the family. The *'enata* can be grouped on the two sides of the *ipu* to symbolize relatives from the two sides of the immediate family. Elements for the immediate family would then go centrally.

On the outside, on the wings of the manta, there are protective symbols as shown in figure 4.9, where elements representing the warrior are highlighted, too.

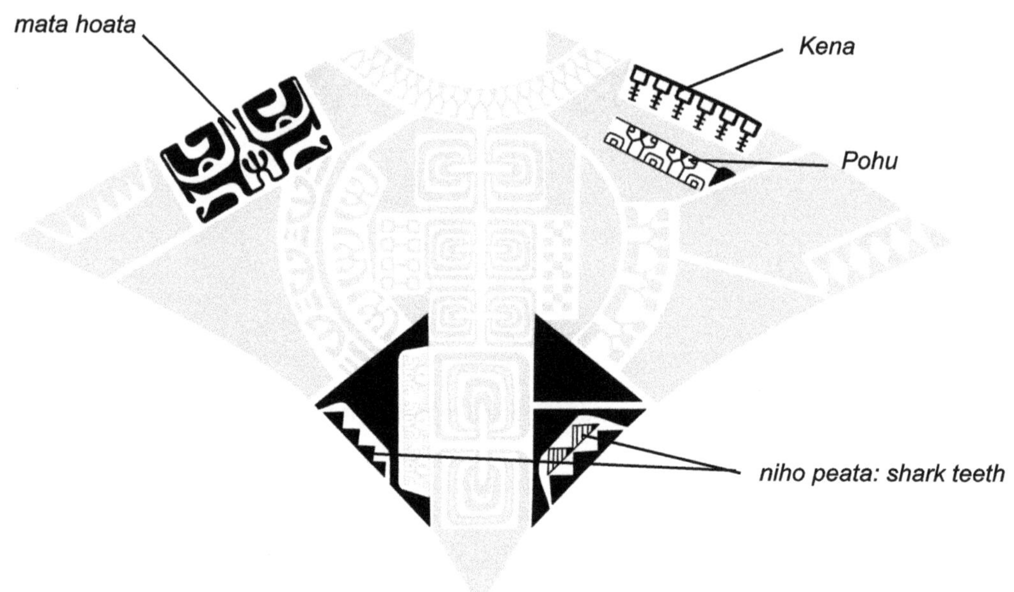

Fig. 4.9: Protective symbols.

Kena and Pohu are legendary warriors and, together with the *mata hoata* and the shark teeth, they bring protection to the family.

The last elements incorporated into the design (fig. 4.10) are the *vai o Kena*, the bonito tail, and the pandanus flower motifs symbolizing prosperity and tradition.

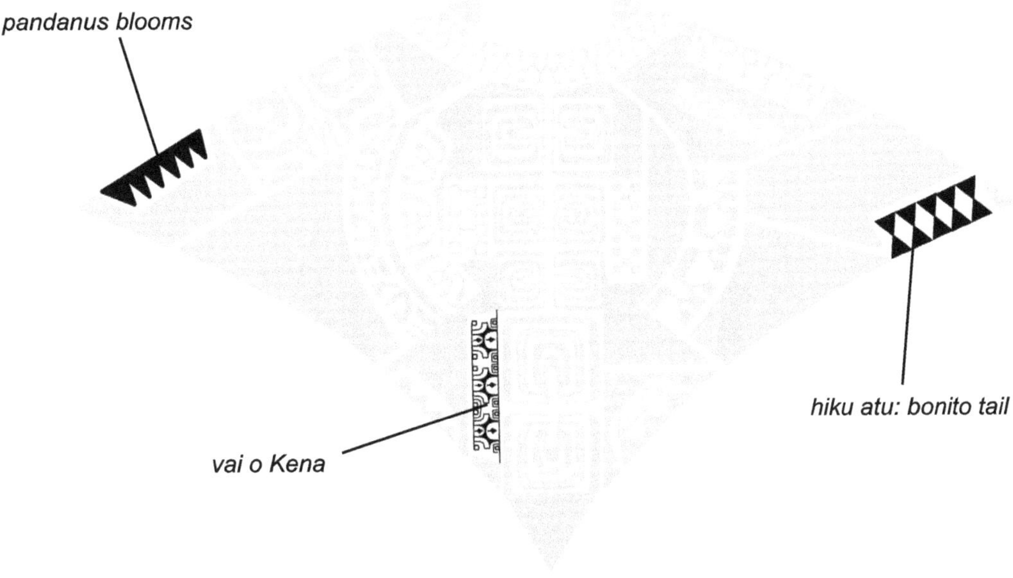

Fig. 4.10: Prosperity symbols.

The *vai o Kena*, or “bath of Kena”, represents a natural pool where the hero bathed. Some natural pools were considered sacred, highly *tapu*, and only people with very high *mana*, like chiefs for instance, were entitled to enter them. On this account, the motif representing the pool of Kena is a symbol of high status.

Half sleeve

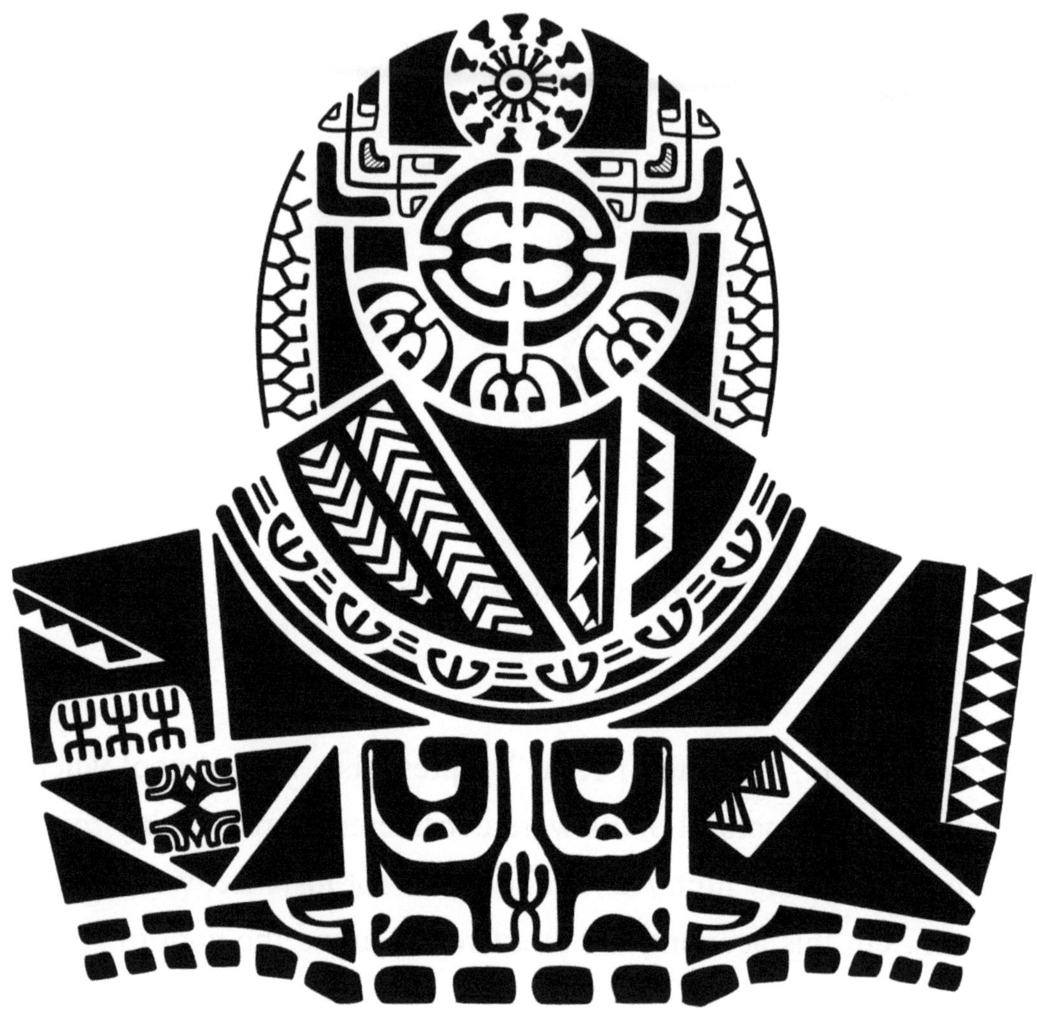

Request: *a half sleeve representing a family that left in search of fortune and is now going back to the island of the ancestors.*

The main themes incorporated into this half sleeve tattoo are family, protection, voyage, and prosperity. Figure 4.11 below shows the elements related to family.

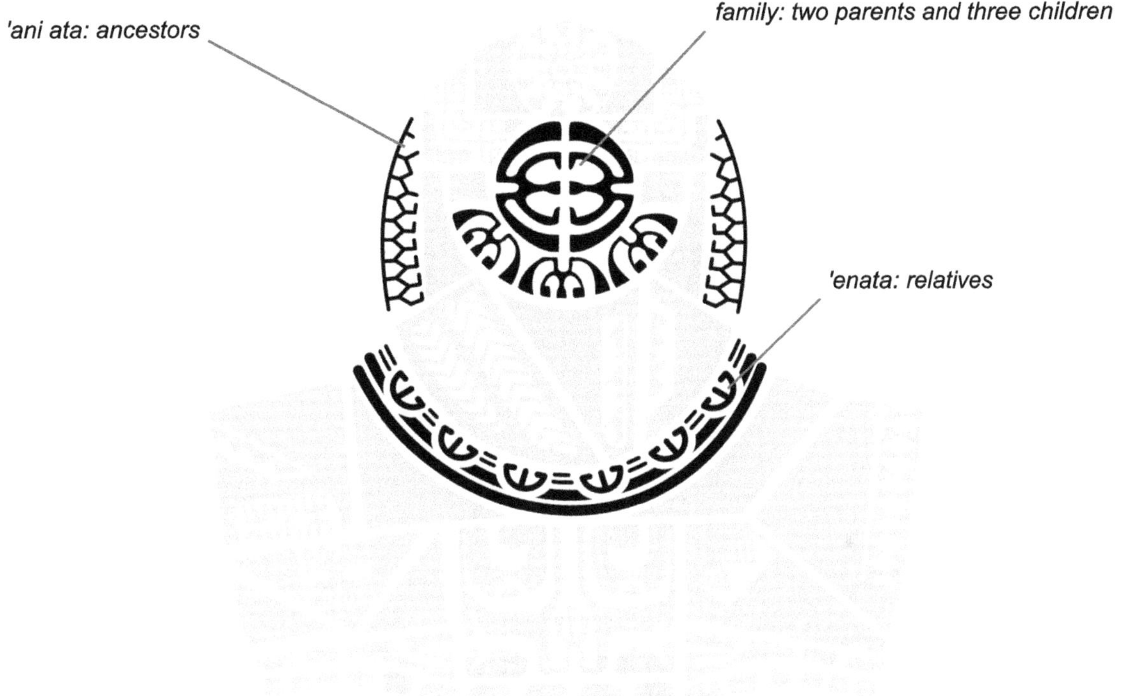

Fig. 4.11: Family-related elements.

Compared to the Samoan version of this design from the previous chapter, the extended family theme is less developed, with a single row of elements positioned below the family, symbolizing their support, and with *'ani ata* motifs on the sides to represents ancestors protecting and guiding the *'enata* in the middle, where two bigger facing elements symbolize the parents and three minor elements below them represent their three children. This is not necessarily the rule, and the family theme can of course be extended and developed further at will, but we preferred to follow the general structure with protection and warrior qualities being the main subject, as shown in figure 4.12.

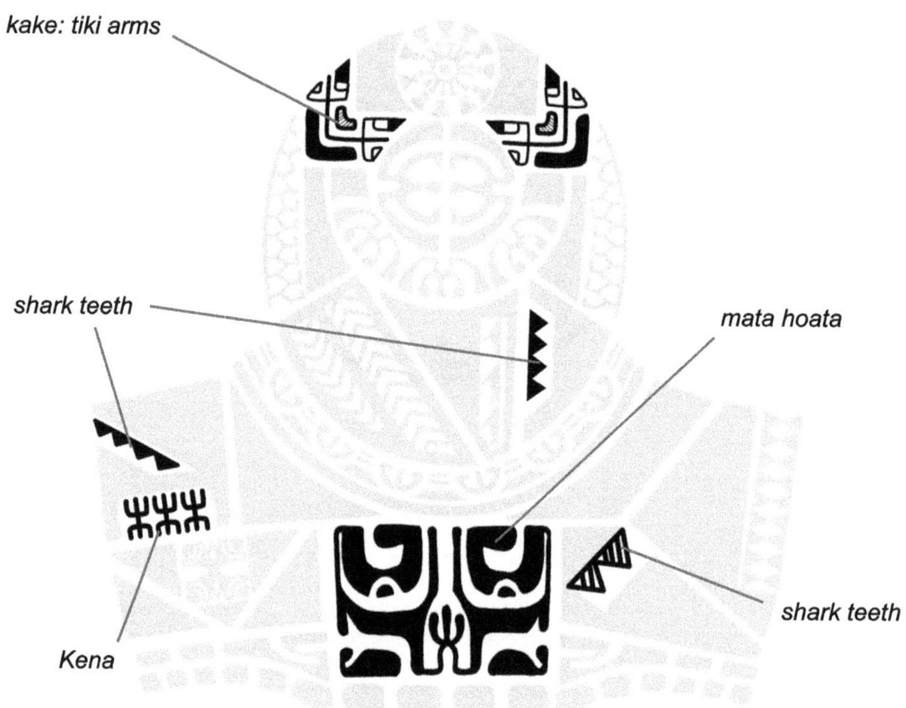

Fig. 4.12: Protection and warrior symbols.

The *mata hoata* at the base represents a protector, like the *tiki* arms on top holding the couple. Kena is a mythological hero, famous for his cunning, strength, and courage, and his symbol was included to bring these qualities to the tattoo and, ultimately, to its bearer. Shark teeth symbolize fierceness and strength.

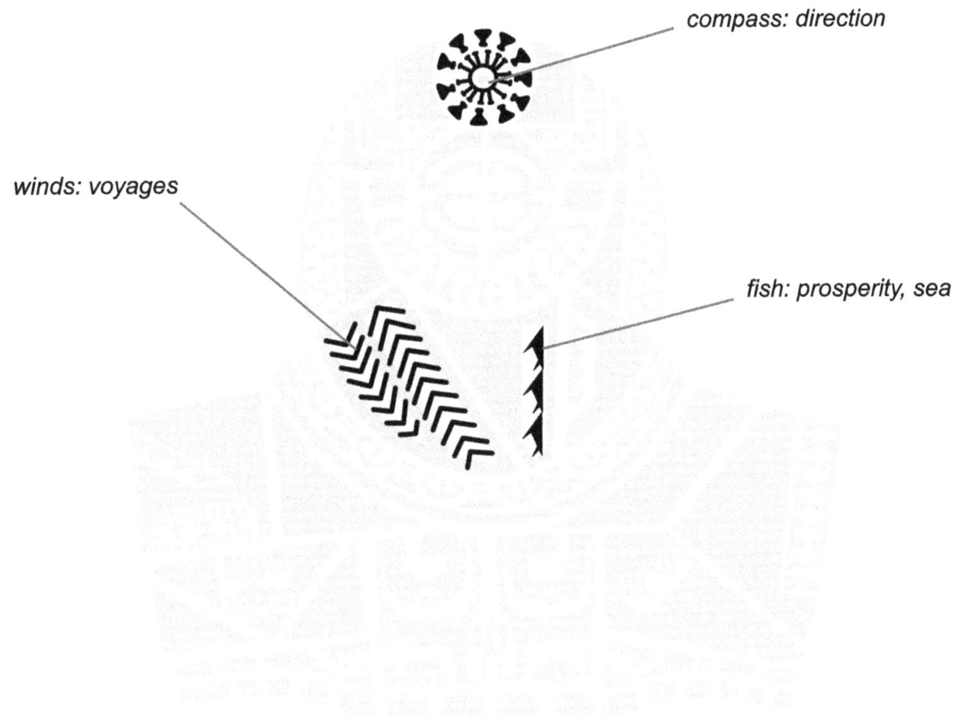

Fig. 4.13: Voyage theme.

The two zigzag-like motifs highlighted in figure 4.13 symbolize winds blowing in opposite directions, and they represent the voyage that led the family away in search of prosperity (the row of fish, which can also represent the voyage by sea), and the voyage that is leading them back. The compass on top represents the goal to be reached, and it also gives them direction never to lose their way, never to forget where they come from.

Prosperity and status are represented by the *vai o Kena* and by the bonito tail motif. Finally, the row of stones at the base marks steps along this voyage and represents achievements and lessons learned, which became the foundations used by the family upon which to build their new life.

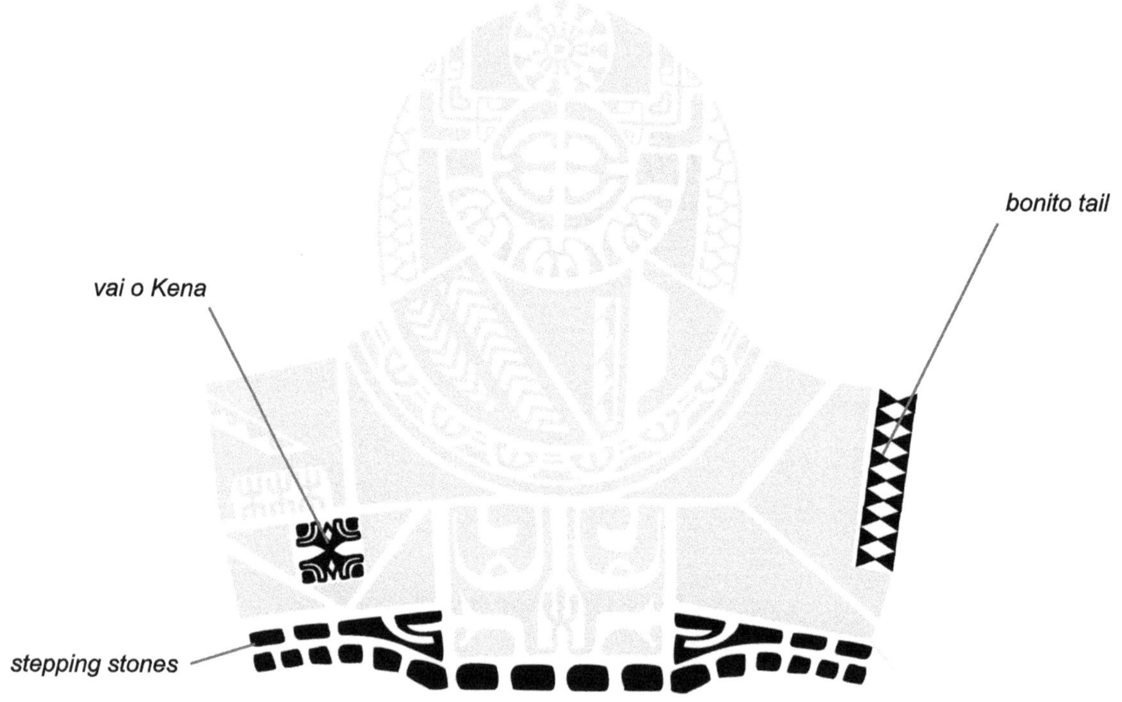

Fig. 4.14: Achievements.

Band

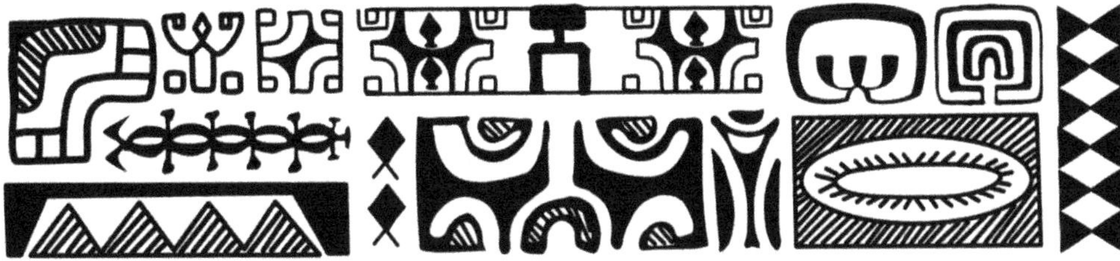

Request: *ankle band for a woman representing protection and tenacity to pursue and achieve every goal in life.*

The symbol that we used to represent the goals to be reached is the *vai o Kena*, but we added Tefio in the middle, the wife of Kena, to symbolize a woman, femininity. Other symbols of prosperity are the bonito tail motif and the fish.

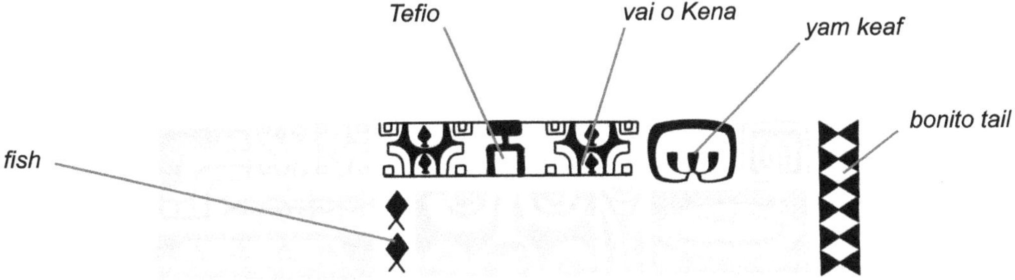

Fig. 4.15: Prosperity and status to be reached.

Figure 4.16 shows the struggle to face adversities in order to achieve one's goals: the moray eel on the right symbolizes difficulties and protection from them, while the centipede, the hero Pohu on the left, and the shark teeth all symbolize a fighting spirit.

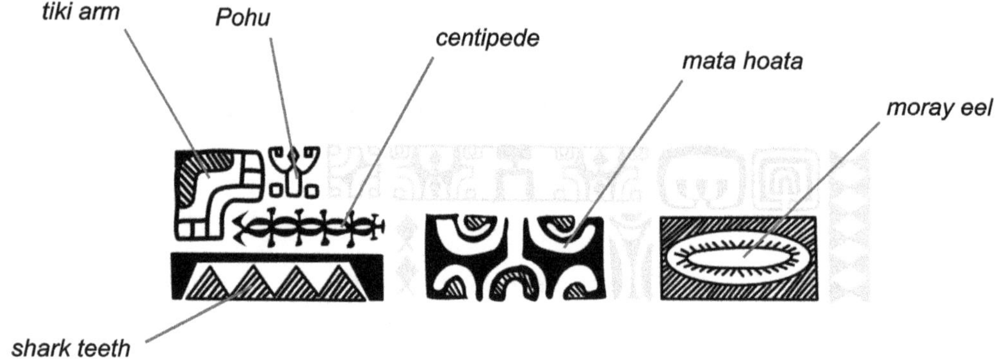

Fig. 4.16: Protection from adversities.

The *tiki* arm and the central *mata hoata* were added to give protection along the voyage, which is represented by the bird.

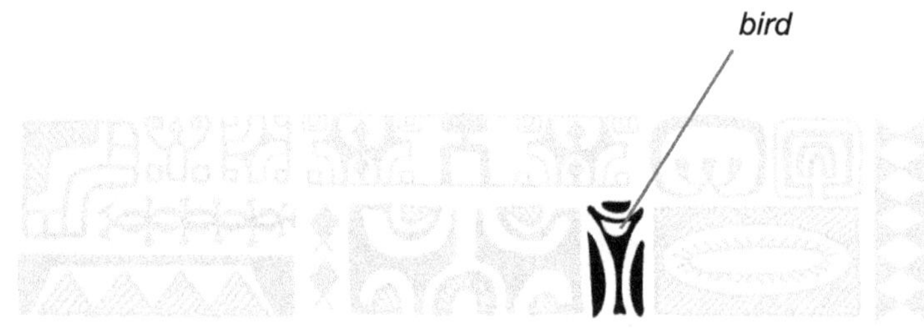

Fig. 4.17: Voyage.

Finally, on the sides of the *vai o Kena* there are two elements: an *ipu* representing fertility and empowerment, and a *hope vehine* for femininity.

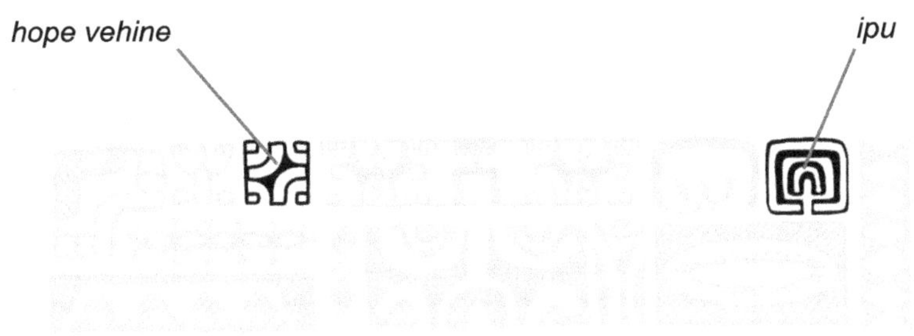

Fig. 4.18: Femininity.

Elements in women's tattoos tend to be lighter than men's counterparts. By using dashed fillings instead of solid black, the overall look becomes lighter and more intricate.

Ho atu, ho mai

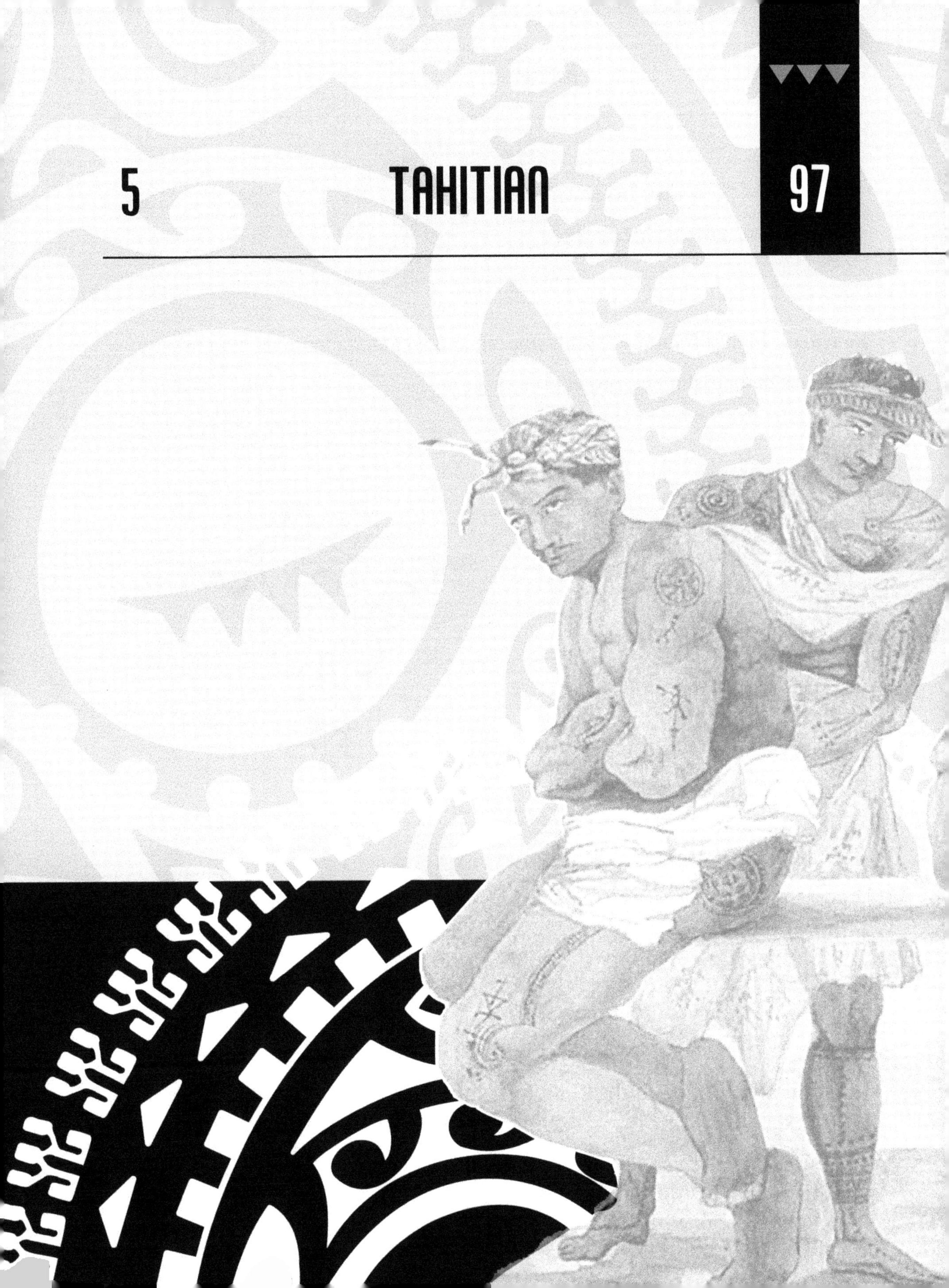

5

TAHITIAN

“Ho atu, ho mai.”
—*Give and you will receive*.

Features: highly figurative, with smooth and rounded elements, naturalistic.
Purpose: embellishment, protection, origins.

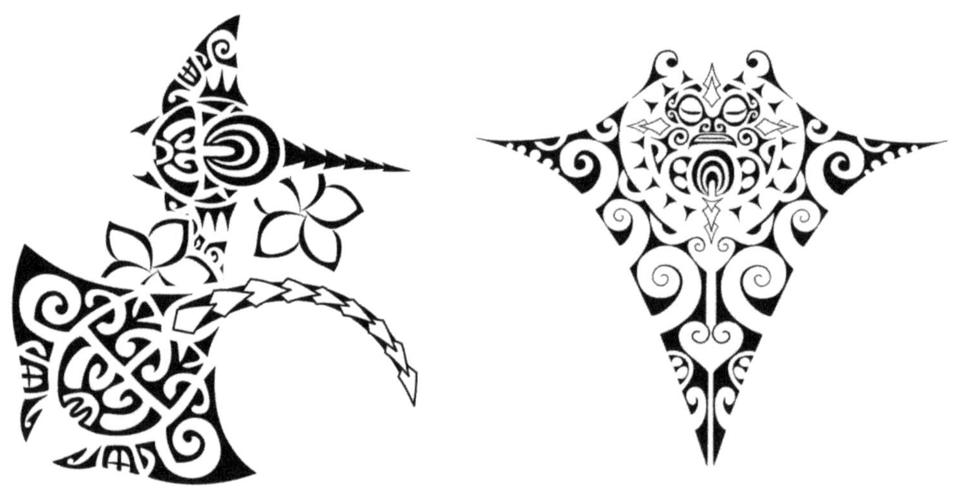

Fig. 5.1: Tahitian tattoos, also known as modern Polynesian.

i. about the style

The Society Islands are a part of French Polynesia and they include Tahiti, Moorea, and Bora Bora (among others), with Tahiti being the largest.

Originally, Tahiti and its archipelago had their own tattoo tradition, comparable to the ones from Samoa and the Marquesas, with similar visual elements and symbols. This is evident in the few drawings that have survived from the reports of early explorers.

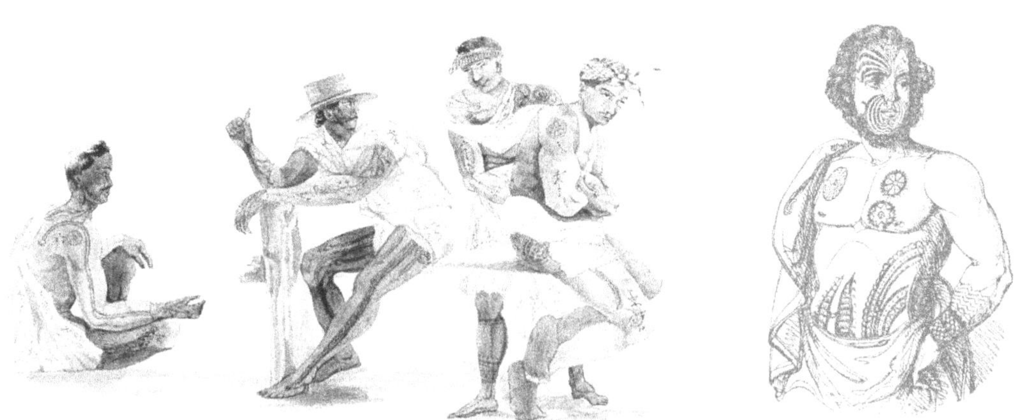

Fig. 5.2: (a) Tahitian tattooed men from a drawing by Duperrey, 1826, (b) John Rutherford's body tattoos, after an unknown artist drawing, 1890.

As the Society Islands were among the first to be discovered in the Pacific Ocean, they also underwent a heavier degree of interference from European explorers and suffered the greatest changes in terms of culture and traditions.

Europeans helped unify the whole archipelago under a single monarchy, thus earning the favor of the ruling family, who soon converted to Christianity. This led to a situation where missionaries had a great influence upon the royalty, a circumstance that did not facilitate the preservation of the native cultural wealth, causing instead the loss of a great part of it. In 1819, Pōmare II introduced the first Tahitian Legal Code, which strongly reflects the influence of missionaries and marks an abrupt and crucial change from the past, banning nudity, dances, chants, and tattooing, virtually causing them to disappear from the islands.

At this time, one group of people known as *ario'i* had been playing an important role in handing down traditions. They were artists, historians, priests, and keepers of the traditional lore, and they traveled from island to island to propagate and teach stories, dances, songs, and traditions, keeping them alive and living off the offerings that they were given as a reward for their performances. Both sexes were equally represented within the *ario'i* and they were highly revered, enjoying a prominent role in society. They used tattooing as a means to indicate their status within their ranks, with eight specific body areas tattooed according to the eight different grades they were organized into, with the two higher grades only accessible to people of royal blood, or *ari'i*. The *ario'i*, being the keepers of traditions, rose up against the prohibitions. Due to their prestige and authority, it wasn't long before tensions developed between natives and the new settlers. This led to a period of war that ended in 1842 with the French permanently taking control over the islands and their cultural identity.

Tattooing in particular was almost entirely abandoned and ended up disappearing, nearly causing the loss of all the symbols along with their meanings. Only a limited number of symbols survived, handed down in *tapa* clothing decorations.

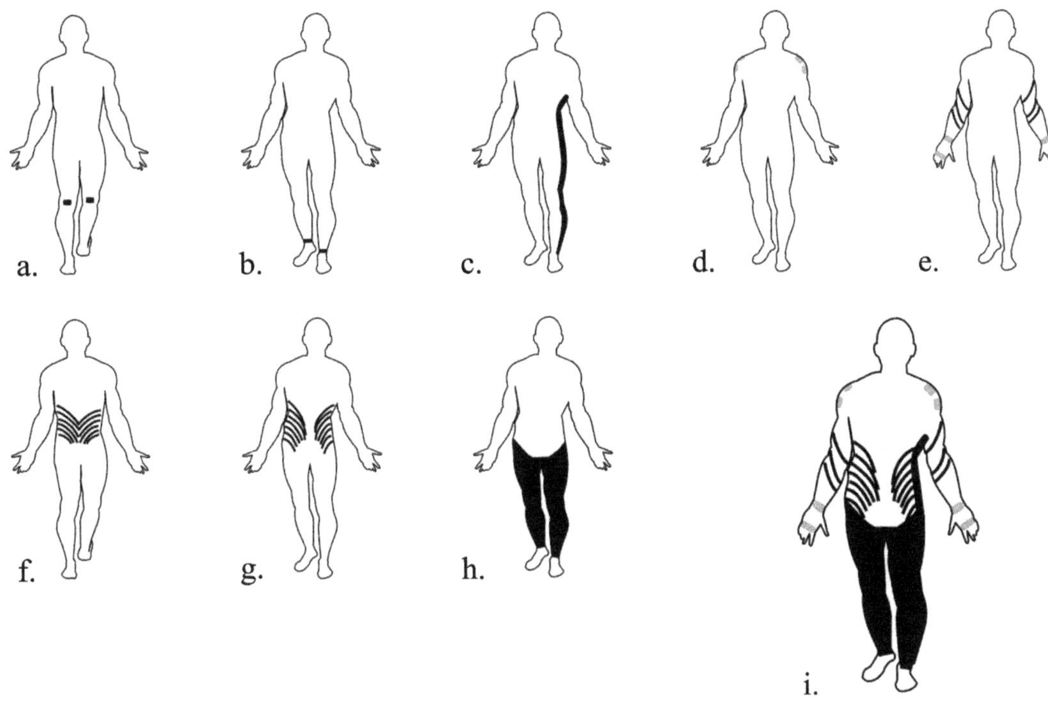

Fig. 5.3: Ario'i tattoo positioning.
(a) 8th grade, apprentice: tara tutu, "pointed horn", behind the knee.
(b) 7th grade: ohe mara, "seasoned bamboo", a circle around the ankle.
(c) 6th grade: atoro, one stripe down the left side.
(d) 5th grade: hu'a, "small", two or three light marks on the shoulders.
(e) 4th grade: oti'ore, "unfinished", light marks on the knuckles and wrists, heavier ones on the arms and shoulders.
(f) 3rd grade: taputu, "gathered together", a series of curved lines radiating upward toward the sides of the torso from the lower end of the spinal column to the middle of the back.
(g) 2nd grade: harotea, "light colored print", bands running crosswise on both sides of the body from the armpits downward toward the front.
(h) 1st grade, high chief: avae parai, "blotted legs", solid black from ankle to groin.
(i) 1st grade, complete tattoo, front view.

Very few copies of the original designs survived to testify that tattooing was once practiced and common on the islands. In the images of the *ario'i* tattoos we can notice the similarity between the original Tahitian style and Samoan and Marquesan traditions, including the bands of parallel curved lines on the sides of the hip converging toward the groin (fig. 5.3.f and fig. 5.3.g).

Unfortunately, this is a small heritage compared to all the lore that has been lost. With the renaissance of Polynesian tattooing during the last decades of the twentieth century, Tahitian artists found themselves limited with little or no material to work with. They searched, dug, reorganized what they had, and transformed it into something new, tapping into other Polynesian styles, mainly Marquesan, as it was initially the best documented one, and eventually Samoan, which have been blended with modern influences and Western art. Finally, a very figurative and creative style was developed that appealed to the taste of people from all over the world, thus contributing to its popularity.

Many factors have fostered the success of this style: it is not limited to specific positions on the body or bound by strict rules in its composition; the use of modern tattooing machines makes it accessible to anyone; the style is very pictorial and the elements easily recognizable despite still retaining a Polynesian look, which makes it unique and appealing; and, perhaps the most important aspect, as the style is not strictly traditional, it is not restricted to Polynesian natives and has become a favorite souvenir for tourists to bring back home, where others would appreciate the style, thus contributing to its popularity.

Another characteristic of the Tahitian style that makes it so versatile is that there isn't actually a single authentic style: every artist reinterprets the symbols according to their taste and experience, introducing variations like shadings, realistic parts, etc. This results in everyone being able to find an artist whose style matches their personal taste and expectations. Elements that are not truly Polynesian can even be integrated into their work, designed to blend seamlessly into the tattoos, making them even more personal.

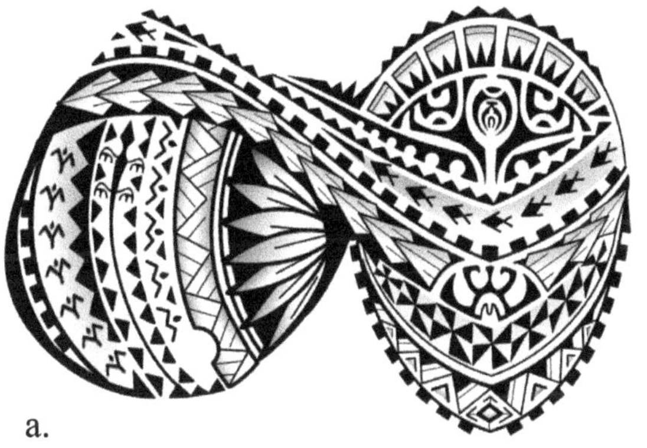

a.

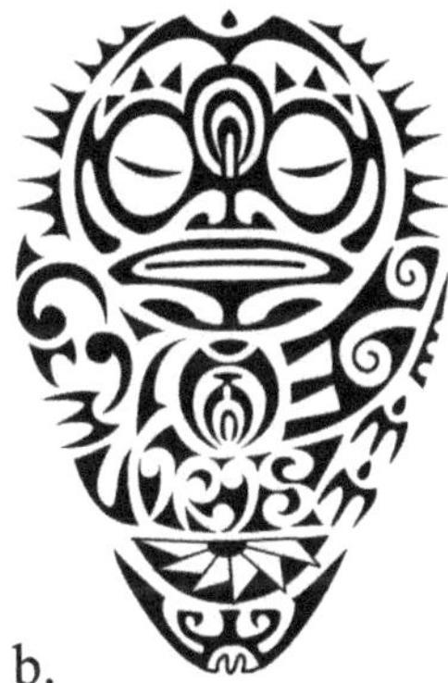

b.

Fig. 5.4: Examples of custom modern Polynesian tattoos.
(a) Samoan inspired, with added shadings. (b) Name inclusion (Iris).

One peculiarity of this style is the presence of images within images. Basic elements make up small designs, and small designs join together to form bigger shapes that result in intricately detailed tattoos, as shown in figure 5.5, where smaller animals are woven together to form the main turtle design:

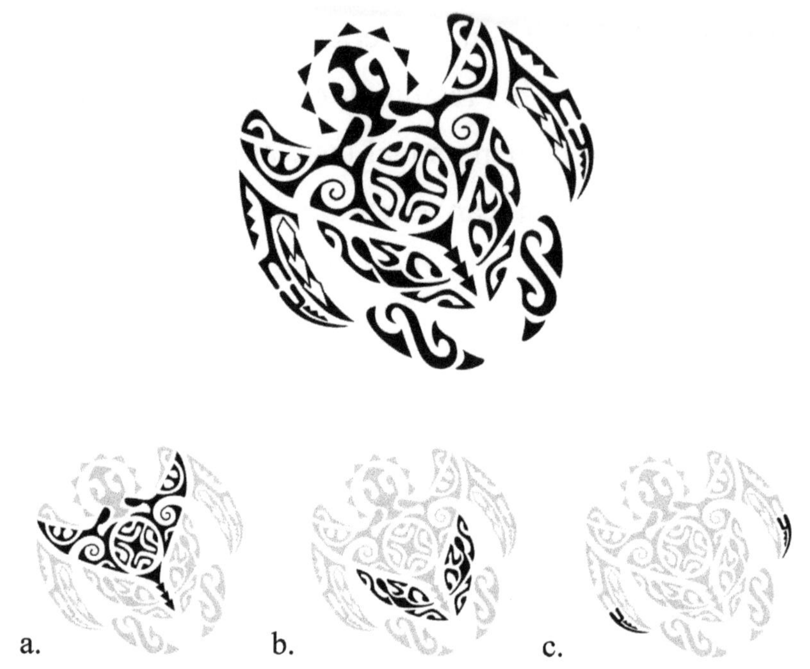

Fig. 5.5: (a) Manta, (b) lizards, and (c) moray eels.

ii. elements

Modern Tahitian tattoos are highly figurative. Whilst naturalists aboard the vessels of the early expeditions report that ancient Tahitian tattoos did not include animals, this may not be exact, as we now know that naturalistic subjects have always played an important part in Polynesian tattoos. What is true is that no animal was included in a pictorial, recognizable way until 1777, when Bligh noted the inclusion of horses into Tahitian tattoos, followed later by muskets and other elements brought by the foreigners. They symbolized economic assets earned by the chiefs thanks to their relations with the explorers, and they are a good example of how tattoos were adapted to new situations to remain a faithful representation of the life of their bearers. In modern tattoos, animals and nature are prominent and easily recognizable, designed by the union of smaller elements and symbols that are derived from the old designs and integrated with elements from other Polynesian traditions. The following list shows the most common symbols used in Tahitian modern tattooing.

Symbol	Name and Meanings	Variants
▲	**niho mao = shark teeth** *meaning: strength, protection, adaptability* Shark teeth are the base of many designs. In Tahitian tattoos they can be used to represent the sun when placed along a circular path. Fully designed sharks and hammerhead sharks are often included too.	

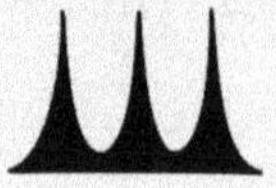

moua = mountain

meaning: stability, islands

Mountains are firm standing points, visible from afar. They symbolize stability and direction, and can represent islands, too.

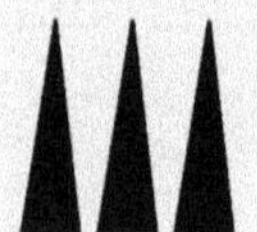

ia = fish

meaning: prosperity

The resources of the ocean were fundamental as a guarantee of prosperity to the islanders.

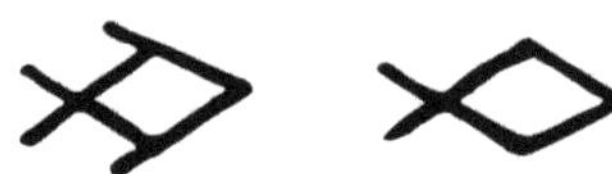

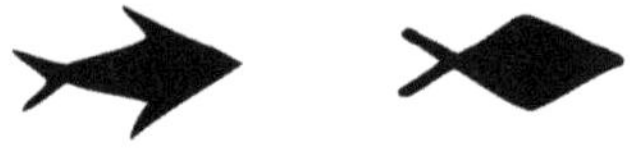

matau = fish hook

meaning: status, wealth

Fish hooks and fishing lines are symbolic of abundance and status.

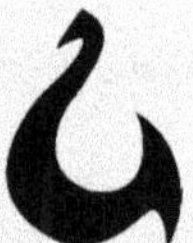

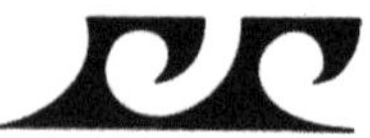

vai / miti = water / sea

meaning: origins, continuity

Waves are also used to symbolize change.

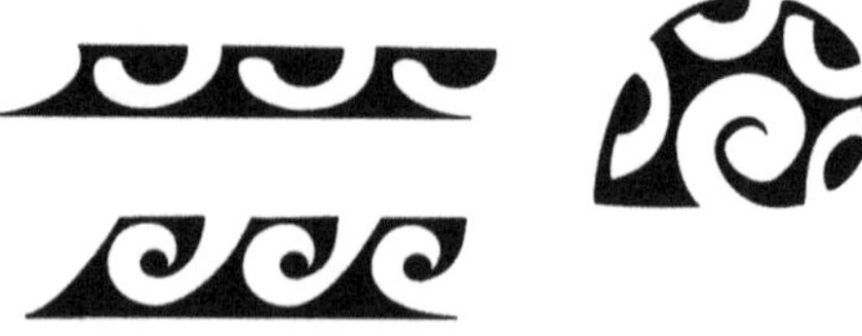

manu = bird

meaning: safe return, voyage

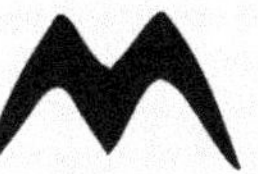

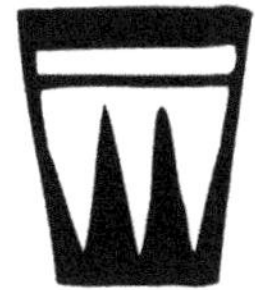

'ao ha'ari = coconut bud

meaning: prosperity

Coconut buds, flowers, and leaves all symbolize prosperity. The coconut was revered as a source of food, utensils, and raw wood.

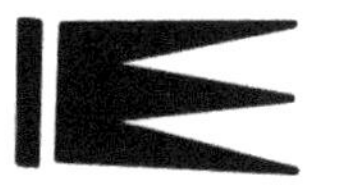
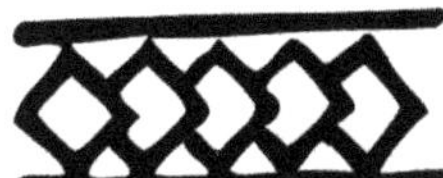

tiare = flower

meaning: beauty, grace, femininity, children

Tiare actually means "flower" in Tahitian. The flowers of tiare, hibiscus, and plumeria are the most represented in Polynesian tattoos.

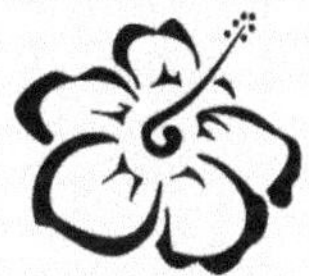

hibiscus
seize the moment, carpe diem

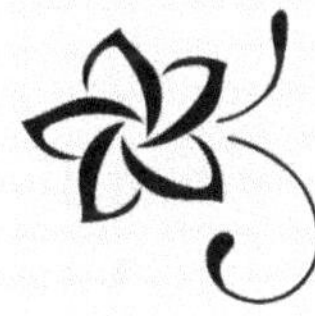

plumeria
children, safe shelter

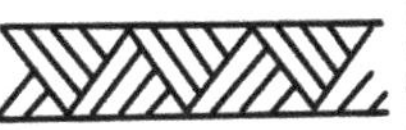

tapa'au = braid made of coconut leaves

meaning: union, community

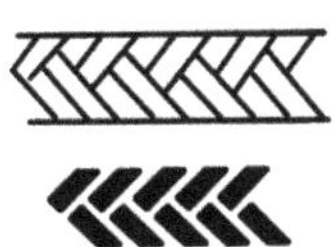

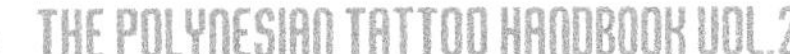

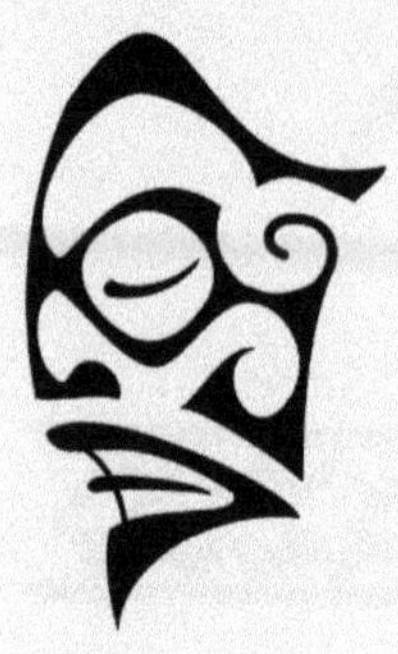

Tiki

meaning: protection, ancestor

The Marquesan *tiki* becomes less stylized and more realistic in Tahitian tattooing.

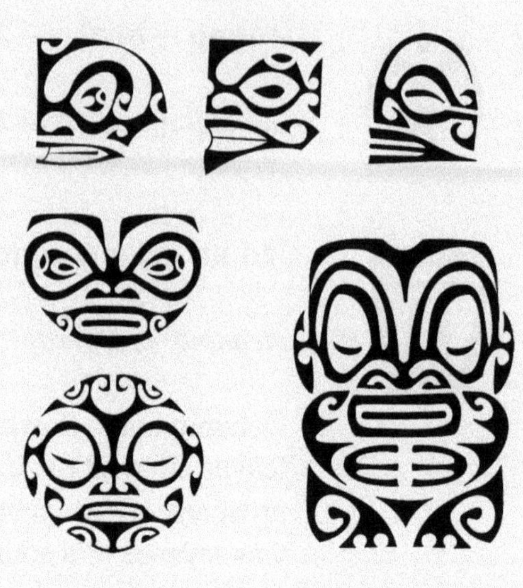

It's common to see parts of the *tiki* alone, like hands and eyes, included in the designs.

tiki hands

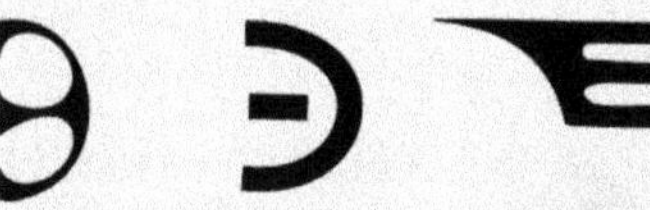

tiki eyes

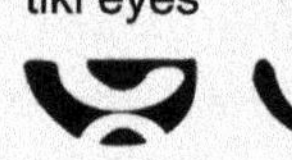

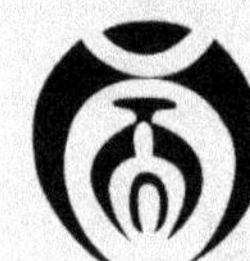

mo'o = lizard

meaning: health, luck, messenger from the gods

Lizards and geckos are often included in a realistic way.

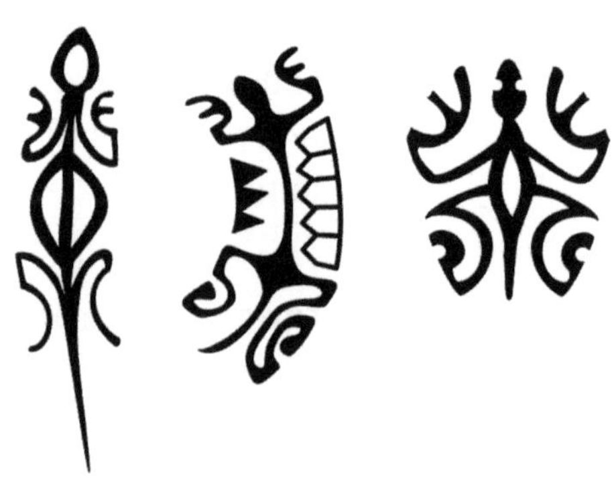

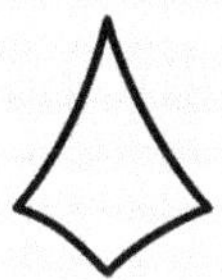

atai = spearheads

meaning: strength, courage

Spearheads represent a warrior, and they symbolize fierceness, strength, and courage.

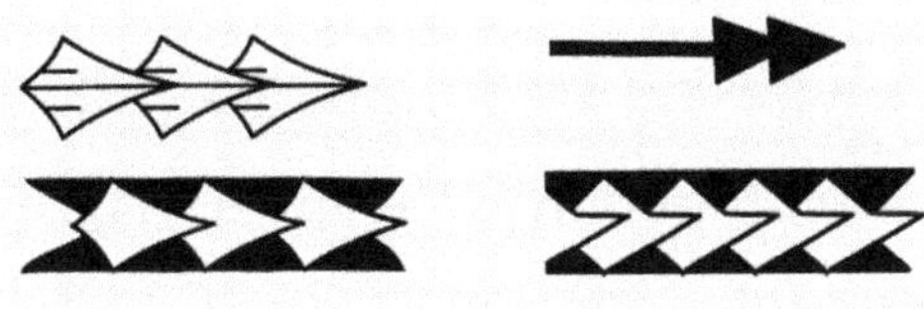

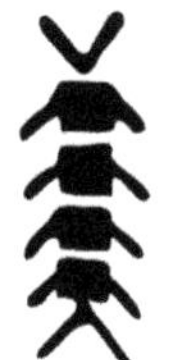

veri = centipede

meaning: fighting spirit

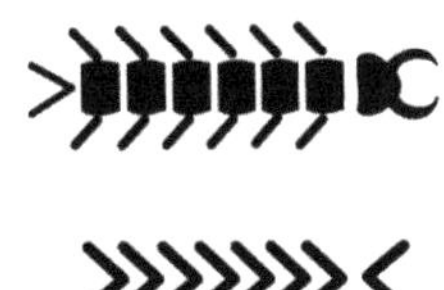

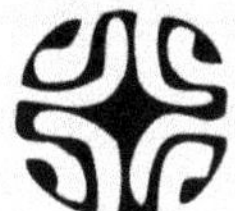

Marquesan cross

meaning: balance, union of the elements

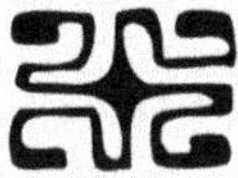

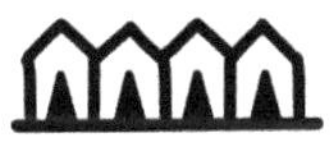

honu = sea turtle

meaning: navigator, union, family

Realistically shaped turtles are often included in the designs, being a common symbol for family.

va'a = canoe

meaning: voyage, adventure, cooperation

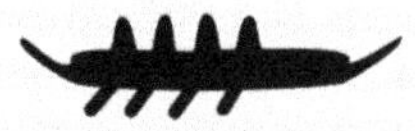

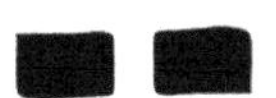

ofai = stones

meaning: achievements

Modern Tahitian tattooing also includes elements from other Polynesian traditions, like the *koru* ("loop", unfolding fern bud) and the *kape* ("eyebrow") from Maori traditions, or the Hawaiian *ala nui o Kamehameha* ("long path of Kamehameha") and the *lō kahi* ("agreement, unity") for example, listed in this book within the corresponding chapters.

Animals often have a primary role in these tattoos, in relation to the concept of spirit animals, to give protection or as a means of including their characteristics and passing them on to the tattooed person. Among the most common animals to be seen in Tahitian tattoos are turtles, sharks, mantas, lizards, dolphins, whales, and birds, but the list goes on. Each animal is often comprised of several smaller symbols and represents a specific aspect or story within the main narrative of the whole tattoo.

Plants are another common theme, with flowers being more predominant in women's tattoos, which also have a lighter look. The style gets reinvented with every new piece, reinterpreted by modern artists as an illustrated story where every element is positioned freely, unaffected by schemes and boundaries. The main element will often give its shape to the tattoo, as shown in the third example of the following section.

iii. tattoo examples walkthrough

In the first two examples of this section we kept the same stories and shapes of the corresponding designs from the first two chapters, to make it easier to see the differences between the three styles. The third design holds the same meanings of the other bands, but freely develops on them to show the possibilities of this style.

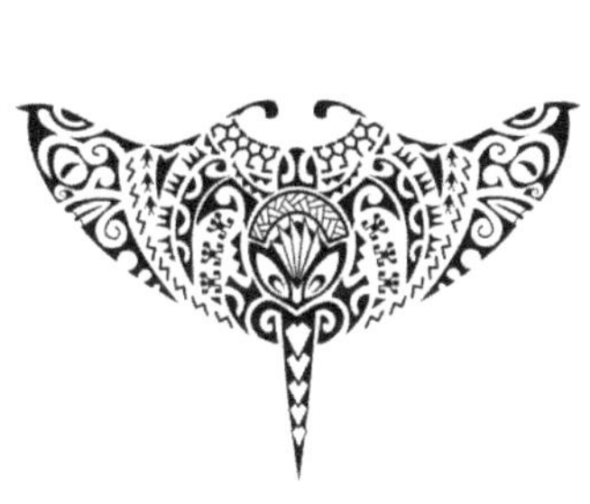

Upper back manta, man

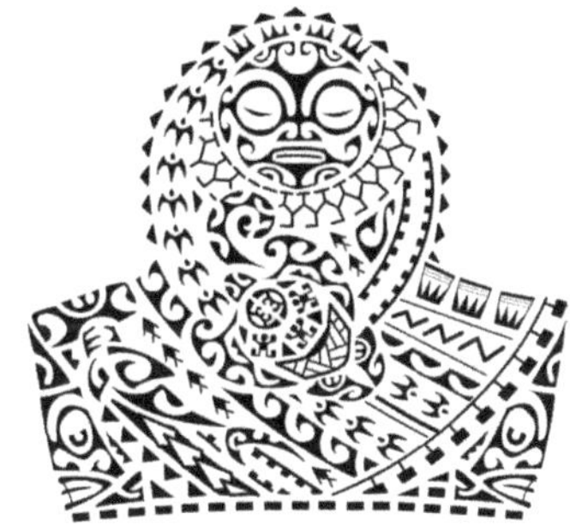

Half sleeve, man

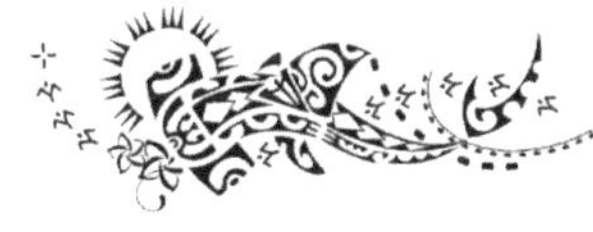

Band, woman

Upper back manta

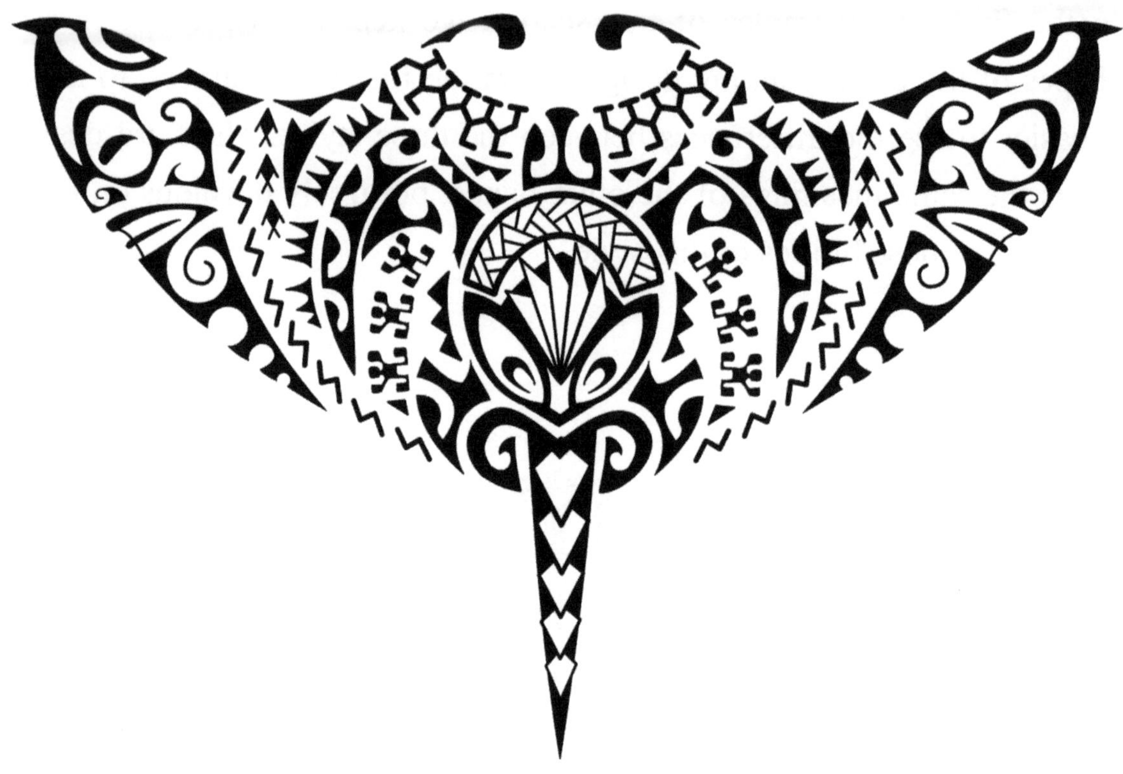

Request: *a manta for the upper back representing the centrality of family and traditions, and protection to the family.*

Once again the elements related to family were incorporated in the center of the design to symbolize their importance. The turtle represents the immediate family, with close relatives under its wings, and the Samoan

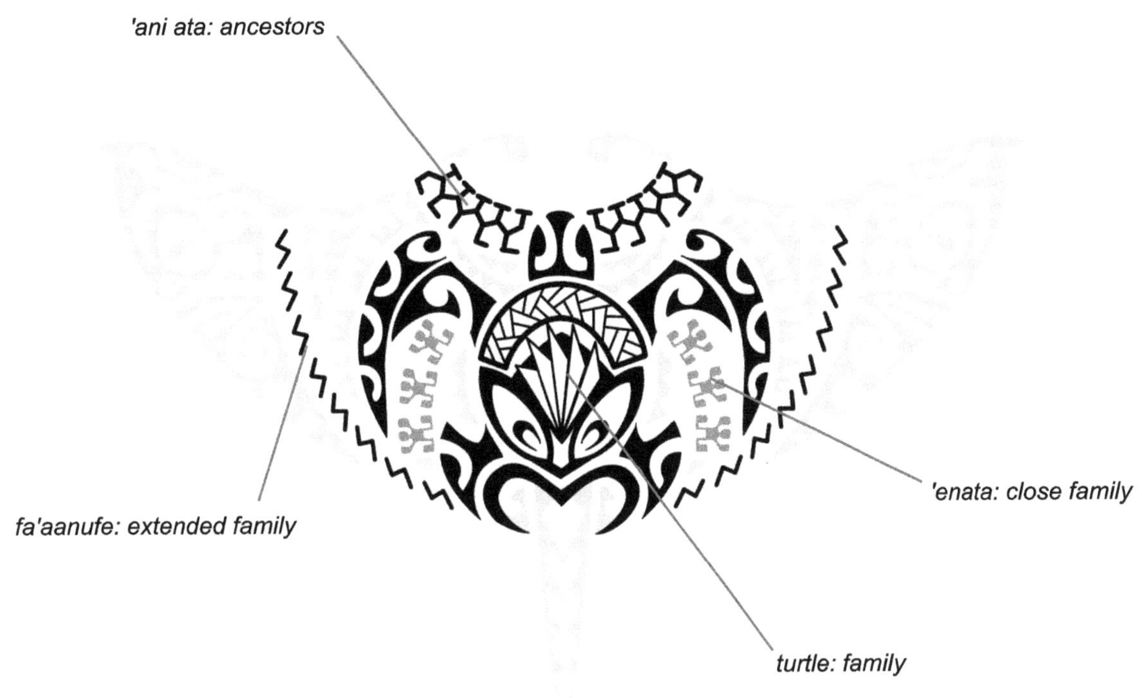

Fig. 5.6: Family-related elements.

fa'aanufe motifs around them represent the extended family. The *'ani ata* motif on top represents the ancestors guarding them all. The *'enata* were placed under the front flippers of the turtle to symbolize the protection ensured to the close relatives. Family also represents a source of joy and stability, symbolized by the sun made of mountains that surrounds the whole family, as shown in figure 5.7. The fish next to them are symbolic of prosperity.

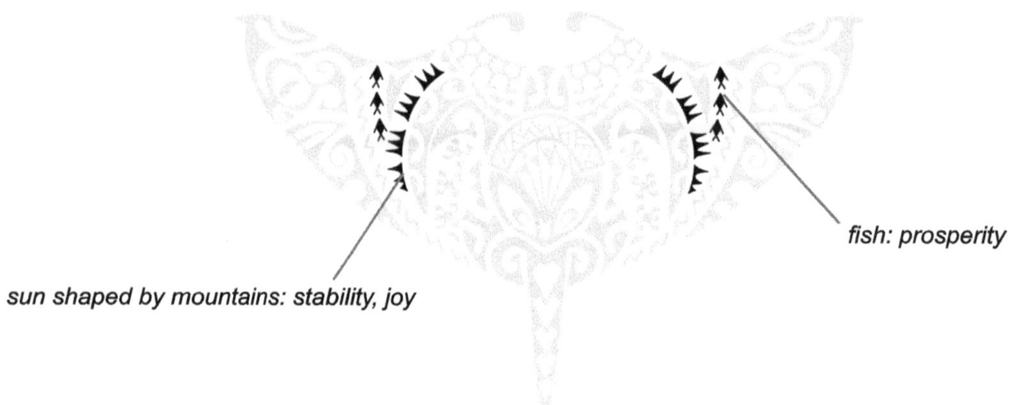

Fig. 5.7: The sun shines on the family.

Figure 5.8 shows how the shell of the turtle was designed using flax leaves surrounded by a braid. They are both symbolic of unity, with the braid made by weaving fibers together like the relations between family members. As a braid, which is much stronger as a whole than its fibers

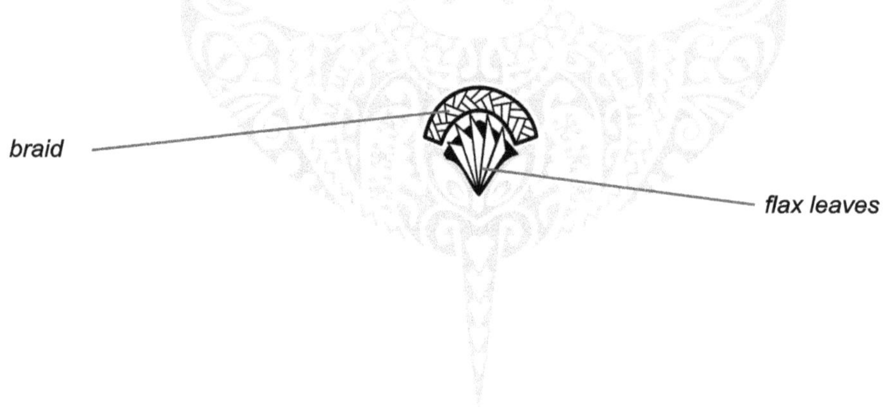

Fig. 5.8: Family union.

separately, a community is much stronger than its single elements, and the more fibers are joined together, the stronger the cord will be.

Another important element is protection, represented by the two *tiki* figures placed externally on the wings of the manta, which enclose the family, guarding it from all sides. Another protective element is the face of a *taniwha* (it will be discussed further in the Maori chapter) that shapes the lower half of the shell, as shown in figure 5.9.

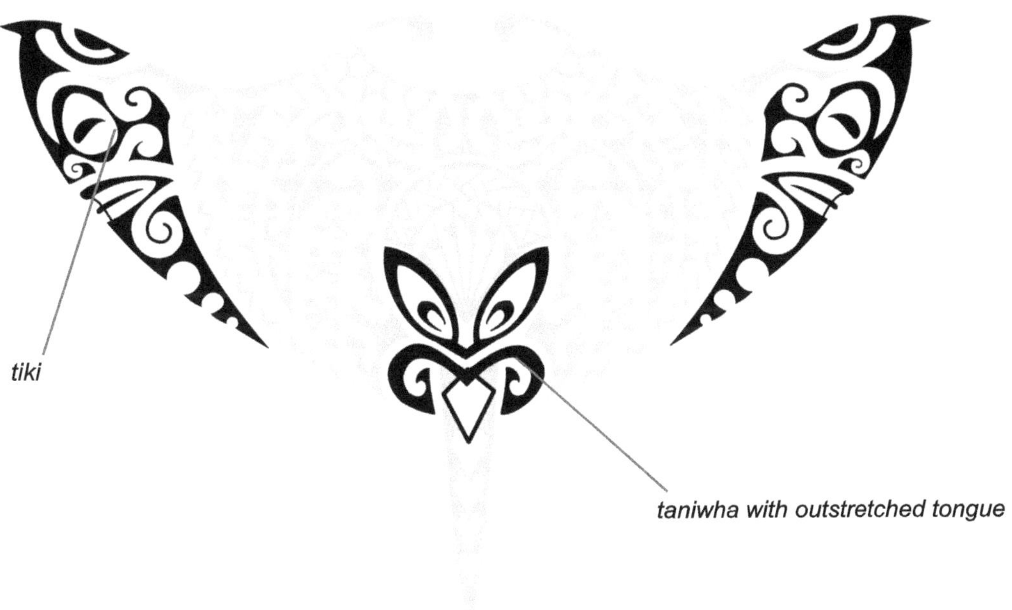

Fig. 5.9: Protective spirits.

The last theme included relates to the warrior, as shown in figure 5.10.

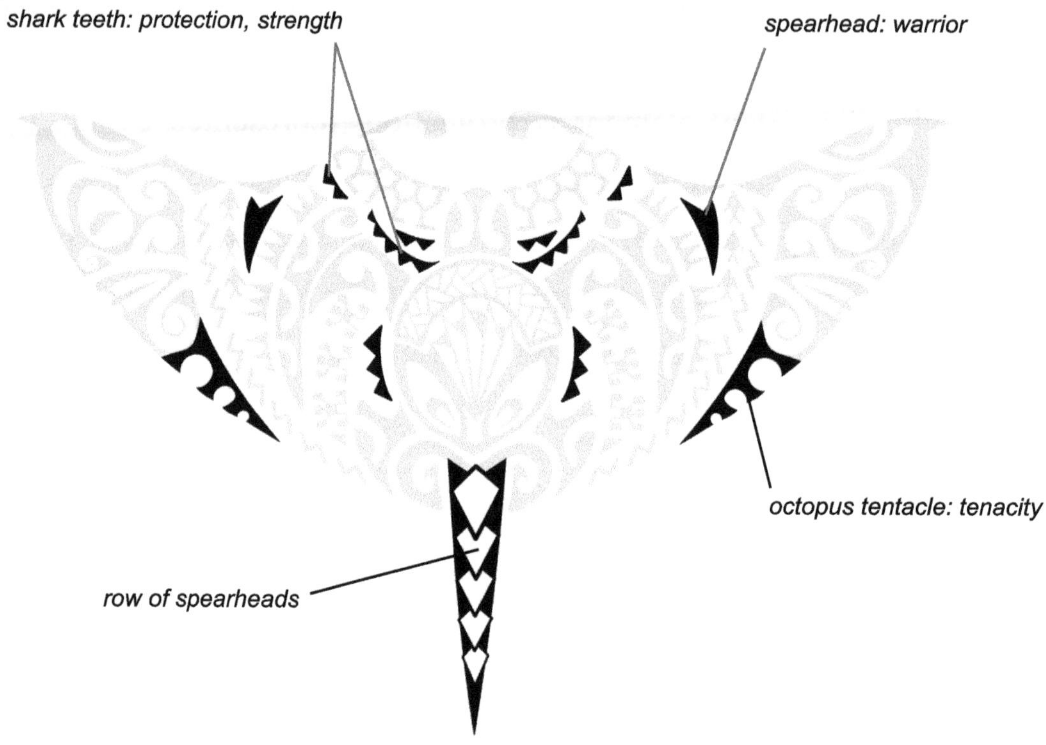

Fig. 5.10: Warrior qualities.

Spearheads are symbolic of the warrior who protects his family, while shark teeth and the octopus tentacles symbolize tenacity and adaptability. Keeping family-related elements central and surrounding them with warrior and protective symbols is a common way to structure a tattoo that aims to bring protection to the family.

Half sleeve

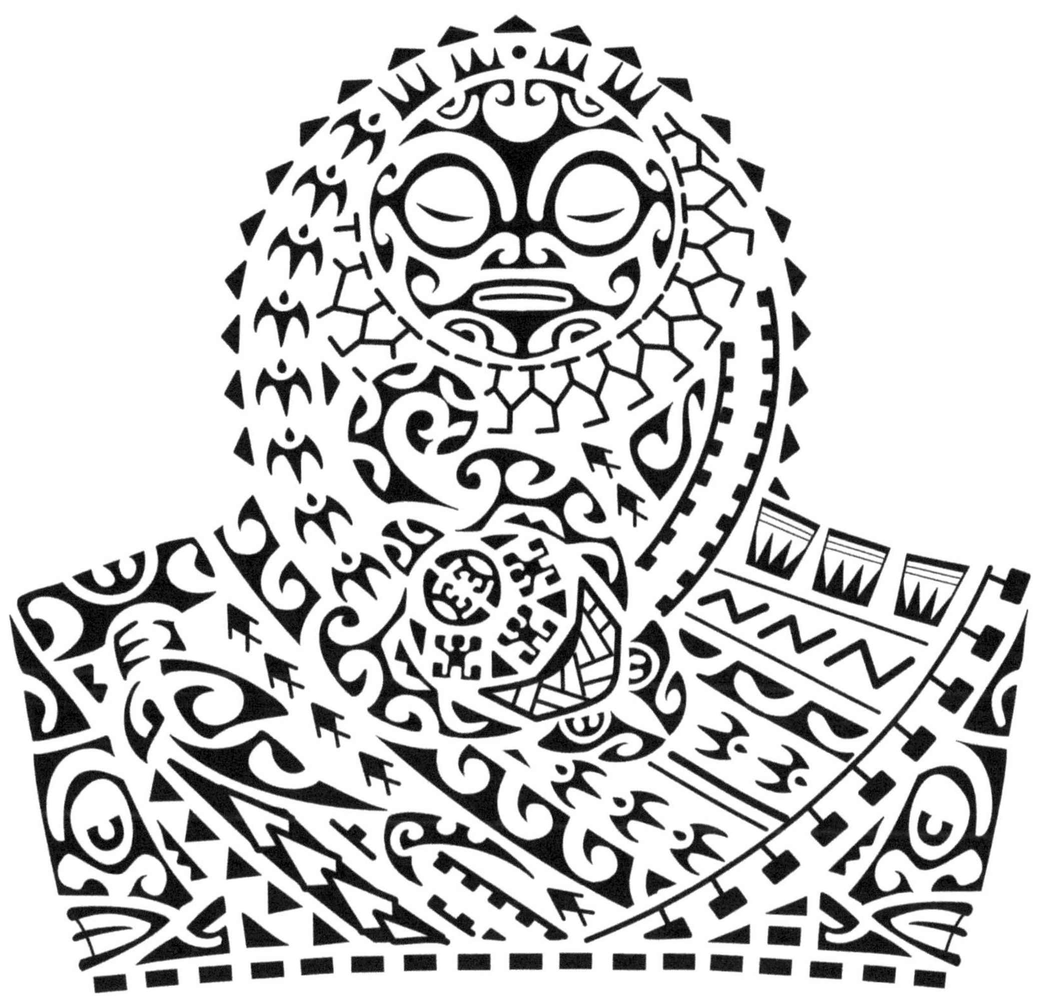

Request: *a half sleeve representing a family that left in search of fortune and is now going back to the island of the ancestors.*

This design includes three composite animals, as shown in figure 5.11: a turtle, a hammerhead shark, and a manta.

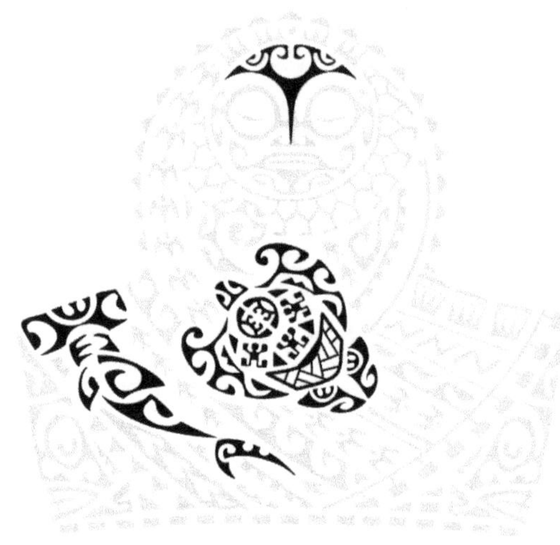

Fig. 5.11: Turtle, hammerhead shark, and manta.

The turtle was chosen to symbolize family, the hammerhead shark represents a warrior, tenacity, and determination, and the manta symbolizes freedom.

The turtle is moving along the path shown by the row of birds (see fig. 5.14), with the hammerhead shark on its side as a protector, while the manta on top represents the freedom waiting at the end of the voyage. The family-related elements are shown in figures 5.12 and 5.13. The turtle includes five *'enata*, two of which are coupled to represent the parents, and the other three are placed around them for their children.

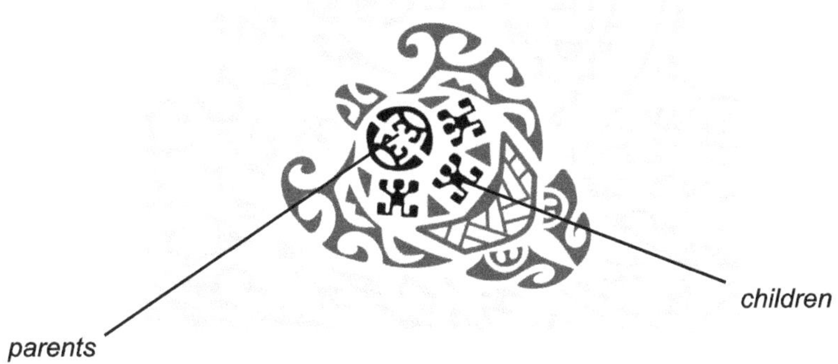

Fig. 5.12: Close family.

The *'ani ata* motif above the turtle, surrounding the face of the *tiki*, represents ancestors guarding the family from above while the *fa'aanufe* motif behind the turtle represents the extended family left on the island.

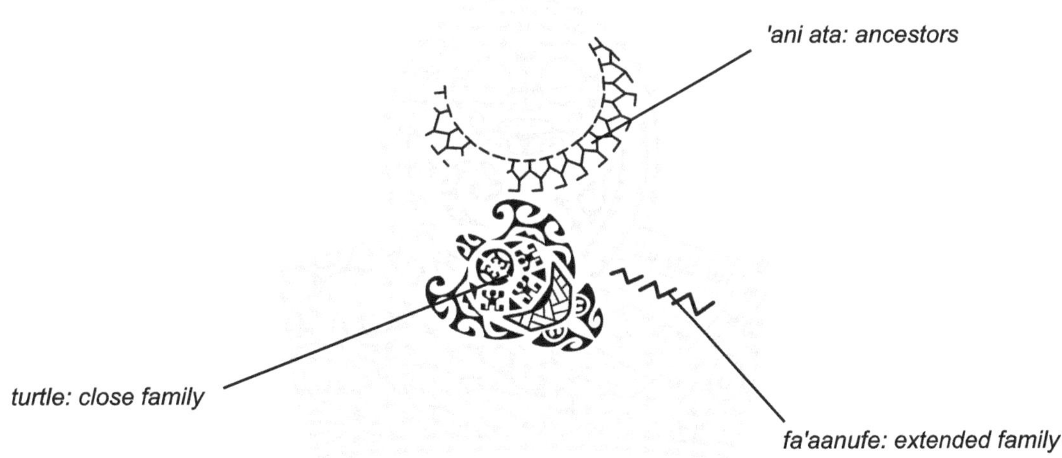

Fig. 5.13: Family-related elements.

The voyage theme is represented by two rows of birds: a shorter one that goes backward, opposite to the direction of the turtle, representing the first voyage that brought the family far from their homeland, and a

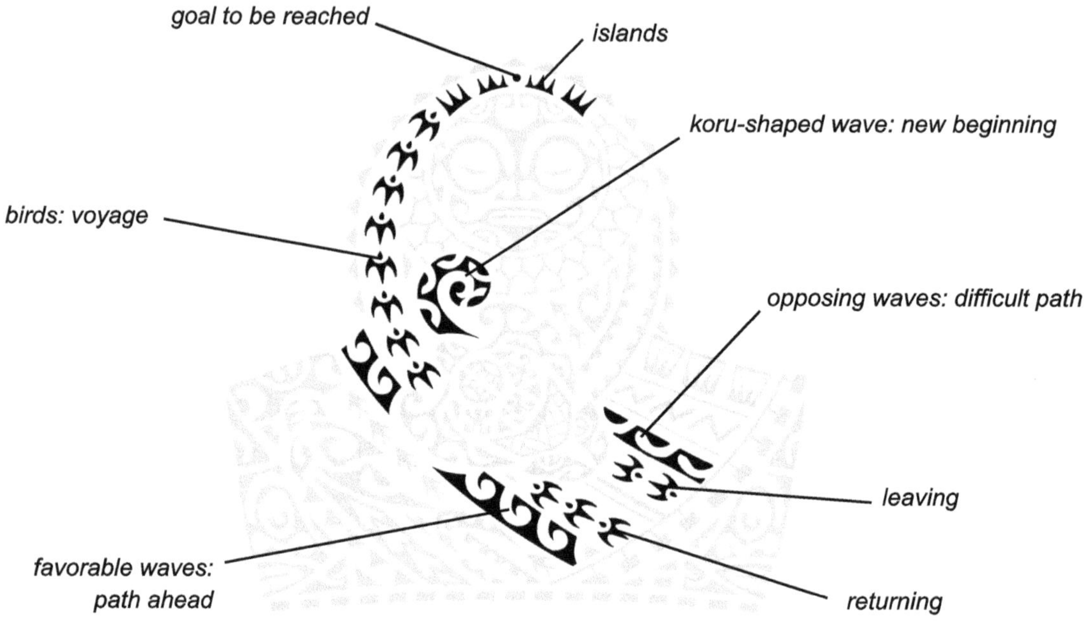

Fig. 5.14: Voyage theme.

longer one that goes forward ahead of the turtle marking the path to the land of the ancestors. The dot in front of the manta symbolizes importance, the goal to be reached, and the mountains on its sides symbolize islands.

Both rows of birds are flanked by waves. They flow against the turtle on the first voyage (showing difficulties) and along with it on the voyage back, symbolizing a positive change leading to a new start, as represented by the *koru*-shaped wave in front of the turtle. (We'll describe the *koru* in the Maori chapter.) The motif of the path of Kamehameha placed in the past, near the beginning of the voyage, symbolizes the difficult challenges that caused the family to depart.

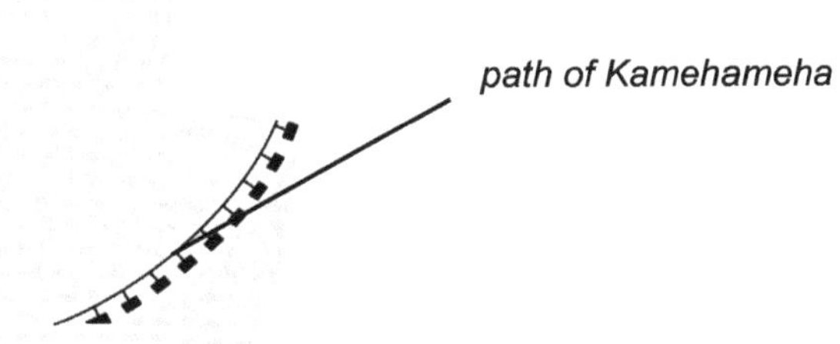

Fig. 5.15: Path of Kamehameha. Difficult challenges.

Two *tiki* figures on the sides of the tattoo join around the arm, and together with the third *tiki* placed centrally on top of the shoulder, they bring protection to the family from all directions.

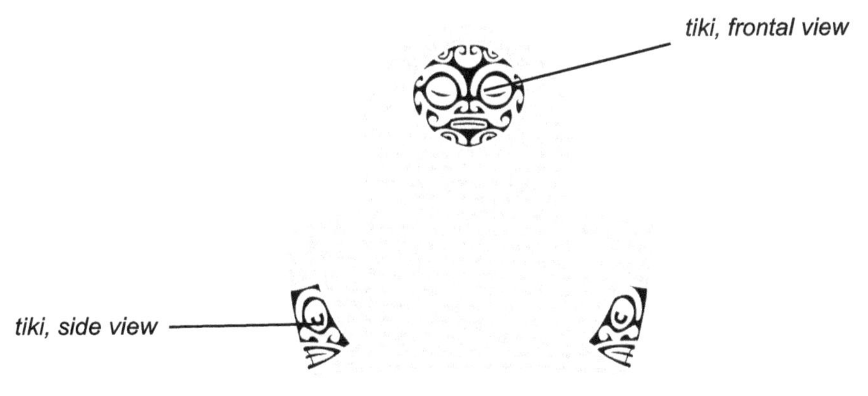

Fig. 5.16: Protection from all sides.

The line of stones at the base represents achievements, which brought prosperity (the coconut leaves, the fish, and the fish hook), stability (the mountains on top), and success (the sun encircling the shoulder, also symbolizing joy and eternity).

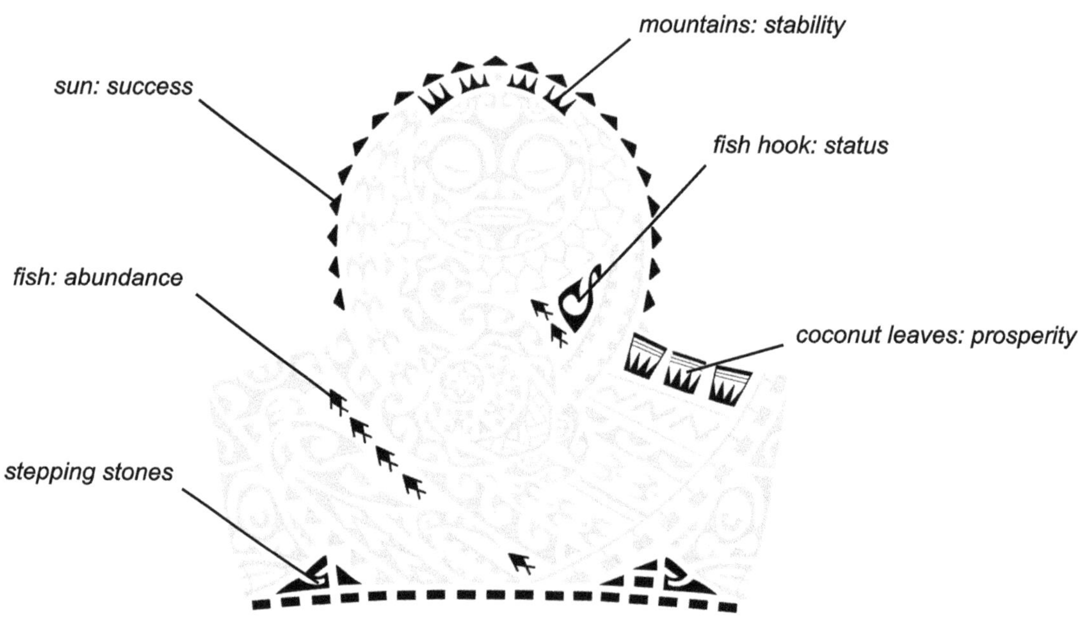

Fig. 5.17: Achievements.

Band

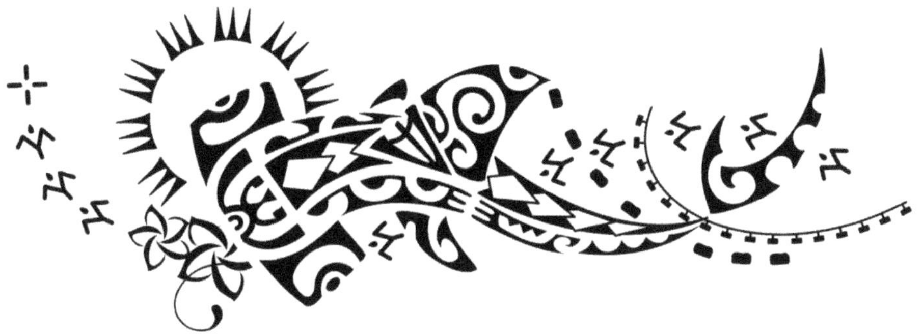

Request: *ankle band for a woman representing protection and tenacity to pursue and achieve every goal in life.*

The greatest strength of modern Tahitian tattoos is probably their versatility. The shape and position of these tattoos are not strictly coded and they can help define the meanings, like in this example where the band is not straight-edged, giving life and movement to the design, with the main element being a hammerhead shark.

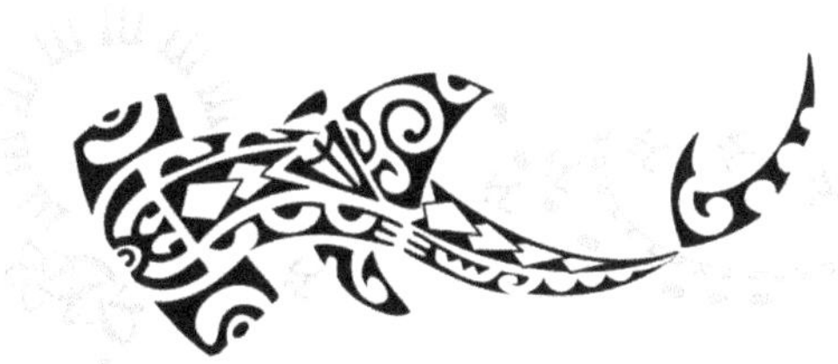

Fig. 5.18: The hammerhead shark (tenacity, strength).

The hammerhead shark is a symbol of tenacity and strength, and it represents the warrior who fights to reach the desired goals. A female *'enata* holding spearheads above her head extends this concept, ending with an octopus tentacle symbolizing tenacity and adaptability. All these characteristics are needed to face any challenge, turning it into a new achievement as shown in figure 5.20, where the trials of the path of Kamehameha become stepping stones, new marks along the voyage that leads to success.

Fig. 5.19: Warrior symbols.

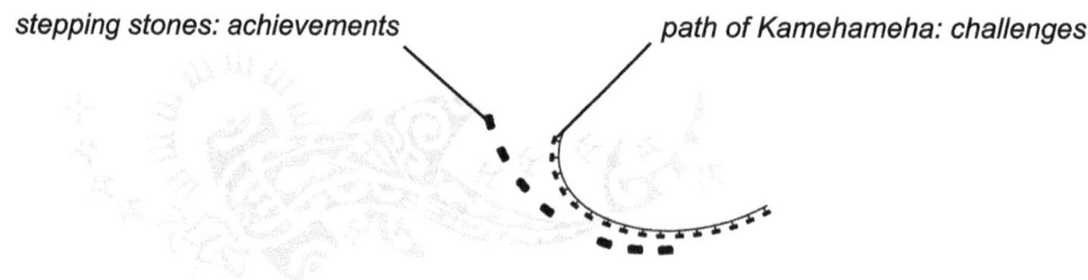

Fig. 5.20: Turning challenges into achievements.

The row of birds represents the voyage, with a star at its end to symbolize the goal ahead, the fixed point at the end of the path. The sun nearby symbolizes success, with mountains for stability.

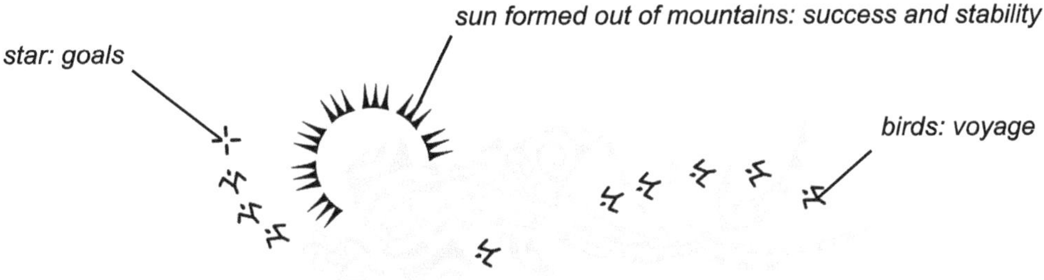

Fig. 5.21: The path leading to the desired goals.

The hammerhead shark includes several protection symbols: a *tiki* face on the back fin, *tiki* eyes for the shark, *tiki* hands, and plumerias, which symbolize femininity and safe shelter.

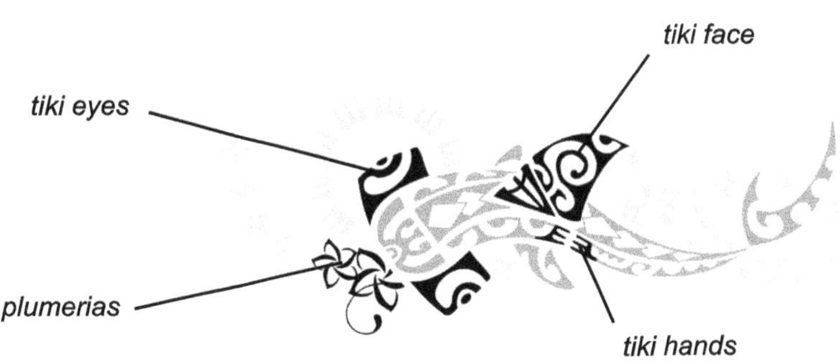

Fig. 5.22: Protection symbols.

'A'ohe pu'u ki'eki'e ke ho'ā'o 'ia e pi'i

"No cliff is so tall it cannot be climbed."

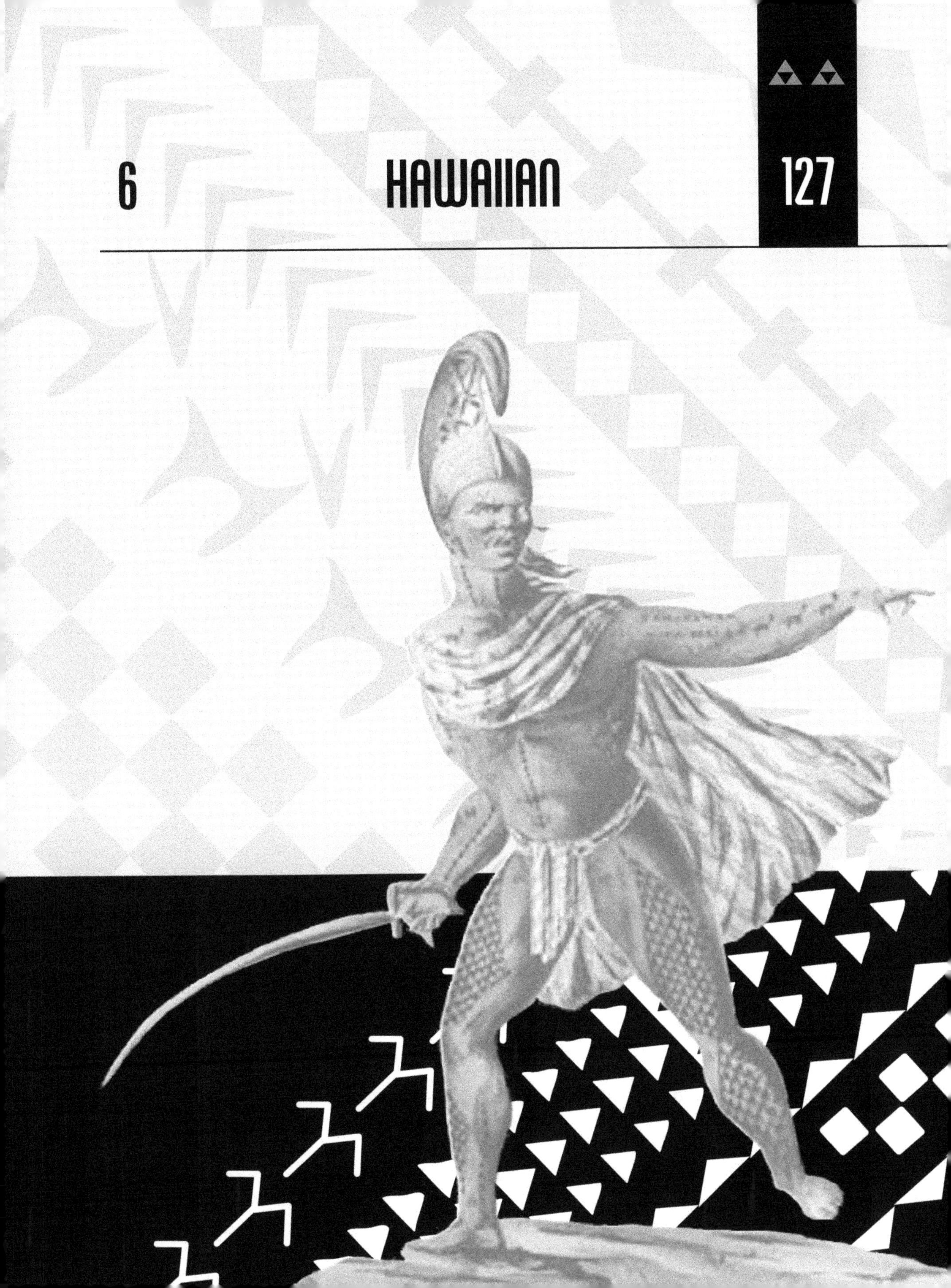

6 HAWAIIAN

" 'A'ohe pu'u ki'eki'e ke ho'a'o 'ia e pi'i."

—***No cliff is so tall it cannot be climbed***:

Any goal can be achieved.

Features: originally highly geometric, currently more figurative.

Purpose: embellishment, protection, community.

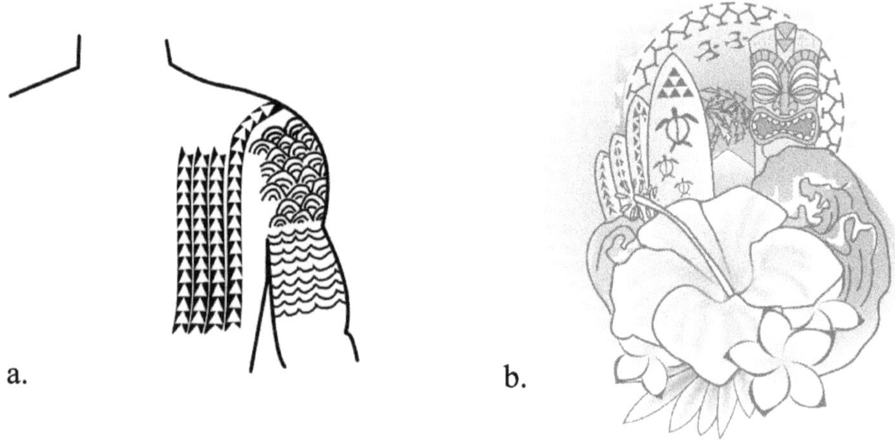

a. b.

Fig. 6.1: (a) Hawaiian traditional tattoo after Webber, 1778, and (b) modern "tiki" tattoo.

i. about the style

Hawaiian tattoos unfortunately shared the same fate of Tahitian tattoos, being abandoned after the arrival of missionaries and the conversion to

Christianity of a great part of the population.

Similar to what happened in the Society Islands, the whole Hawaiian archipelago was unified into a single kingdom. In Hawai'i this was achieved by Kamehameha I, who subdued the other chiefs in battle or through alliances. In the beginning this did not affect the system of beliefs of the Hawaiian people, as Kamehameha was a high priest by birth, son of a king, and a keeper of traditions who strove to preserve the culture. After his death though, the old political system crumbled, and so did most of the autonomy and lore that had been preserved against European and American influences. The art of traditional tattooing in particular, which had already undergone some changes by including foreign elements, met with an ever stronger opposition from missionaries, and it was eventually marginalized and abandoned.

The invention of the tattoo machine in the United States by the end of the nineteenth century made it easier and quicker to get a tattoo, and sailors traveling to Polynesia were the perfect match for this new trend. Artists like Sailor Jerry settled in Honolulu over the following decades and popularized a style known as "old school", where classic maritime themes like ships, swallows, and nautical stars, to name some of its most iconic designs, blended in with Polynesian themes like hula dancers, tropical islands, and palms. This revived colorful style became immensely popular among the American soldiers based in Hawai'i during World War II, consolidating itself as the recognized local style and spreading throughout Polynesia to the USA and to Europe, marking the tattoo scene during almost three decades. When the old school style started to lose momentum during the second half of the twentieth century, Hawaiian tattoos evolved again to include designs rich with floral elements, surf culture themes, and references borrowed from the so-called "*tiki* culture" and its imagery, as well as copies of ancient petroglyphs.

When traditional Polynesian tattooing had its revival toward the end of the twentieth century, the Hawaiians found themselves with almost no sources to refer to, until scholars and artists alike started to research the reports from the early explorers and the mummified remains found on burial grounds on the island of Hawai'i, to find information on ancient traditional designs.

The drawings by Choris (Kotzebue expedition, 1816) and William Ellis (Freycinet expedition, 1819) represent the most valuable resources to gain an insight into the ancient symbols and to help identify some of them along with their significance. Unfortunately, they do not record the meanings of all of the depicted symbols, and in some cases tattoo artists had to resort to the identical designs known from *kapa* clothes decorations in order to have clues about their significance.

Other important sources were the writings left by John Papa I'i and Samuel Kamakau, who described the life and customs of the Hawaiian society around the mid-nineteenth century, and also the works of Kenneth P. Emory and Sir Peter Buck. We must notice though that all these last works were produced in a time when the Hawaiian way of living had already undergone great changes following the conversion to Christianity.

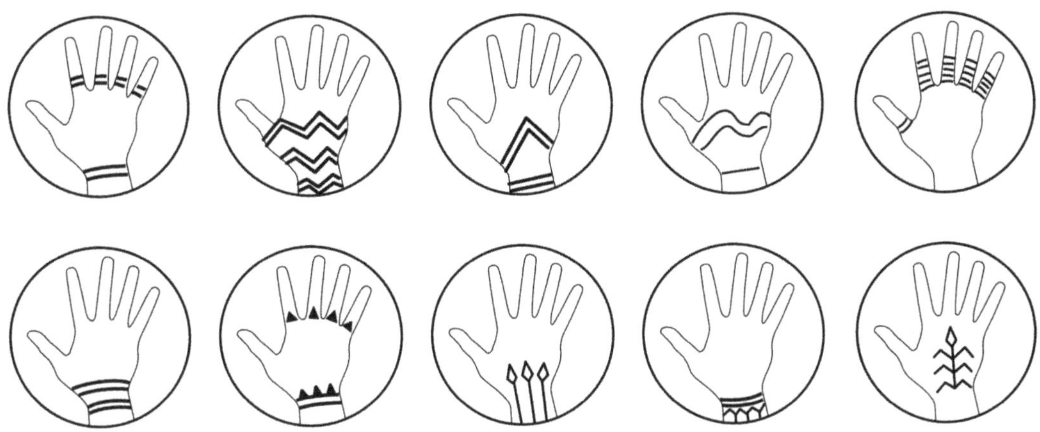

Fig. 6.2: Female hand tattoos. After a drawing by K. P. Emory, 1946.

Hawaiian motifs, like all Polynesian designs, possess several layers of meaning (*kaona* in the Hawaiian language), and their inherent significance may depend on the position of the symbols, on their orientation, and on their association with other elements of the tattoo.

Over the last decades, Hawaiian native artists like Keone Nunes have played a fundamental role in revitalizing the art of tattoo tapping in its more traditional form and significance, becoming a reference to the Hawaiian community in much the same way as the Sulu'ape family has been to the Samoan one.

Even more important than this process of regaining the symbols has been the process of regaining a cultural identity. Hawaiian tattoos represent a heritage, a foundation, and a way of looking at the past to shape the future. A Hawaiian word, *kuleana*, identifies this concept: it is translated as “a two-way responsibility”, and has a deep meaning to it. It embodies the strong relation that exists between all things, the people, and the ancestors. For example, if people care for the land, the land will care for them. We are all interconnected, and the wealth and well-being of the land is our own wealth and well-being. A symbol representing this is shown in figure 6.3. It’s called *lō kahi*, which means “unity, agreement”, and it is shaped by three connected triangles representing the world of people, the world of spirits, and the land. They are three parts of a single entity, and all of them are related and equally important. The white triangular shape left in the middle of the symbol represents light emerging through darkness, tradition, and balance between *pō* and *ao*. Its ubiquity in Hawaiian patterns is a testimony of its importance.

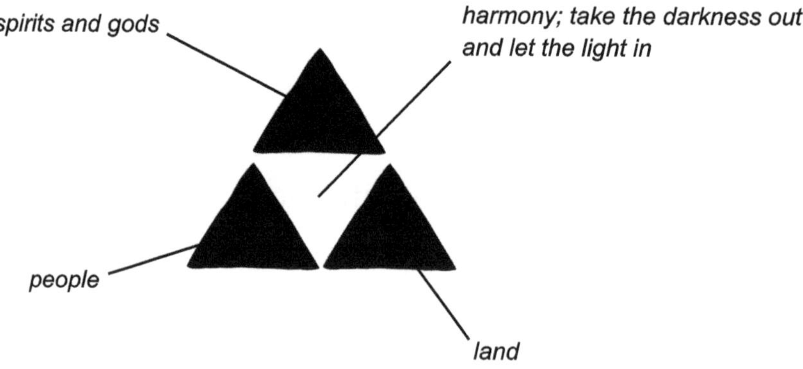

Fig. 6.3: Lō kahi, balance and unity. Black symbolizes pō and white represents ao.

Currently, modern and traditional styles coexist in Hawai'i, with the latter being the subject of this chapter.

Hawaiian traditional style, as reported by early explorers, was highly geometrical, based on the repetition of basic patterns, and asymmetrical in its nature, although balance was usually sought between the sides of the body (tattoos on the left upper torso may be balanced by other designs on the right lower torso, for example). As we have seen in the Marquesas, asymmetry was considered a god-like feature and gave warriors a dramatic aspect meant to strike terror into enemies. It has also been noted that the body parts of the warriors being tattooed often correspond to the parts of the body that were not shielded in battle, suggesting the protective purpose of such tattoos.

Men were usually more tattooed than women, and the extension of their tattoos depended much on the island where they lived, to the extent of having half of the body completely tattooed in solid black from head to foot in the case of a group of warriors from the island of Maui.

One of the motifs that appears most frequently in the notes and drawings from various early explorers is a checkered pattern called *papa konane,* or *lau hala*. It is often positioned across the chests of men as a breast plate. *Papa konane* is the name given to the board used in a Hawaiian game similar to checkers, while *lau hala* refers to the taro leaves used to weave mats. Depending on the intention of the tattoo artist, and on the personal experience of the person receiving the tattoo, the design may inherit one or the other meaning.

ii. elements

Ancient Hawaiian tattoos were based on the repetition of very geometrical basic elements, usually arranged in rows. Triangles, arcs, and chevrons are the most recurring shapes, consistently appearing as the foundation of a great part of the elements. This simplicity of forms reinforces the theory that the Hawaiian style and motifs remain the closest to the original ones, having undergone fewer changes than others by means of external contacts and intercultural influences.

Symbol	Name and Meanings	Variants
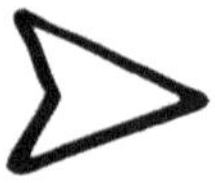	**maka ihe = spearhead** *meaning: duty to protect and to provide, protection, a warrior* This spearhead represents a harpoon, and as such it symbolizes being able to provide for the family. As a weapon it is also representative of warriors, and a symbol of protection.	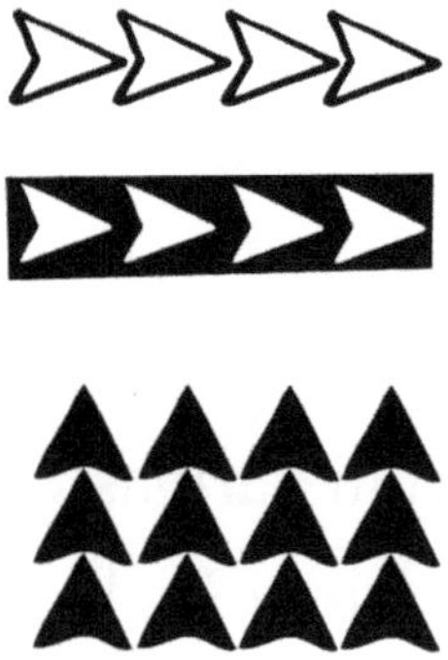

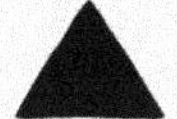

niho manō = shark teeth

meaning: protection

Shark teeth around the ankle are a protective symbol stemming from a popular legend (see vol. 1).

niho niho: *row of teeth*

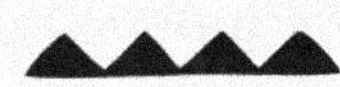 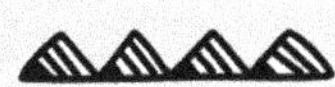

When repeated in several rows they can also symbolize abundance.

papalua: *double*

 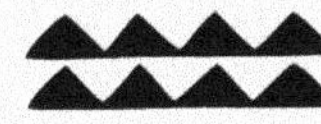

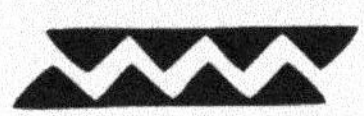

Infinite patterns called *niho mano* can be created, but their use in certain combinations is restricted to specific families.

niho mano: *many teeth*

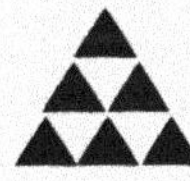 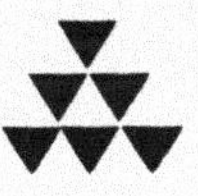 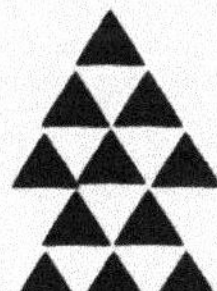

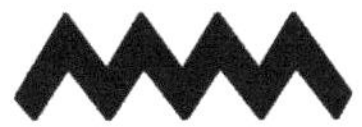

mauna = mountain

meaning: separation, seclusion

Mountains were believed to be home to the gods.

This design can be used to represent a valley enclosed between mountains.

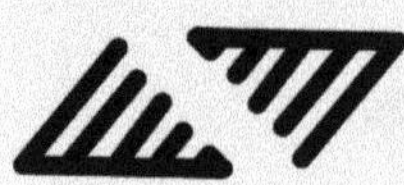

ku pipi = to place thickly together like taros in rows

meaning: community, union, abundance

lei hala = taro garland

meaning: wisdom, a rite of passage

Such garlands were given to the young during rites of passage, and they were also worn by chiefs and priests as a symbol of wisdom.

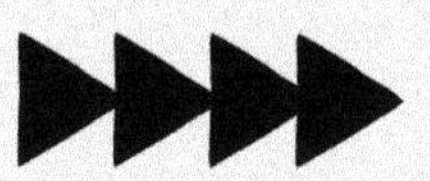

pua hala = taro blossoms

meaning: posterity, descendants, abundance

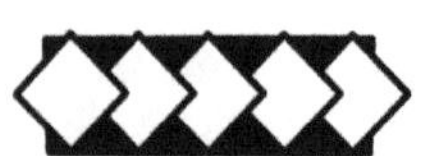

lauloa = long leaf

meaning: foundation, prosperity

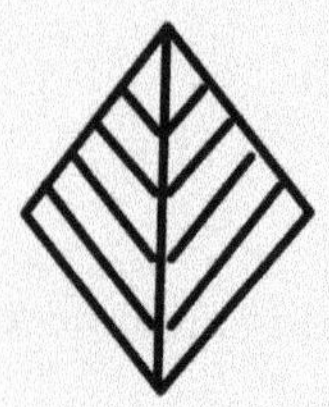

kumu = base, origin

meaning: origins, prosperity

This symbol represents the base of a tree, right above the roots, giving stability to the plant.

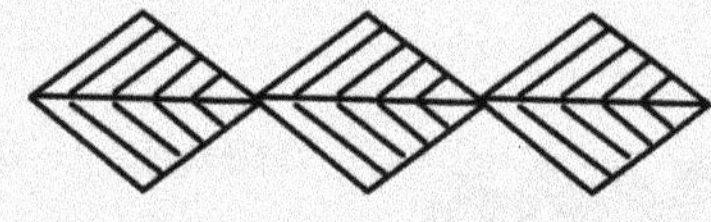

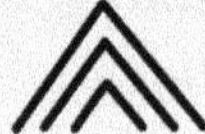

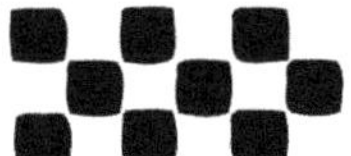

lau hala = taro leaf

meaning: protection, union

This pattern, often worn across the breast, mimics a woven mat, made strong by the tight union of its composing fibers.

It is also known as *papa konane*, a board game similar to chess, which symbolizes thinking before acting.

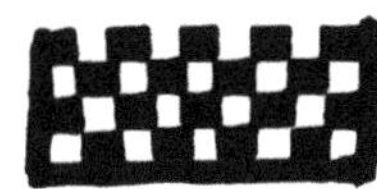

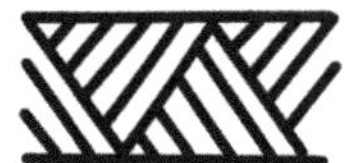

papa konane: *konane board*

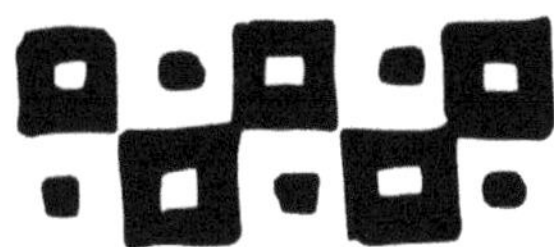

māhā 'upena = fishing net

meaning: providing, prosperity, unity

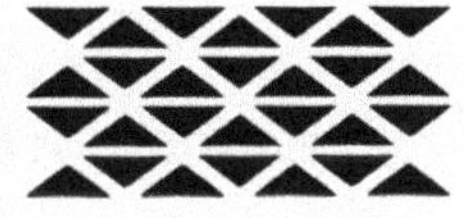

kapua'i = steps

meaning: footprints of the ancestors

This is derived by the footprints of the golden plover (*tuli*, a sacred bird and a messenger of the god Kanaloa).

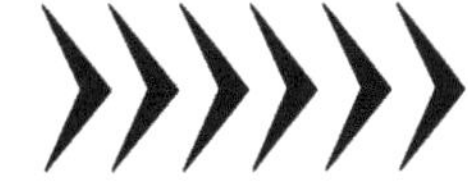

'anuenue = rainbow

meaning: connection to the gods, messenger

'Anuenue, the rainbow maiden, was a messenger for her brothers, the gods Kāne and Kanaloa.

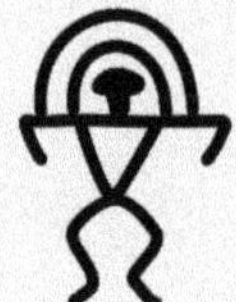

kai = ocean

meaning: origins, ocean

The source of life of the Polynesian people, and also their place of rest.

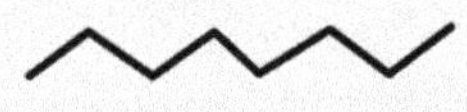

anuhe = worm

meaning: people

hulu = feathers

meaning: status, high rank

Feathers were treasured to make chiefly cloaks, and the feathers of the red-tailed tropic bird were especially sought after, as red was the color reserved for royalty.

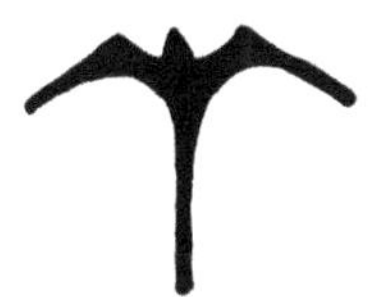

koa'e'ula = red-tailed tropic bird

meaning: a traveler who safely returns home

The red-tailed tropic bird is a revered bird whose feathers were reserved for the high chiefs.

Birds are among the symbols that can be used to represent people. Another common element for people is a small square:

 a person

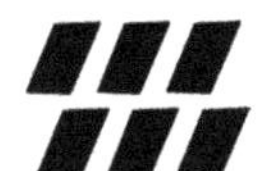 a family

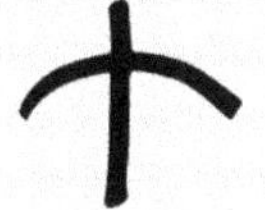

koa'e = tropic bird

meaning: family members, safe return

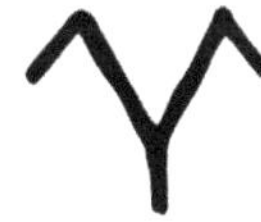

manu = bird

meaning: divine connection, travel

frigate bird:
a voyager

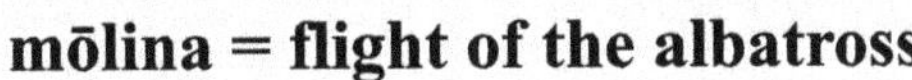

mōlina = flight of the albatross

meaning: longevity, patience, perseverance

pe'ahi = fan

meaning: status, prestige, protection from death

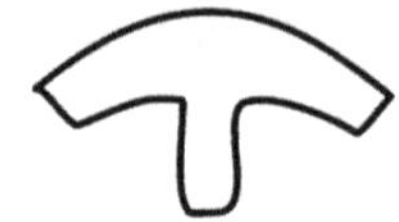

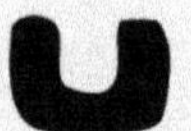

wa'a = canoe

meaning: seaman, connection to the ocean and to ancestors

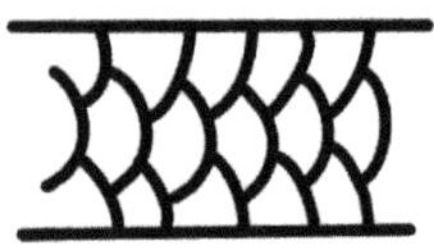

uhu = parrot fish

meaning: headstrong, stubborn

The parrot fish teeth are arranged tightly on the outside of the mouth, in a sort of parrot-like beak that allows them to crunch corals in search for algae.

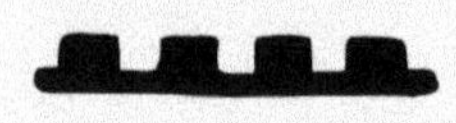

pikapika o ka he'e = octopus suction cups

meaning: tenacity, ability to gain and retain knowledge

It's also known as *pilipili he'e* ("octopus tentacles").

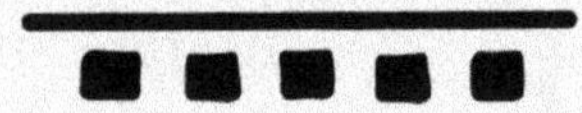

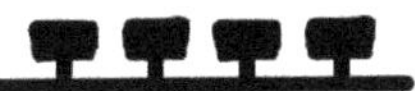

ala nui o Kamehameha = Kamehameha's great path

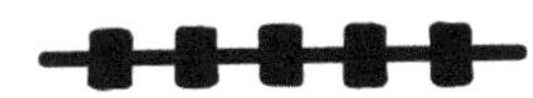

meaning: a difficult path that leads to success

The elements added along the line symbolize the challenges and trials found along the path.

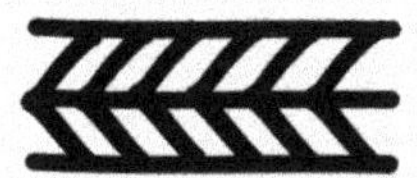

nā iwi puhi = eel crest

meaning: protection

kuhanu = breath of Ku

meaning: balance, light emerging through darkness, creation

Ku is the Hawaiian god of war, and he is related to the dualism of life and death.

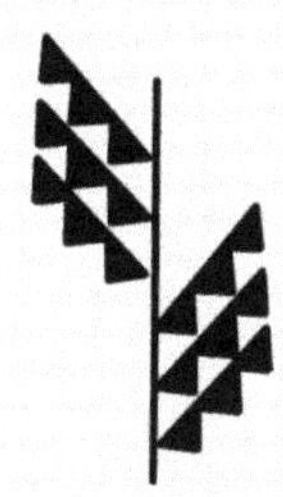

kupukupu = fern

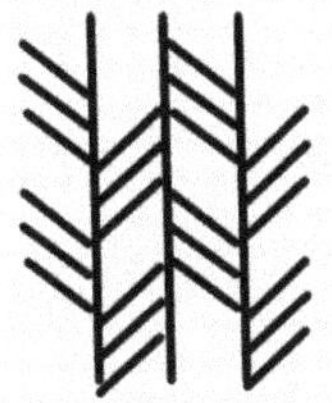

meaning: growth, descendants, to ascend

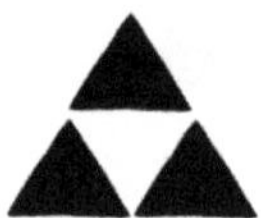

lō kahi = unity, agreement

meaning: harmony, balance

hōaka = crescent

meaning: possibly used to symbolize tradition, lineage

pō = darkness, night

meaning: deep knowledge, sacredness

Other elements that sometimes are included in traditional tattoos are ancient petroglyphs such as the following:

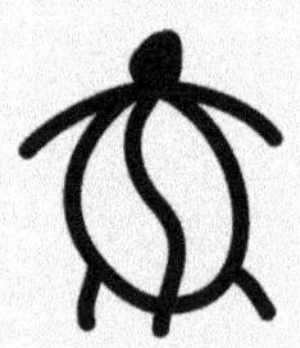

honu / ea = turtle

meaning: family, navigator, protection, longevity

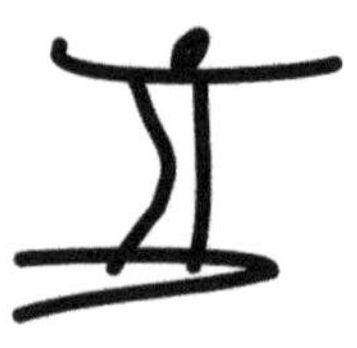

paka = to slide on a wave

meaning: surfer, connection to the ocean

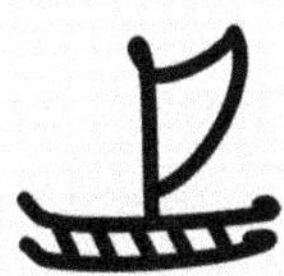

wa'a kaulua = double-hulled canoe

meaning: seafaring, voyages, connection to the ocean

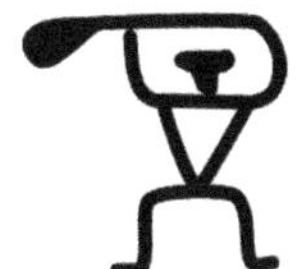

kupe = person with the steering paddle

meaning: direction, guide, leader

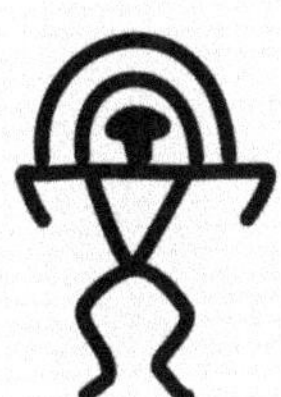

'Anuenue = the rainbow maiden

meaning: messenger of the gods, protection

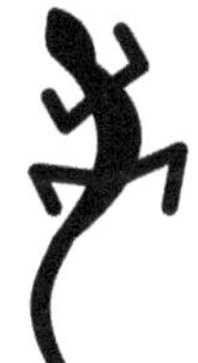

mo'o = lizard

meaning: protection, communication with the gods, intuition

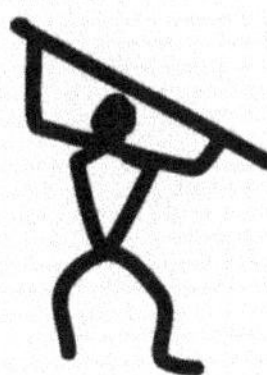

pahelo = to throw a spear

meaning: ability, hunter, to provide

iii. tattoo examples walkthrough

The three tattoos explored in the previous chapters are here redesigned using Hawaiian motifs in a traditional style. As it is immediately evident, the repetition of rows of basic elements is a strong feature of this style, where dark and light areas are mutually balanced and equally important, representing the balance between *pō* and *ao*, darkness and light, the realm of spirits, from where all knowledge comes, and the world of the living.

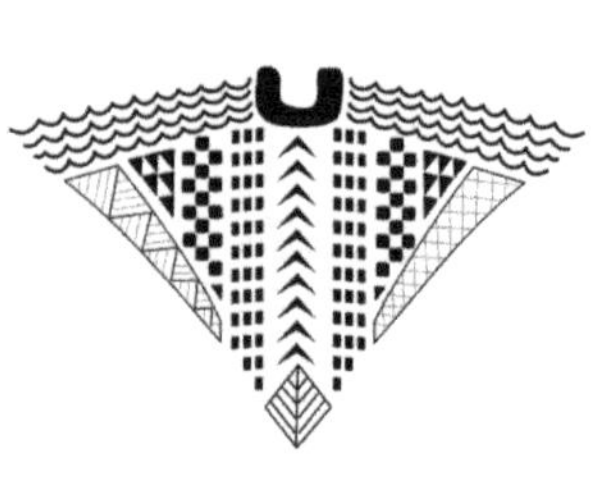

Upper back manta,
man

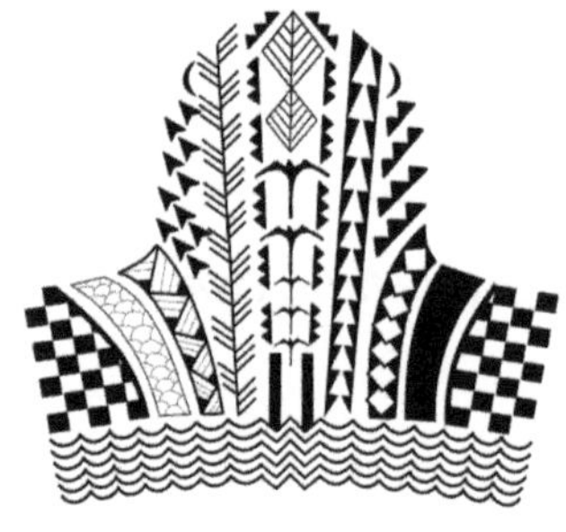

Half sleeve,
man

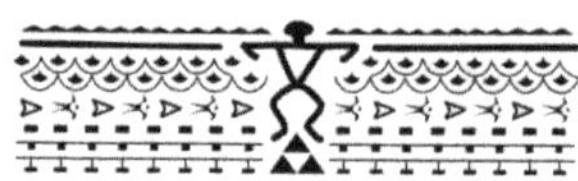

Band,
woman

Upper back manta

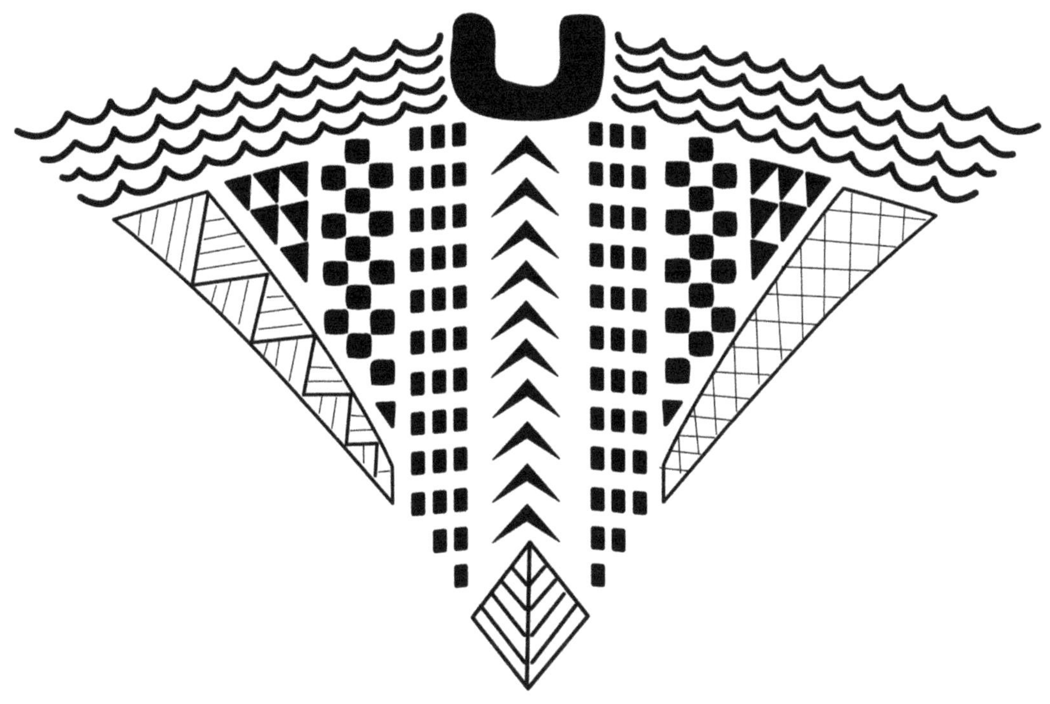

Request: *a manta for the upper back representing the centrality of family and traditions, and protection of the family.*

The predominant theme of this tattoo is family, represented as a whole unique entity extending from the very first ancestors to the present. We maintained the ancestors' central position, as this concept is a constant throughout the whole Polynesian area. Figure 6.4 shows the *wa'a* on top surrounded by the ocean, representing the canoe with which the ancestors crossed the ocean reaching Hawai'i. Their deeds set the roots of the new culture, positioned at the base of the tattoo to give it stability.

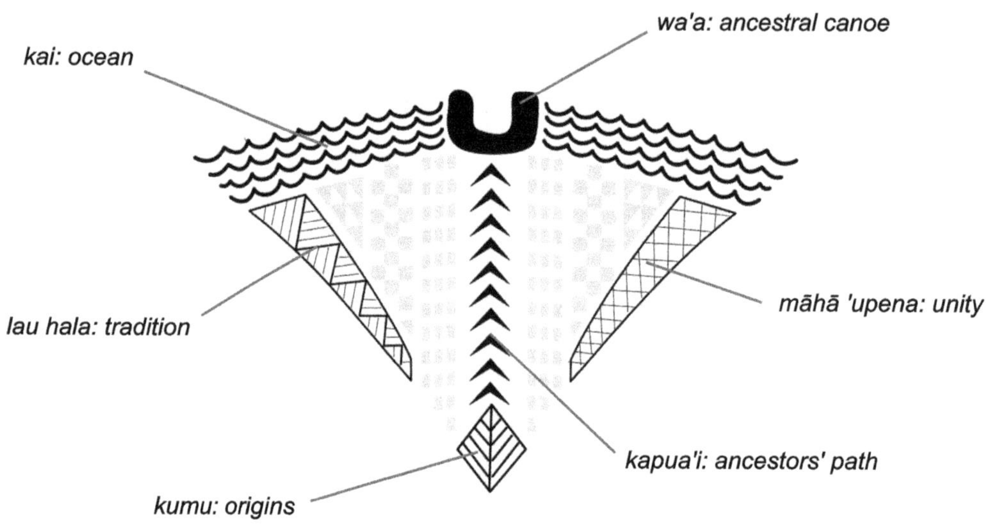

Fig. 6.4: Ancestors and traditions are the backbone of the family.

On the sides of the ancestors' path, embracing the family in the middle, there are two motifs representing tradition and unity, the founding values of Hawaiian society. All the people who take part in raising and educating the young are part of the *'ohana*. This groups together the extended family formed by parents, relatives, friends, and educators.

The square elements placed in rows on the sides of the ancestors represent the members of the family, who bring their knowledge and experience in order to make the family stronger.

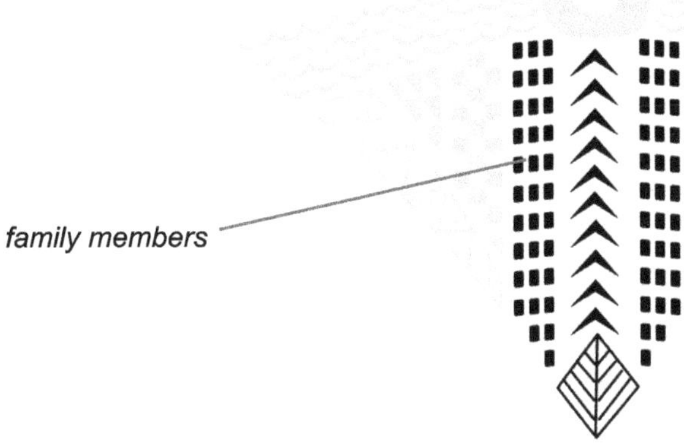

Fig. 6.5: The whole family.

The remaining elements symbolize protection and unity.

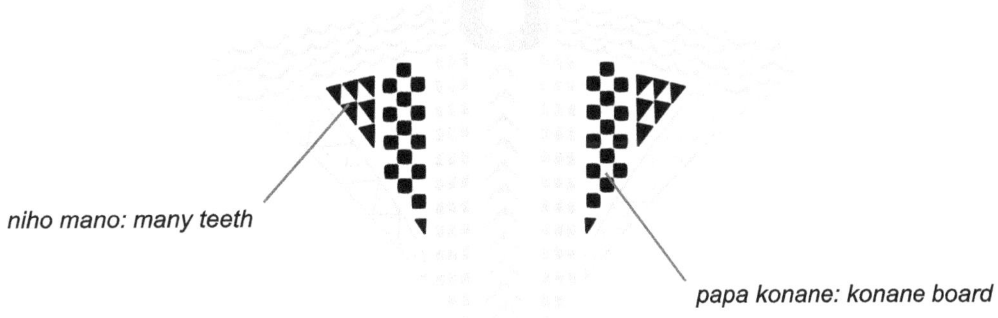

Fig. 6.6: Protection and unity.

Half sleeve

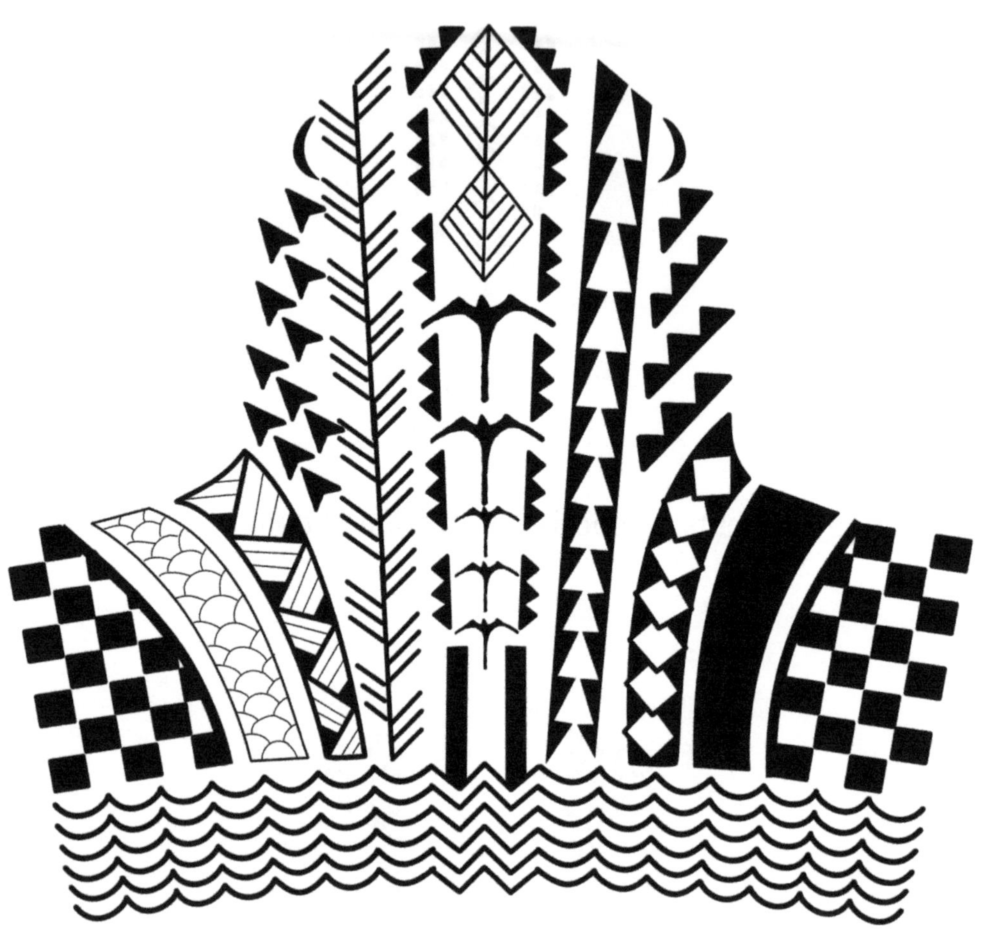

Request: *a half sleeve representing a family that left in search of fortune and is now going back to the island of the ancestors.*

Traditions and family are two deeply interconnected concepts in Polynesia, with traditions being the means by which family lore is preserved and handed down to the next generation. Family is not just the union of its living members, it's a single line that joins them together with the ancestors in the past and the descendants in the future. It can be seen as a tree, where ancestors are the roots and the young are the branches: to grow strong and tall a tree needs good roots, well into the ground. The stronger the roots, the taller the tree can grow.

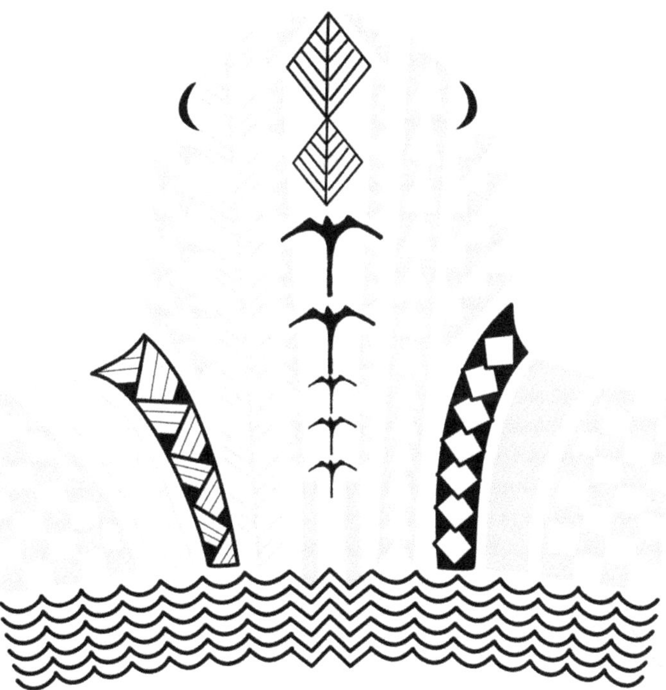

Fig. 6.7: Family and tradition.

Birds are symbolic of voyages and safe return, so we used five of them to represent the five members of the family that have traveled, leaving the rest of the extended family behind (represented by the *anuhe* motif at the base, which is enclosed within the ocean motif).

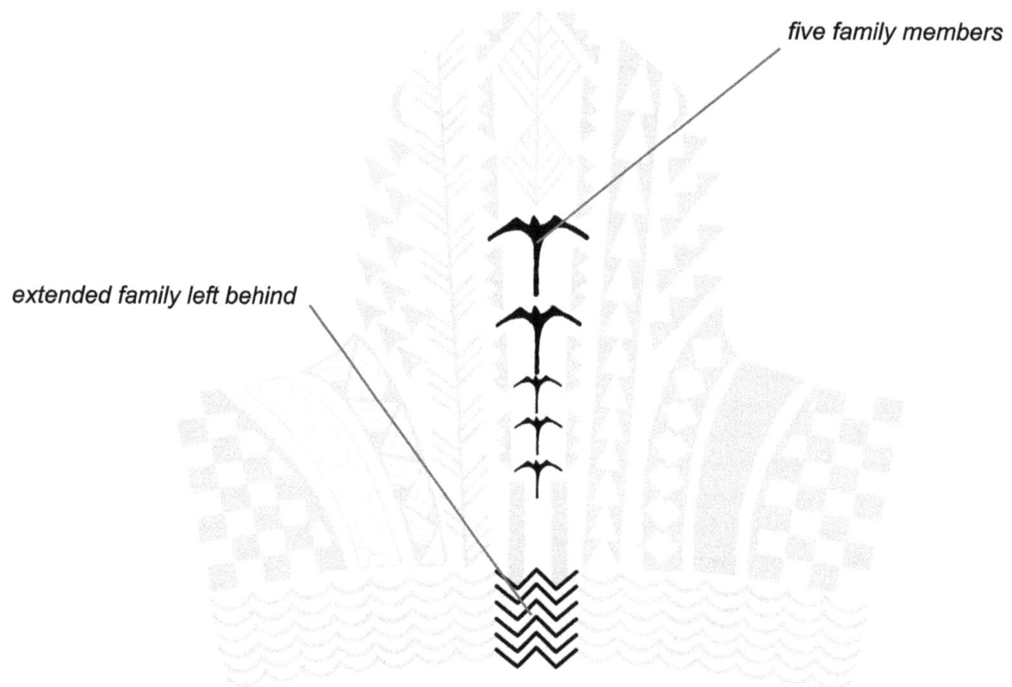

Fig. 6.8: Family-related elements.

The ocean itself symbolizes both the place they came from (their origins) and the ocean that was crossed in search of a new life. The birds are flying toward the *kumu* symbols on top, representing both the prosperity found and the land of the ancestors that is the destination of the voyage back. The crescents on their sides are related to traditions and origins, like the very ocean at the base of the band. The symbols above the ocean shown in figure 6.9 are related to tradition, unity, and prosperity.

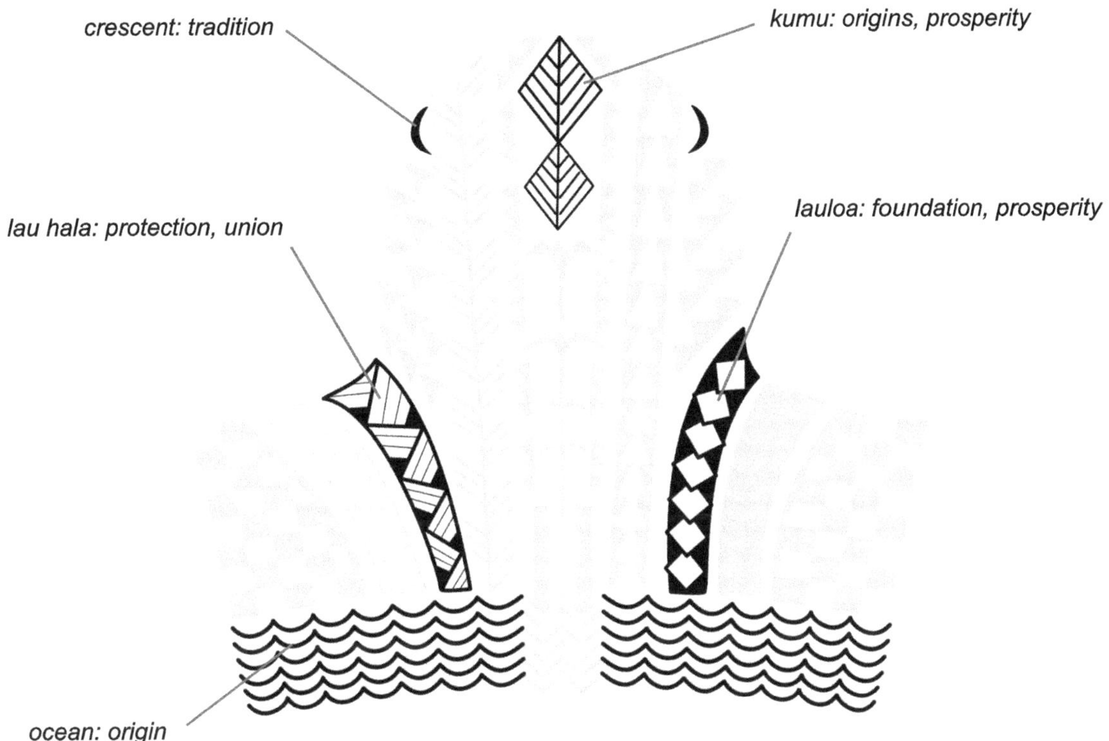

Fig. 6.9: Origins and tradition.

The birds and the ocean are related to the voyage theme too, with the ocean being the place of origin where the extended family still lives. The two lines below the birds, joining them to the extended family, represent the flight of the albatross, *mōlina*, who flies long distances far from land before returning.

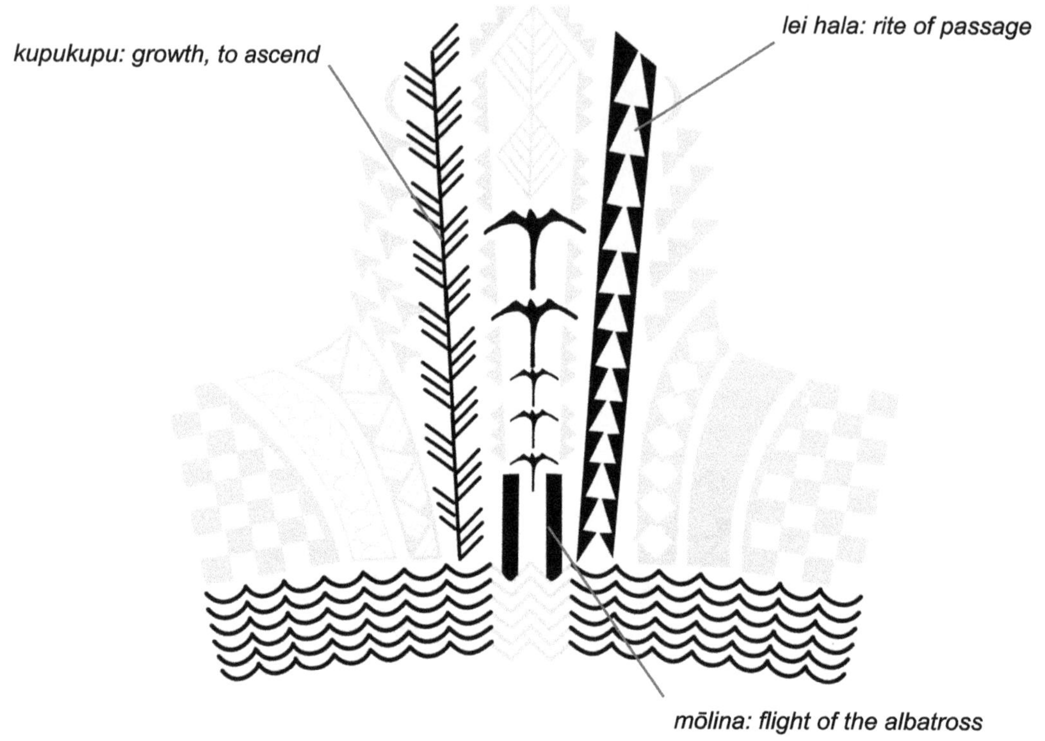

Fig. 6.10: Voyage-related elements.

We placed two more rows of elements on the sides of the birds, relating to the voyage. They symbolize the change that took place, the growth and improvement (*kupukupu*, the fern) brought by the voyage, seen as a rite of passage (*lei hala*, the taro garland) for the family.

On their sides, as well as on the sides of the armband, we placed protective symbols to shield the family from all directions. They are the checkered motif, rows of spearheads, and shark teeth.

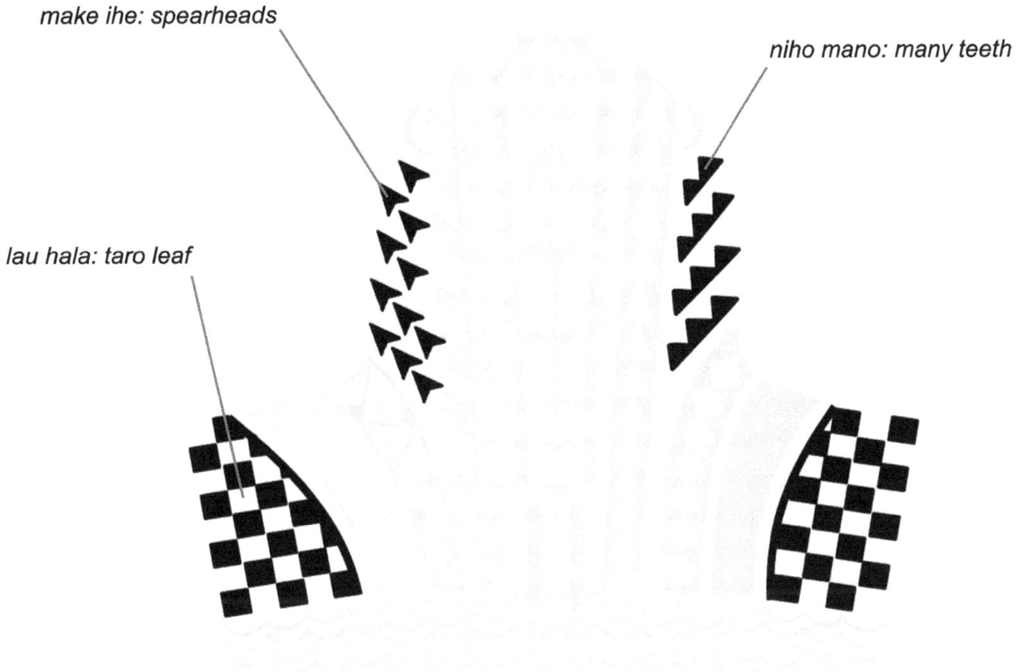

Fig. 6.11: Protective elements.

The last elements, placed on the sides next to the checkered pattern, are a black area in the past and the parrot fish motif in the future. We chose them to symbolize the deep knowledge acquired in the past, which has brought a new view on life, promoting a headstrong and tenacious attitude toward life in the future.

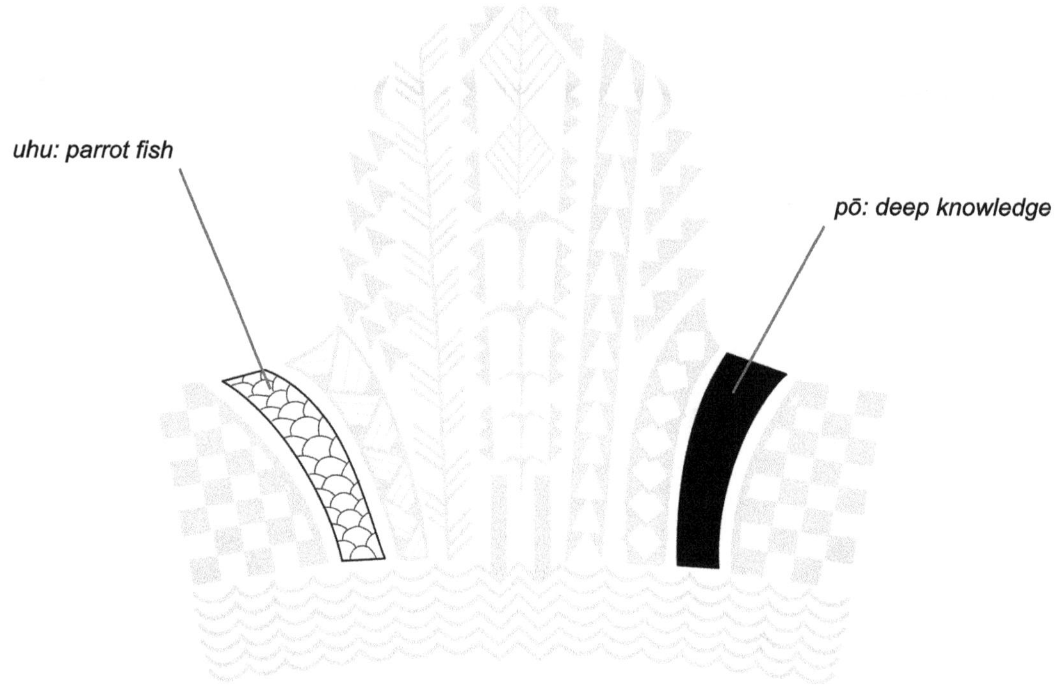

Fig. 6.12: Deep knowledge bringing a tenacious attitude.

Band

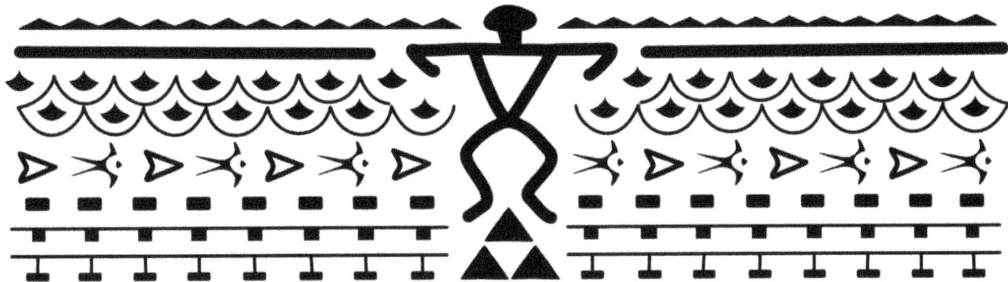

Request: *ankle band for a woman representing protection and tenacity to pursue and achieve every goal in life.*

The central figure of this band represents a woman, and the element below her symbolizes the balance that she found in her life, which gave her the strength to pursue and achieve all of her goals.

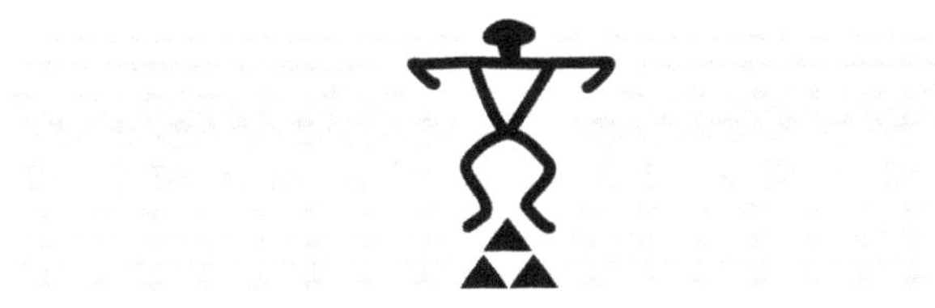

Fig. 6.13: A woman who keeps balance as the base of her life.

From bottom to top, the first three rows of symbols represent the difficult path that leads to success and the tenacity that helps transform each challenge into a teaching, as shown in figure 6.14 below.

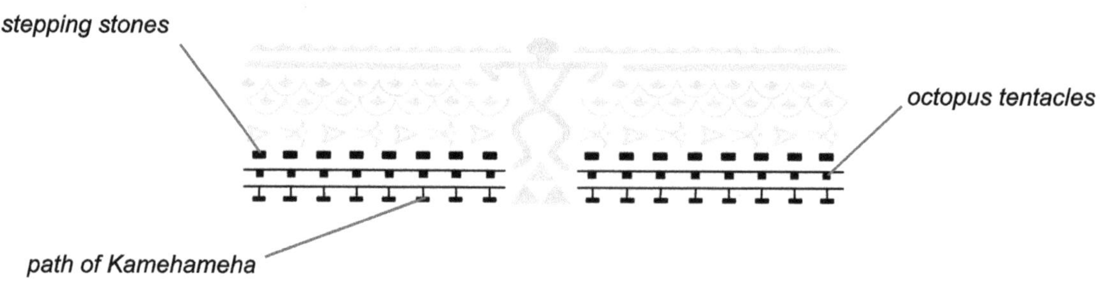

Fig. 6.14: Turning challenges into achievements with tenacity.

The following row includes alternating frigate birds and spearheads to symbolize achieving a higher perspective and a warrior spirit, which bring status and prosperity, as represented by the owl feathers of the next line.

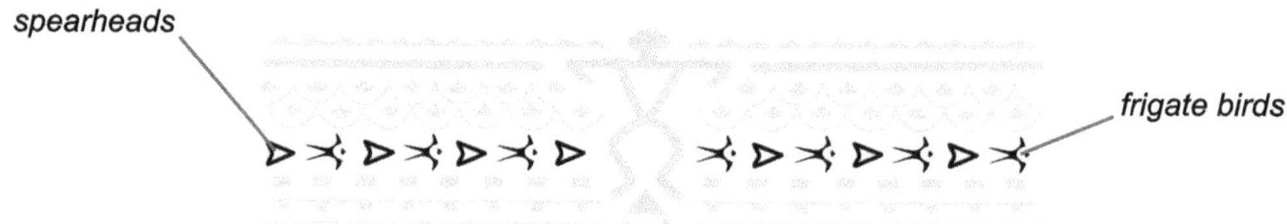

Fig. 6.15: Having a higher perspective and tenacity is the key to achieving success.

Fig. 6.16: A cloak of feathers was representative of chiefs.

The last elements, closing the top of the band, are *niho niho* and *mōlina*, to symbolize protection during voyages:

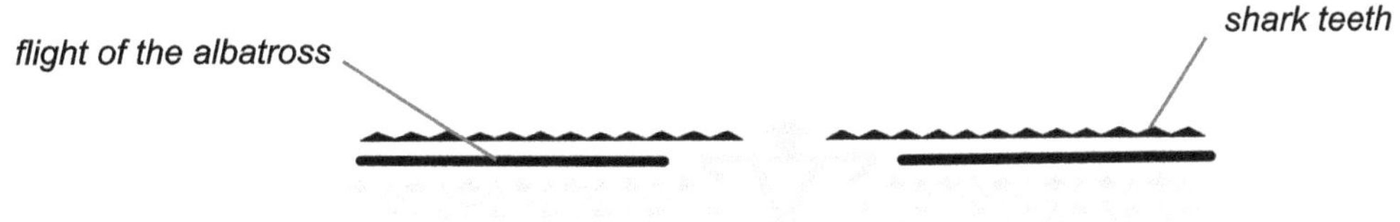

Fig. 6.17: Protection during voyages.

Kaua e mate wheke mate ururoa

"Don't die like an octopus, die like a hammerhead shark."

MAORI

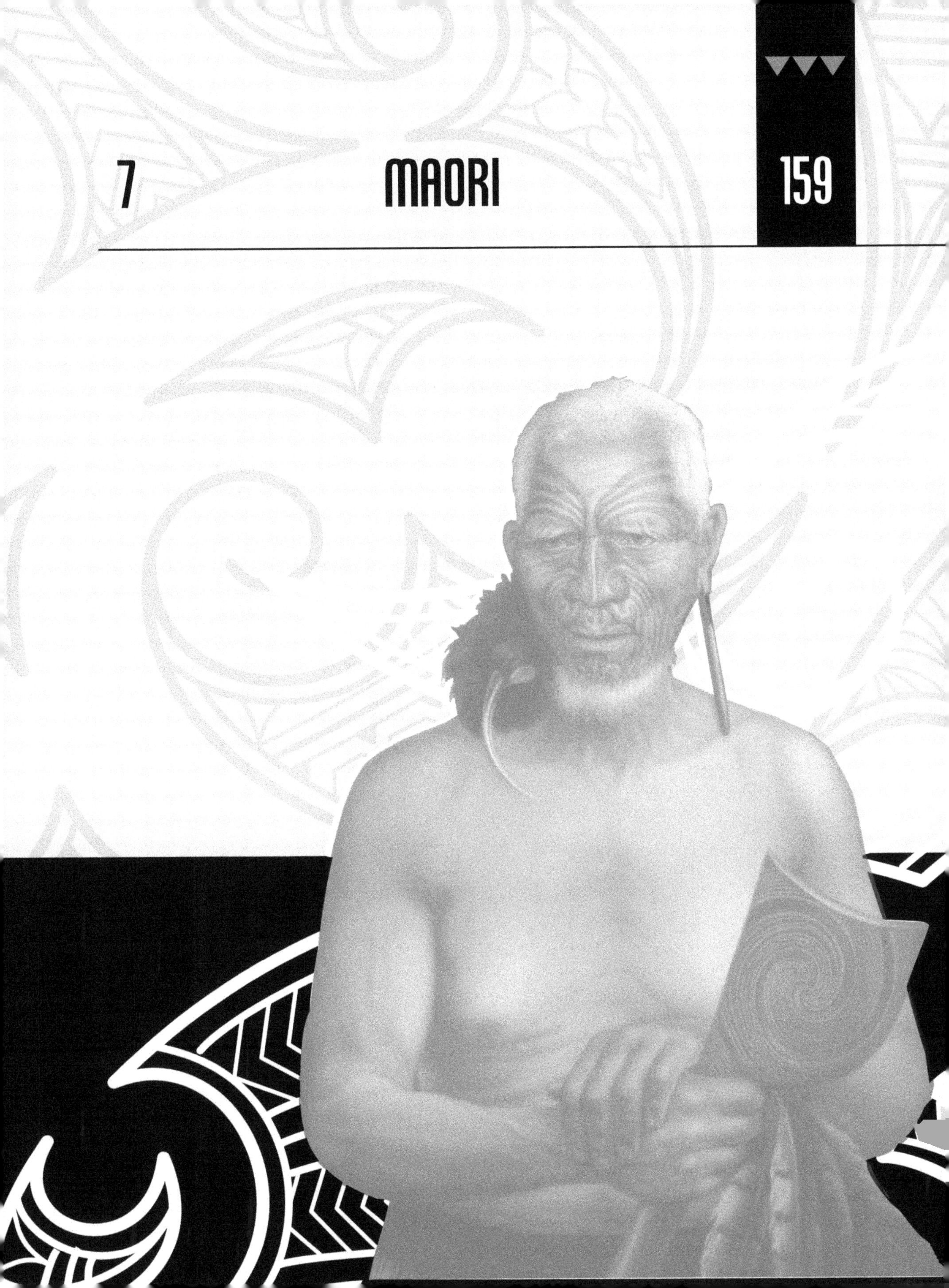

"Kaua e mate wheke mate ururoa."
—***Don't die like an octopus, die like a hammerhead shark***:
Be brave, fight for what you believe in.

Features: rich with round elements, spirals, and intricate fillings.
Purpose: to empower through genealogy, to embellish, to intimidate.

a. 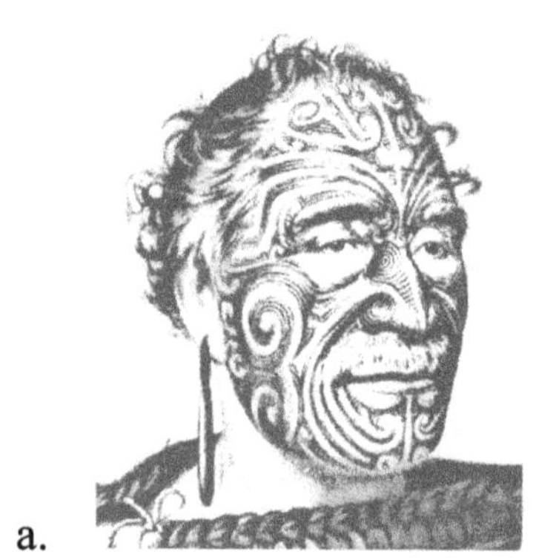

b. 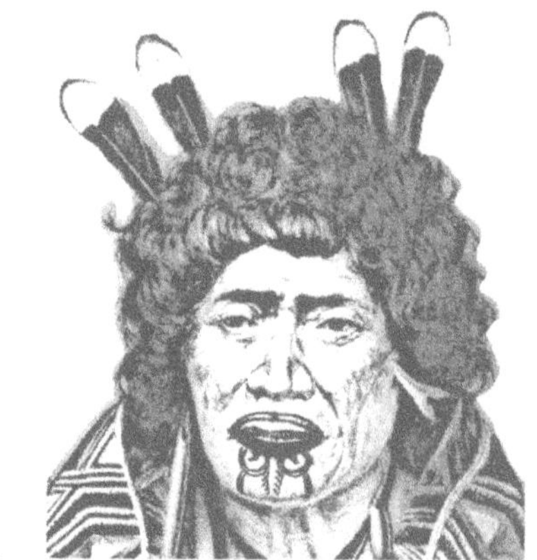

Fig. 7.1: Maori traditional face tattoos from Lindauer, 1890. (a) Male tā moko and (b) female tā ngutu.

i. about the style

Maori tattoos are known the world over thanks to the peculiar, intricate look of the male facial tattoo, called *tā moko*, which is unique to the people of New Zealand. The face was not the only part of the body being tattooed, but it was the one that had the greatest importance, probably due to the fact that the harsher climate caused the body to be fully covered most of the time, with the face being the only part always visible.

The elaborate look of modern tattoos is a relatively recent development of the older geometrical style brought by the Polynesian navigators who colonized New Zealand from Hawaiki, the legendary original homeland now identified as Central Polynesia. Examples of the evolution from this earlier style were described by European explorers during the eighteenth and nineteenth centuries, and some of them can be seen in figure 7.2.

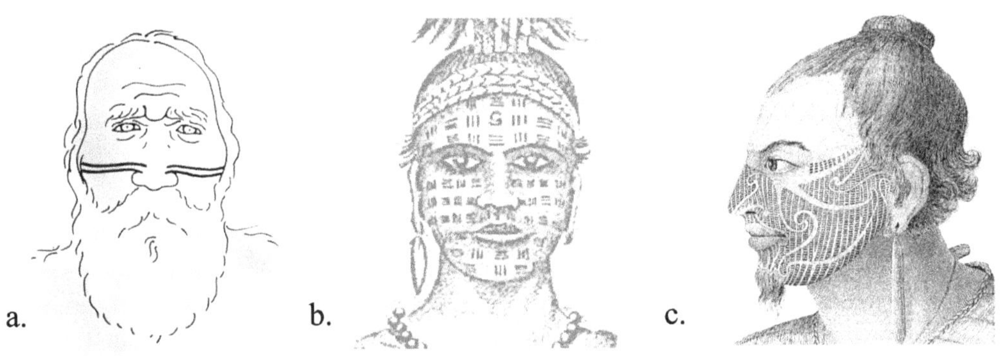

Fig. 7.2: (a) After Cowan, 1910; (b) after White, 1889; (c) after Parkinson, 1769. Motifs (a) and (b), despite being more recent, come from more isolated areas of the South Island, where old patterns may have survived longer; (c) comes from the North Island, where wood carving reached its highest artistic development.

In 1975 S. M. Mead pointed out a similar change in the decoration of

Maori artifacts, and he divided this evolution into three periods based on the names assigned to the different patterns: *moko kuri* (made of straight lines), *puhoro* (straight lines and curved elements), and classic *moko* (curves, spirals, and all the decorative elements we are used to seeing in Maori tattooing and carving).

As in other parts of Polynesia, the tradition of tattooing was abandoned during the twentieth century, discouraged by missionaries and by the rapid changes in the social structure and way of living of the natives. This led to the loss of most of the knowledge related to this art, and we can only infer its original significance from alternative sources. The most important of them is the art of carving, which reached an unprecedented level of artistry in New Zealand. (The inexhaustible supply of suitable timber for building and carving certainly helped in pushing the development of the craft to its stylistic excellence).

Carving statues and houses with tattoo elements became a common way to keep the traditional designs alive when tattooing was discouraged, and it is actually impossible to say exactly which of the two arts has been more influenced by the other, their commonalities being not limited to their symbolism, but also reflected in their material aspects. They both share the same purpose of honoring ancestors and preserving their *mana*, and they can be seen as one unique art yet executed on different mediums. In fact, while tattoos throughout Polynesia were consistently applied by puncturing the skin (which is true for most of Maori tattoos as well), the main lines of the *moko* were chiseled into the skin, creating grooves and furrows on the face that made it look as if it had been carved. The filling patterns of the face tattoo, and the tattoos on other parts of the body, were still applied in the usual Polynesian way that leaves the skin unscarred. Similarly, the meeting houses show both carved and painted elements, with the painted ones usually being decorated using scroll motifs (basic motifs repeating themselves in a continuous pattern) derived from tattoo patterns.

Another strong connection between carving and tattooing lies in their symbolism. We know that meeting houses throughout Polynesia have been built to keep the sense of community strong and to preserve the knowledge of genealogy by depicting ancestors on walls and posts, and we also know that representing ancestors in tattoos was a way to collect their *mana*, passing it on to their descendants.

In New Zealand, where the members of each tribe (*iwi* in the Maori language) can trace their origins back to one of the leaders of the first canoes that brought their ancestors there, the meeting house, or *whare whakairo* ("decorated house") as the Maoris call it, becomes a homage to this ancestry and a way to show the lineage and prestige of the *iwi*. The founding ancestor was carved at the front entrance, and the following generations were carved and painted on the rafters, beams, and side panels inside the house. In the case of the Maori house, this connection was even deeper and the house itself received the name of the founding ancestor, of whom, in fact, it actually became a physical representation: the *koruru* ("carved face") at the head of the gable on the front represents his head, the diagonal bargeboards are the arms and legs ending with elements called *raparapa* ("soles of the feet"), the main ridge pole represents the backbone of the ancestor (*tāhuhu*, "direct line of ancestry"), the rafters are the ribs, called *heke* ("to descend, to be coming"), and the central column is called *poutokomanawa* ("heart of the leader"). The word for the door, *kūwaha*, also indicates the mouth.

Proceeding with our analysis, we can observe how the actual structure and look of the *moko* shares much with the representations of the ancestors on the house posts: carved ancestors are often paired with a *taniwha* (a highly feared and revered guardian, and a very powerful creature), and considering that the facial *moko* may be a similar representation, it is impossible not to note the likeness of its central part with the figure of a *taniwha*, as shown in figure 7.3.

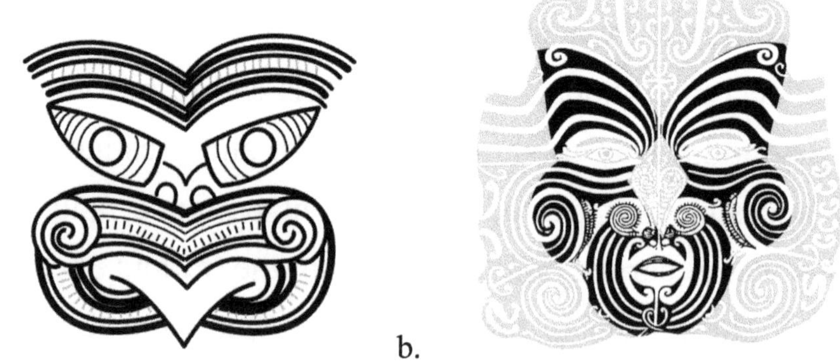

Fig. 7.3: (a) Taniwha face and (b) traditional lines from Te Pehi Kupe's own moko, 1826. Such similarity seems to find another confirmation in the outstretched tongue during war dances.

Incidentally, or maybe not, most grayed parts from the *moko* of figure 7.3, which do not seem to be visually associated with the *taniwha* image, are not representative of ancestors, but of the rank and personal qualities of the person wearing the *moko*, according to the scheme shown in figure 7.4, based on oral traditions and on reports from early Maori historians.

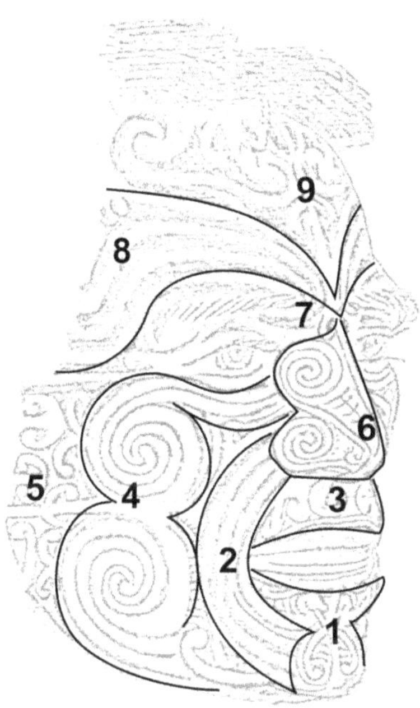

1. 2. 3. chin and mouth area: mana

4. cheeks: birth status and lineage

5. back of jaws: occupation and achievements

6. 7. nose and eyes area: rank in the clan

8. above the brows: position

9. forehead: rank achieved

Fig. 7.4: Despite the lack of absolute certainty, most historical sources and oral traditions tend to agree on these areas and on their significance.

The complete *moko* therefore became a representation of the person wearing it and of their ancestors, unique to that person and to no other, much like an identity card, that chiefs were able to reproduce by heart and which they often used as a signature on deeds contracted with Europeans.

At the same time, it gave the chief the look of a *taniwha*, likening him to the mythical creature in order to strike fear and awe into his enemies, also increasing his spiritual and physical power (to some extent, the *taniwha* was related to fertility, too). The ceremony at the closing of the tattoo process appears to confirm this, as the songs that were sung were related to war and to sexual empowerment. A similar significance also applies to the female facial tattoo, termed *tā ngutu* ("lip tattoo"), which is applied to the lips and chin and whose parts have names strongly related to fertility. High ranking women, such as the first born of high chiefs, also had symbols tattooed on their foreheads.

The *moko* was applied following a strict order, and each of its parts has a specific name, which can slightly vary across the regions of New Zealand. Despite the discrepancies in naming though, all reports agree on the order in which the parts were inked, which is "from the ground up", to use an analogy with house building. This means starting on the chin first, then on the sides of the mouth and below the nose, on the cheeks extending toward the ears, on the nose and below the eyebrows, above the eyebrows, and finally on the forehead. Looking at the significance of each part, it is visually apparent how birth status and lineage are the basis on which the individual builds their own achievements.

While *tā moko* and *tā ngutu* are undoubtedly the most renowned among Maori traditional tattoos, they are not the only ones. Like most Polynesian peoples, Maori too had a traditional tattoo covering the upper part of the legs, from the waist down to just below the knee. It was comprised of large spirals on the buttocks, called *rape*, and of a motif known as *puhoro* ("stormy"), made of joined undulating lines that run across a pattern of straight lines. Two examples of the *puhoro* pattern are presented below in figure 7.5 for both tattooing and *kowhaiwhai* paintings (scroll motifs used in house decoration), showing once again the closeness of these two art forms.

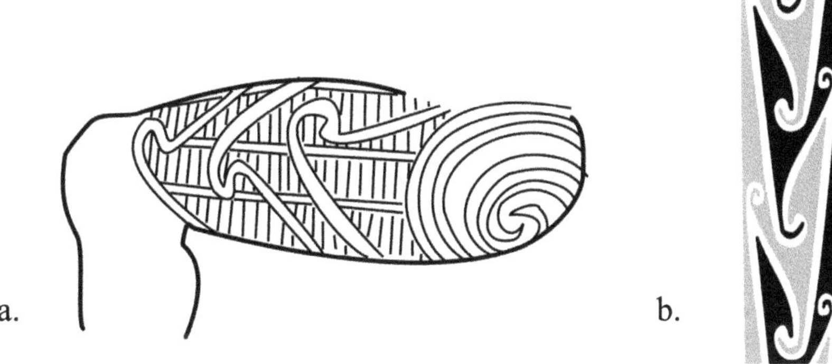

Fig. 7.5: (a) Traditional puhoro tattoo applied on thighs, on arms, or on the face as a filling motif; (b) puhoro pattern used in house decoration, where it was painted as a scroll motif on the beams.

A renaissance in Maori pride has led to a renewed interest in this traditional heritage over the last decades, leading to a resurgence in the use of *tā moko* and *tā ngutu* among men and women respectively. For non-Maori, a similar, more appropriate, type of tattoo is termed *kirituhi* ("painted skin"), which has the same look of the *moko* but does not use *tapu* designs and can therefore be received by anyone.

ii. elements

Nowadays it is not clear exactly which elements originally belonged to tattooing and which ones to house carving and painting, as we have seen that these two arts are intimately related and can be considered as two physical representations of the same art. On this account, *kowhaiwhai* and carving patterns are often regarded as belonging to tattoos too, and are constantly used in Maori modern designs. Other motifs are borrowed from traditional *tāniko* weaving patterns, so we will include some of them at the end of the list that we present in this section.

The distinctive element throughout all Maori arts is the spiral, which is used as a single, double, or composite design.

Another important element, especially in carving, is the human presence. Human and humanoid figures appear consistently on posts and decorative elements to represent ancestors and protector spirits. The *tiki*, the *manaia*, and the *taniwha* are three of them. The *manaia* is a guardian usually depicted with the head of a bird, the body of a human, and the tail of a fish (even if some older ones are depicted with a single leg, from which the tail may have evolved).

Symbol	Name and Meanings	Variants
	haehae = to scratch, to cut up Main lines of the *moko*. They are carved to separate the different parts and to trace the main designs that will be filled by secondary patterns.	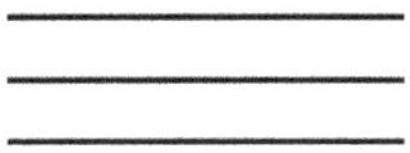
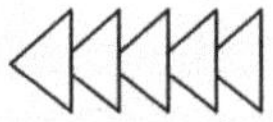	**pākati = dog-tooth pattern** *meaning: protection* It is usually used between two parallel lines.	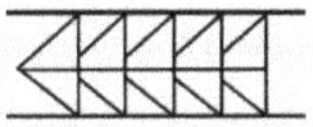 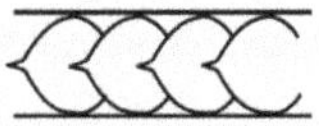 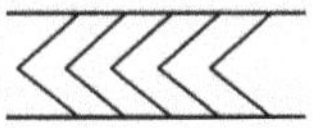
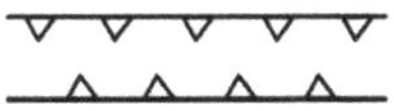	**niho taniwha = taniwha's teeth** *meaning: protection, link to the ocean and to origins, genealogy* Also known as *taratara o Kai* in carving (*taratara* means "barbed, spiky"), it has been noted that it occurs only in regions where the whale design is present (it may possibly be related to Paikea's legend). Each spike is usually associated with an ancestor in the spirals of the *moko*.	

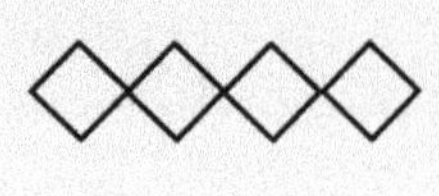

tuarā kuri = dog's spine

meaning: allegiance, loyalty

Usually used between two parallel lines.

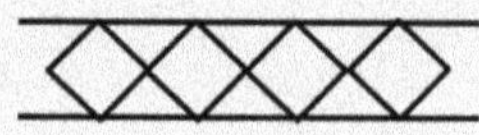

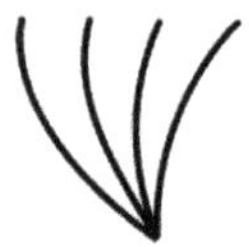

ritorito = flax shoots

meaning: descent, family, protection

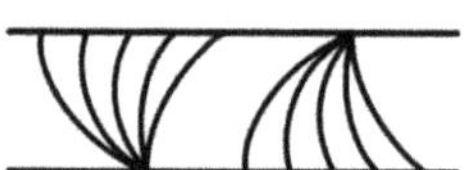

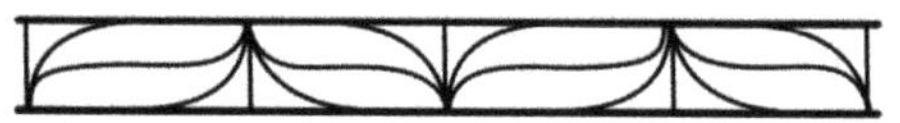

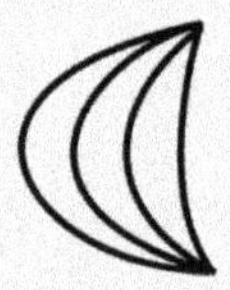

unaunahi = fish scales

meaning: protection

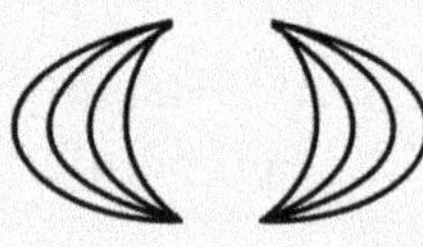

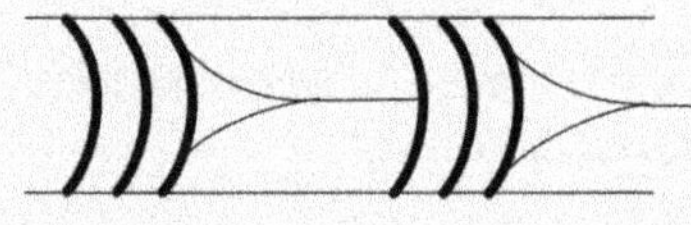

pakura = swamp hen

meaning: descent, family

Often used as a filling next to spirals.

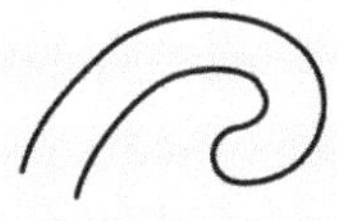

koru = folded, loop

meaning: growth, tradition, new beginning

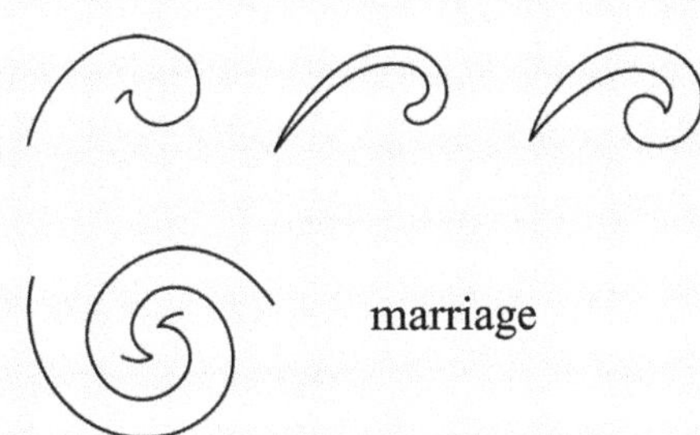

marriage

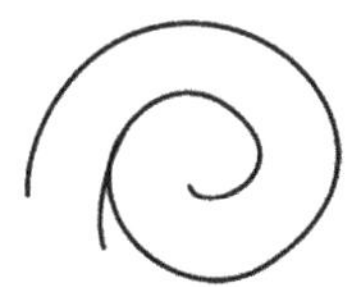

pītau = fern shoot

meaning: growth

takarangi = double spiral
meeting, genealogy

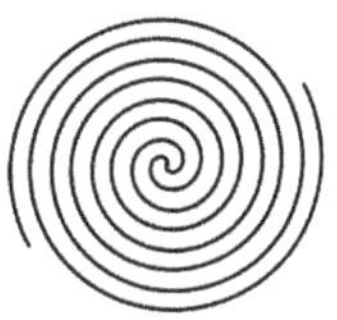

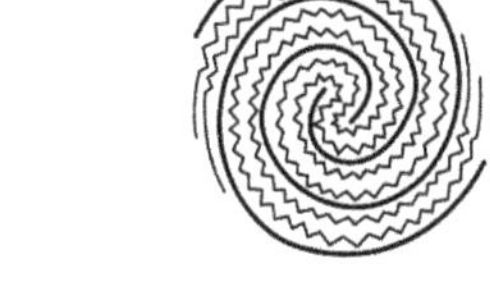

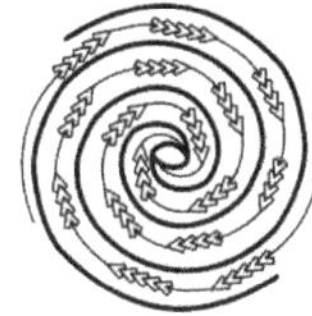

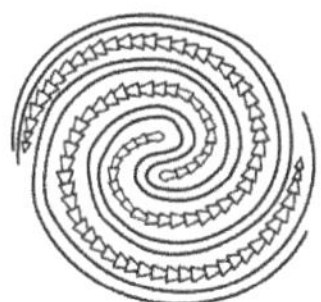

In genealogical lines, the double spiral represents primary descent through a male while the single spiral represents female descent.

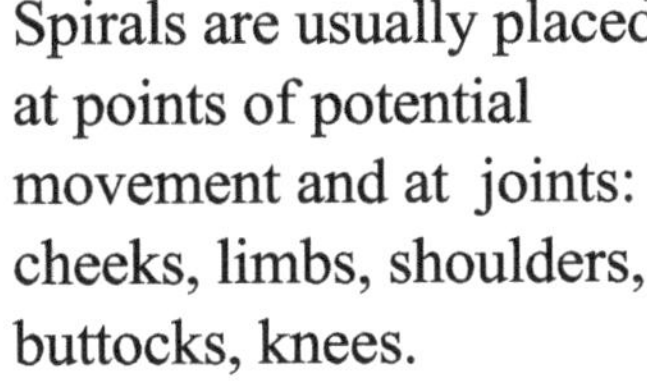

Spirals are usually placed at points of potential movement and at joints: cheeks, limbs, shoulders, buttocks, knees.

Two interconnected spirals, often simplified as a twist, symbolize the union of two people or cultures.

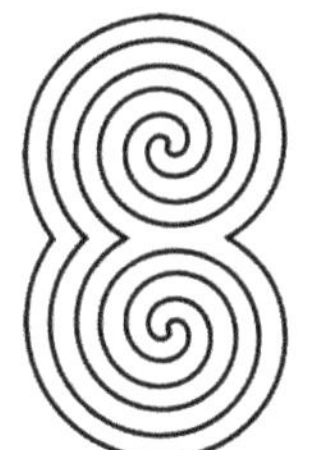

piko rua

A different type of double spiral recalls two interlocked fish hooks and is named *Māui* after the demi-god who fished islands with his magical fish hook.

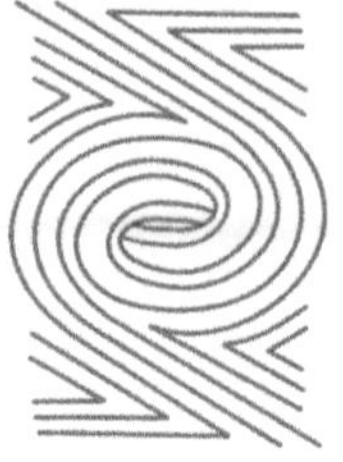

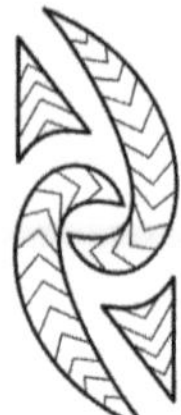

Māui

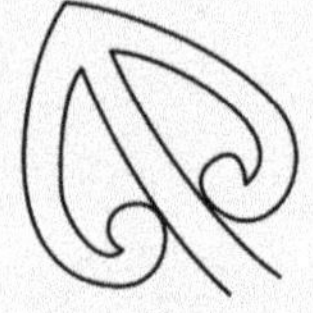

mangōtipi = hammerhead shark pattern

meaning: tenacity, strength

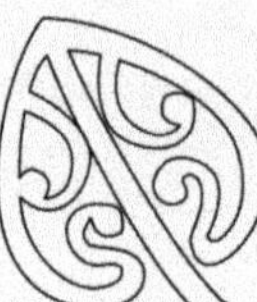

puhoro = stormy

Puhoro is also the name given to the tattoos placed on the body, usually on thighs and arms, which were mostly composed of this motif. It is related to voyages and origins.

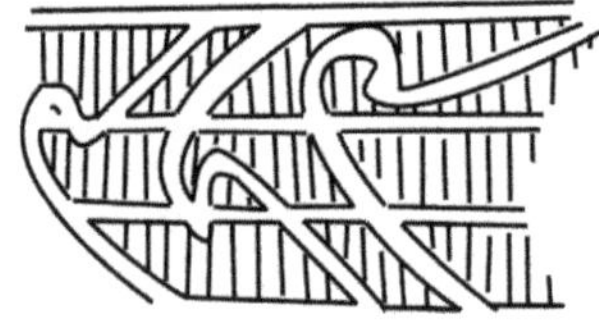

The underlying pattern is called *ahuahu o Mataora*, or "load of Mataora", and it symbolizes a path full of challenges.

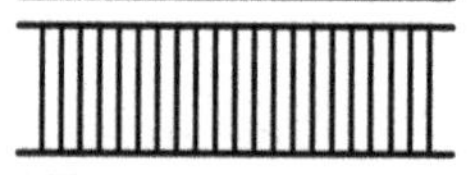

ngaru = waves

meaning: speed, travel

Pattern made by a canoe breaking the waves.

kape = eyebrow

meaning: fierceness

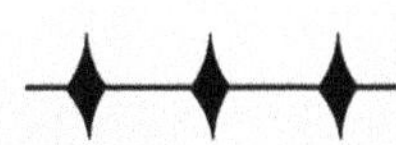

ngau pae = measure marks

steps, achievements

They were originally marks cut in wood with an adze.

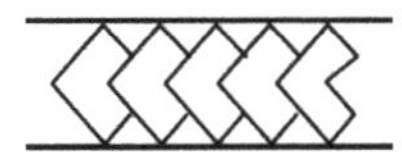

hikuaua = like the tail of the herring

meaning: prosperity

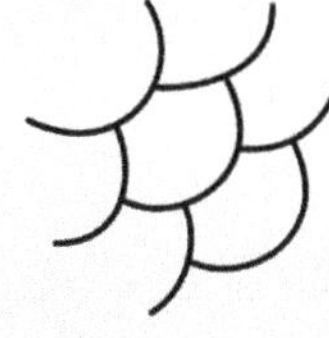

matakupenga = fishing net

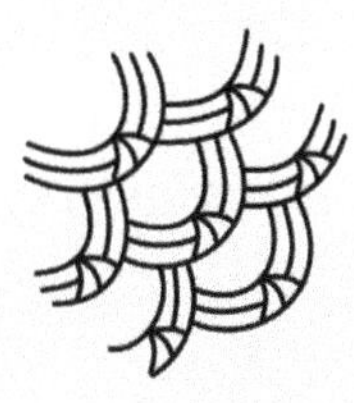

meaning: community, prosperity

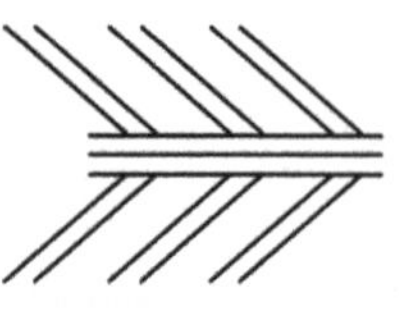

rauponga = leaf of the ponga (silver tree fern)

meaning: community

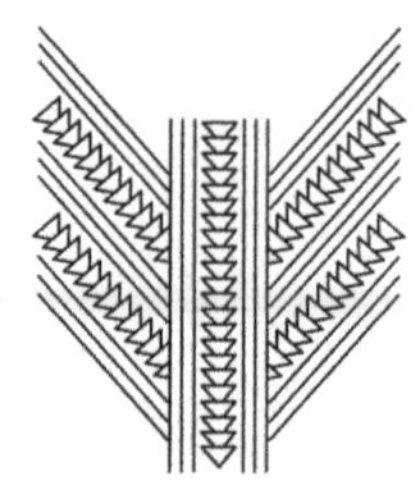

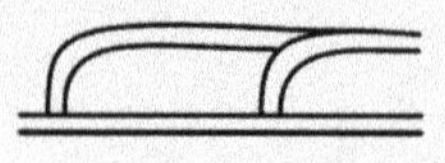

rauponga whakarare = shady fern leaves

meaning: hidden meaning

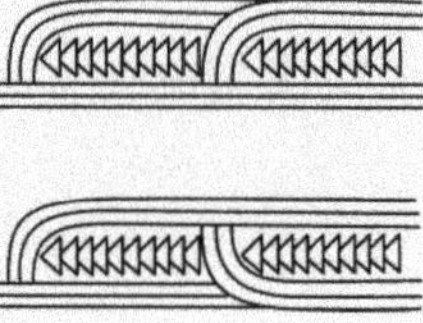

te ara poutama = the path to knowledge

meaning: the steps to knowledge, genealogy

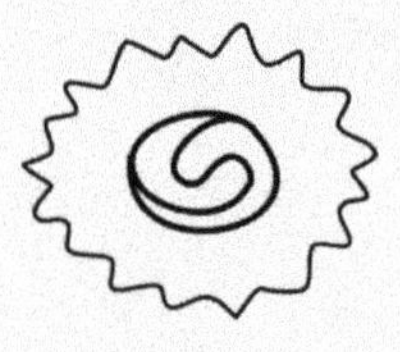

pua wānanga = clematis flower

meaning: to strive for knowledge, healing

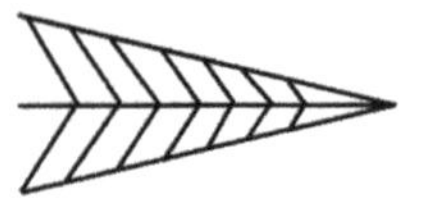

niu = coconut palm

meaning: peace, prosperity

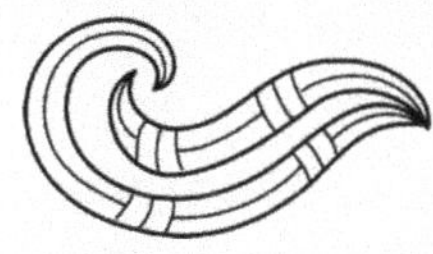

te ha = the breath of life

meaning: breath, essence, sound

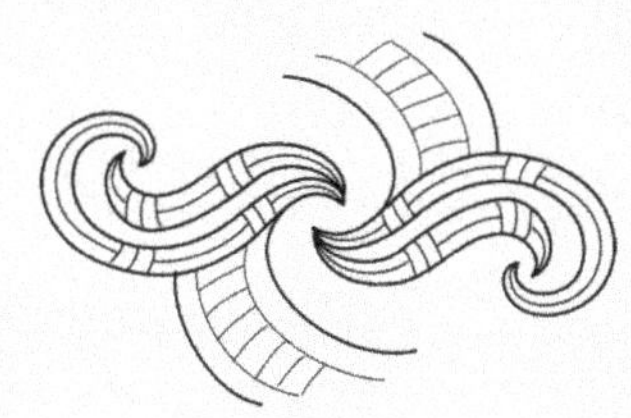

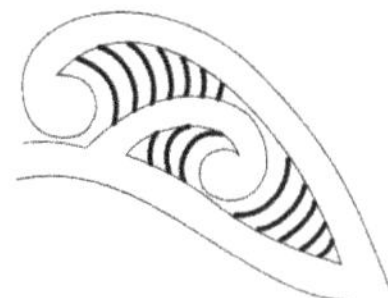

tauira = pattern

meaning: children, learning

Tauira also translates as "pupil" and "example" and is therefore usually related to teaching and knowledge.
It is used in carving and tattooing as a filling pattern between other elements.

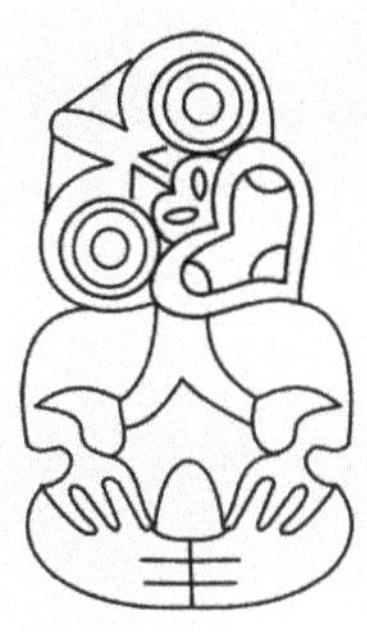

tiki

meaning: ancestor, protection

The *tiki* represents an ancestor. It can be designed with the head straight up or bent to the side. The latter is typically used in jewelry as it allows the carver to optimize the shape of the carved item and is therefore considered a late development of the style. The *tiki* pendant is called *hei tiki*. *Hei* means "to tie around the neck", but it is also used in conjunction with words related to kinship and relationships.

Sometimes, only parts of humanoid figures like this one are included in tattoos, such as the head of the *manaia*, a hand of the *tiki*, or an eye.

taniwha

meaning: power, respect, protection

The *taniwha* is a guardian and a symbol to represent great chiefs. It has a snake-like body with legs, and a mouth full of teeth. These traits make it look very similar to an Asian dragon (a symbol of the emperor), and we can't exclude influences between the two.

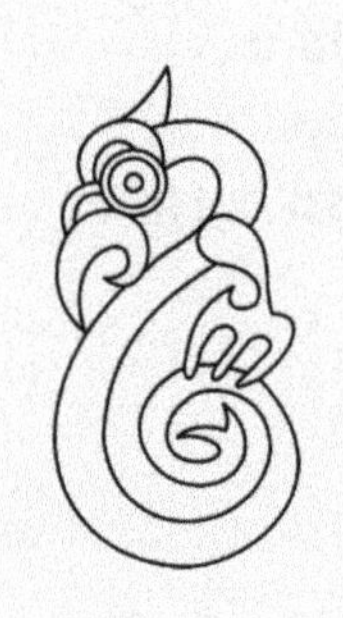

manaia

meaning: protection, guardian

They are usually depicted in profile, as this represents being half in the material and half in the spiritual world, having the ability to cross from one to the other and back.

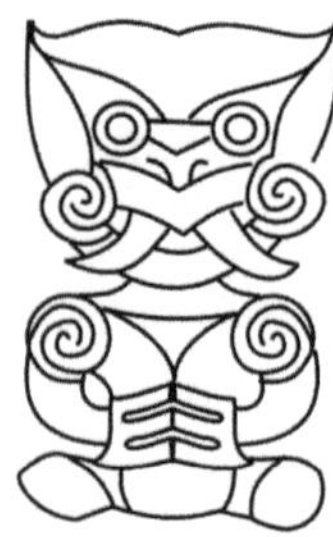

ruru = owl

meaning: guardian, protector, wisdom

While the single outstretched tongue was used to symbolize an act of defiance to enemies, the double tongue, or "split tongue" as it is called, represents great skill in speaking, symbolizing an important orator or a guardian spirit delivering a message.

The following motifs are sometimes included in modern Maori tattoos, and they come from *tāniko* (weaving) patterns:

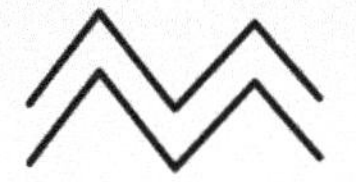

kaokao = on the side of the rising sun / side of a mountain

meaning: strength of a warrior, status

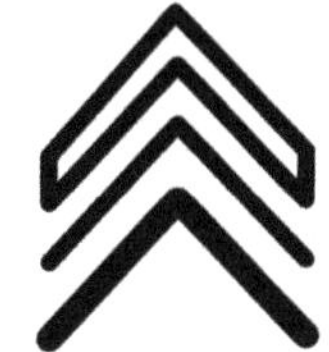

niho taniwha = taniwha's teeth

meaning: protection, family houses within the tribe

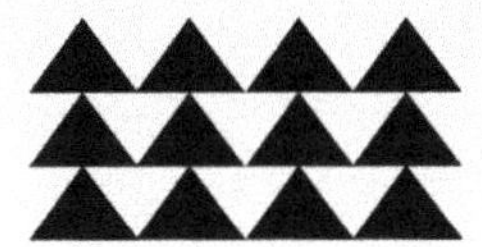

niho niho = small teeth

meaning: protection

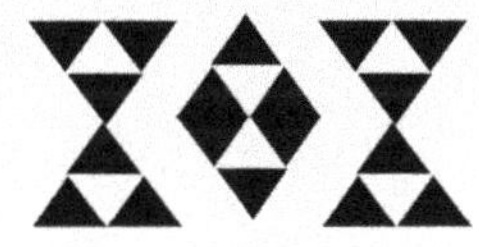

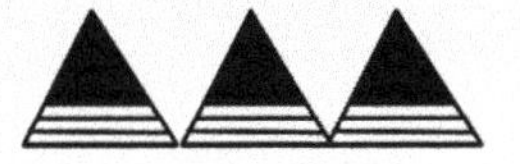

pātiki = flounder

meaning: prosperity

iii. tattoo examples walkthrough

This chapter shows a Maori *kirituhi* interpretation of the three tattoos explored in the previous chapters. The use of thin lines and spiraling motifs is the characteristic trait of this style.

While carving makes great use of bas-relief to create patterns of light and shadow (darkness and light, *pō* and *ao*), you'll notice here that tattooing relies on dense fillings made of thin lines to emphasize the blank patterns cut out of the designs, giving them the same importance of the inked parts.

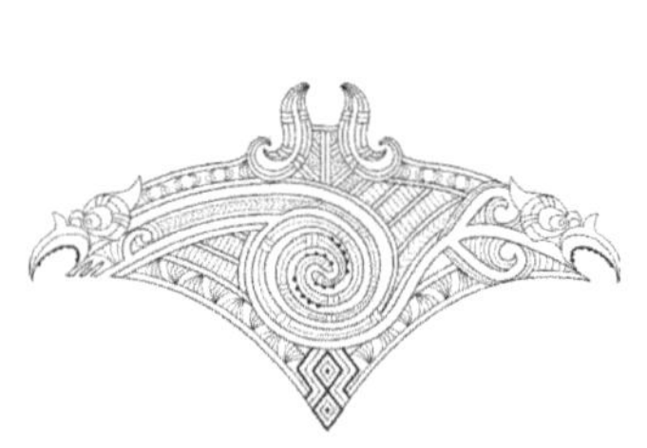

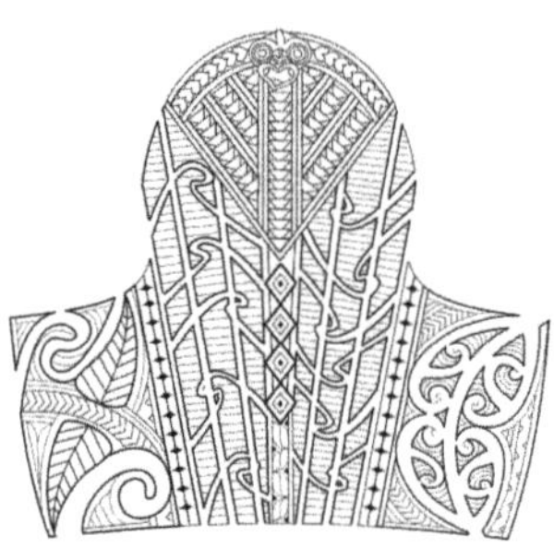

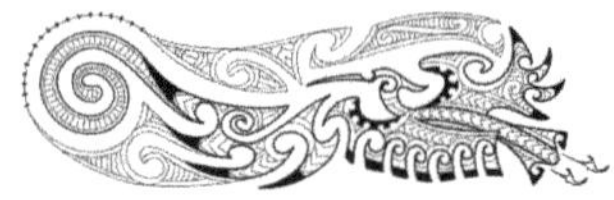

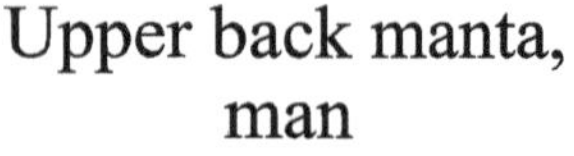

Upper back manta, man

Half sleeve, man

Band, woman

Upper back manta

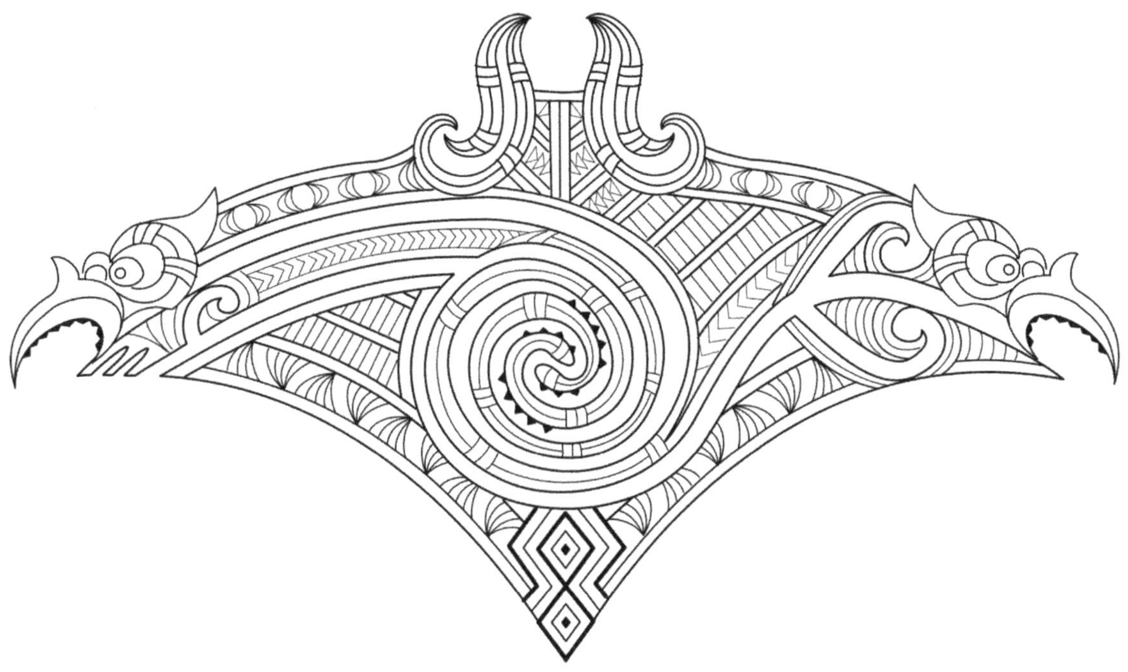

Request: *a manta for the upper back representing the centrality of family and traditions, and protection of the family.*

Family remains the predominant theme of this tattoo, as it was in the previous chapters, with a great double spiral in the center symbolizing the union of man and woman to form the family. The left part of the tattoo is connected to the woman, with a *koru* to represent that she is the bringer of new life, and the right side of the tattoo is connected with the man, with a *mangōtipi* (hammerhead shark motif) representing his tenacity and warrior spirit. Having female-related elements on the left and male-related elements on the right was a common practice in Maori tattooing.

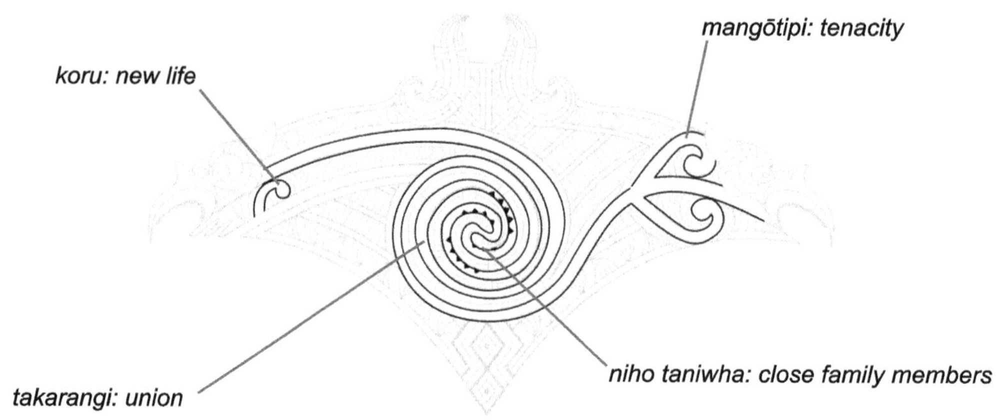

Fig. 7.7: The two people forming the family and their closest relatives.

There are a few small triangles divided into four groups within the double spiral, two on one branch of the spiral and two on the other. They were added to represent the members of the families of origin of the two people symbolized by the spiral, as community and lineage are of great importance in Maori culture.

Above the spiral, between the two symbols representing the breath of life

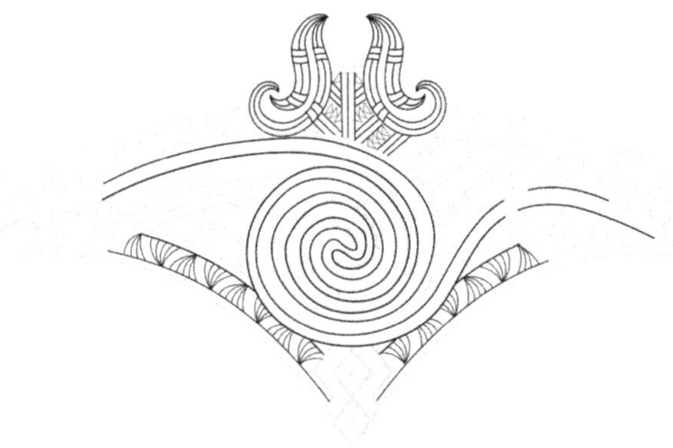

Fig. 7.6: Family belongs to the wider context of the community.

that shape the mouth of the manta, the silver fern motif, or *rauponga*, symbolizes the community and the connection to the ancestors.

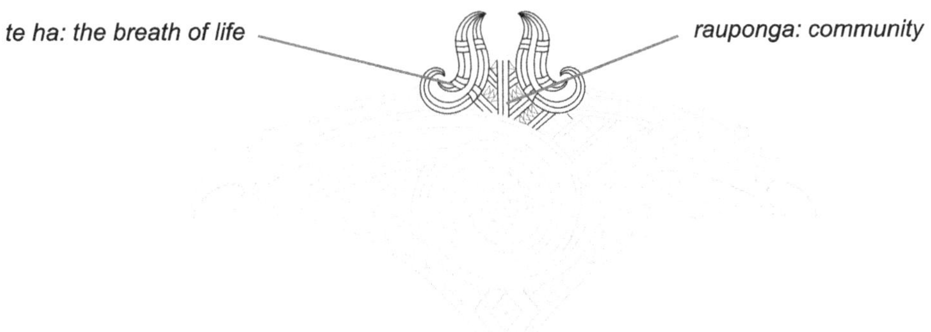

Fig. 7.8: Origins and community elements.

The *ritorito* motif represents family, with the offspring in the middle protected by the parents on the sides and by the grandparents on their outside.

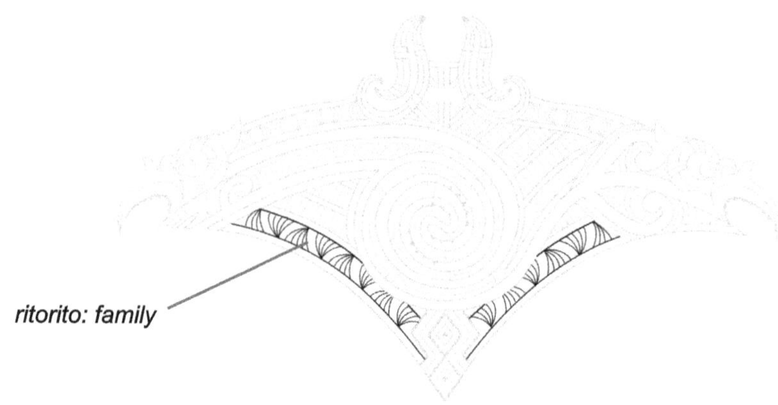

Fig. 7.9: Ritorito embodies the concept of family, with parents protecting their children, keeping them safe in the middle.

The flax plant was considered sacred, and legends tell how humans and flax have common origins and belong to one same line of descent. Maoris would never cut the central leaves in order to guarantee the life of the plant, and similarly, children guarantee the life of the community.

The two *manaia* figures on the tips of the wings looking to the sides are two ancestors, guardian spirits protecting the family.

The element at the base of the manta is the flounder motif enclosed between two *te ara poutama* patterns to symbolize knowledge bringing prosperity to the family.

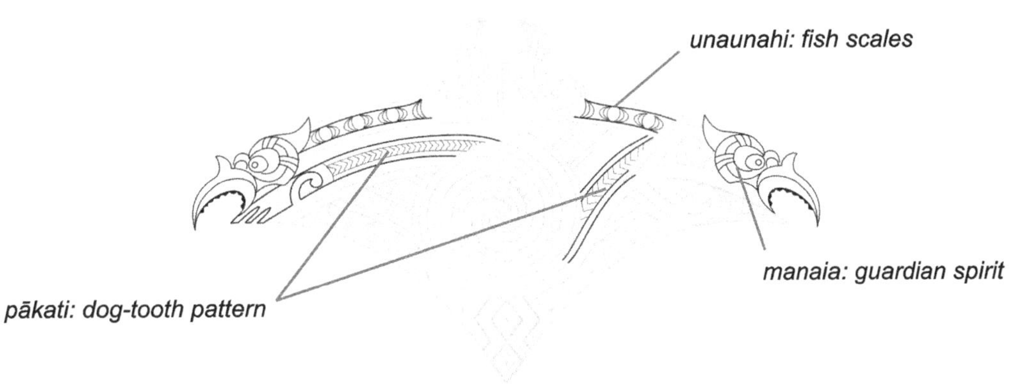

Fig. 7.10: Protection to the family.

The *ahuahu o Mataora* motif on the sides of the double spiral represents the challenges that the family faces along the way.

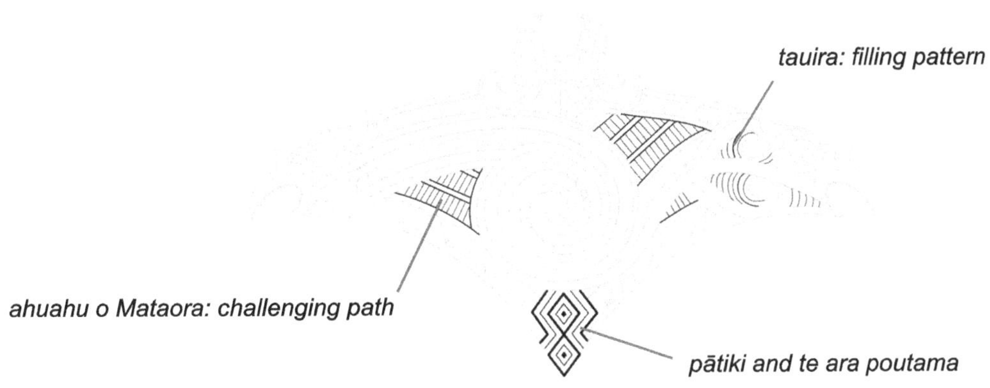

Fig. 7.11: The challenging path to prosperity is conquered through knowledge.

Half sleeve

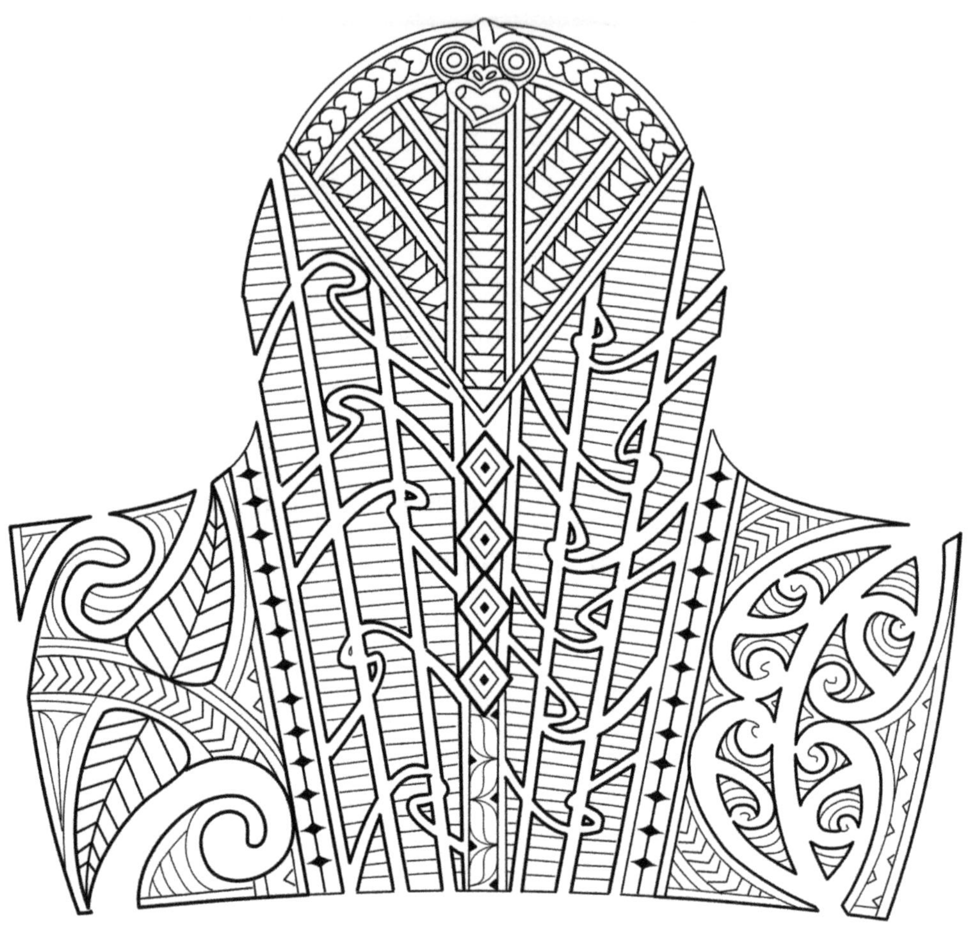

Request: *a half sleeve representing a family that left in search of fortune and is now going back to the island of the ancestors.*

Family remains central in this design, but only the small *ritorito* element in the center represents it as an entity, with five small teeth of *taniwha* to represent its five members. The remainder of the tattoo reveals the family members' characteristics and attitudes, following the concept that our actions define who we are.

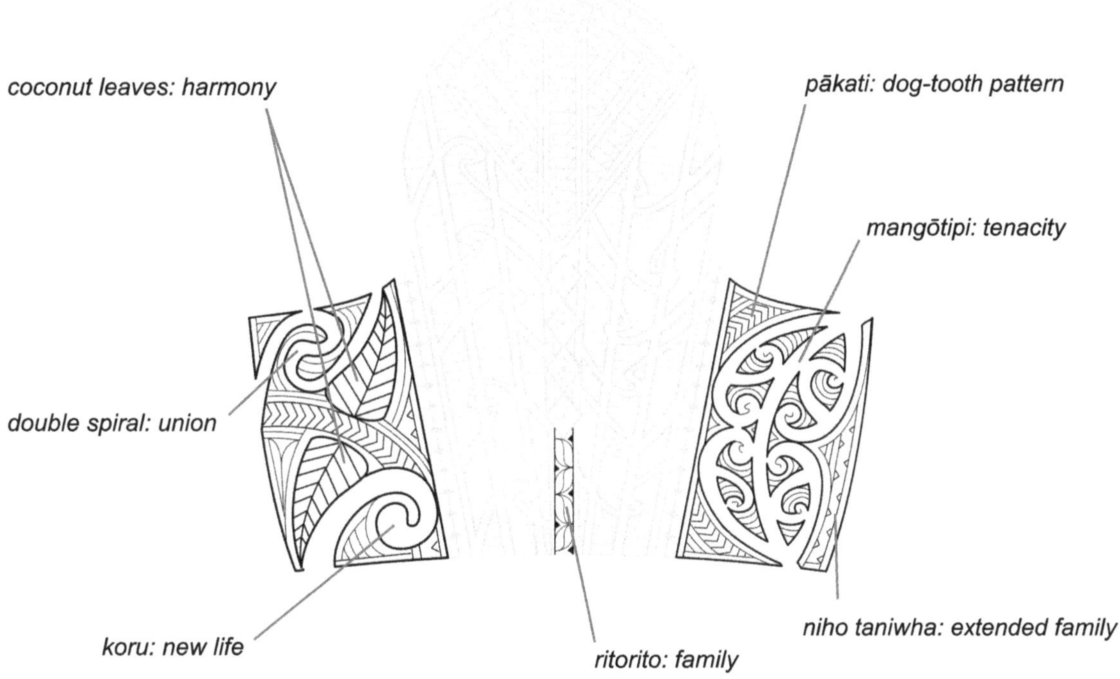

Fig. 7.12: Family and its related elements. They appear as open patterns in the design.

On this account we designed a hammerhead shark motif on the right to symbolize the tenacity and fighting spirit that guides the family through the challenges encountered along the voyage, and a double spiral on the left to symbolize union, while the coconut leaves represent how the family stayed united, working in harmony toward their common goal. The row of *taniwha* teeth on the right, on the back of the arm and therefore related to the past, symbolizes the extended family left behind. The dog-tooth pattern used to join all the elements brings protection to the family.

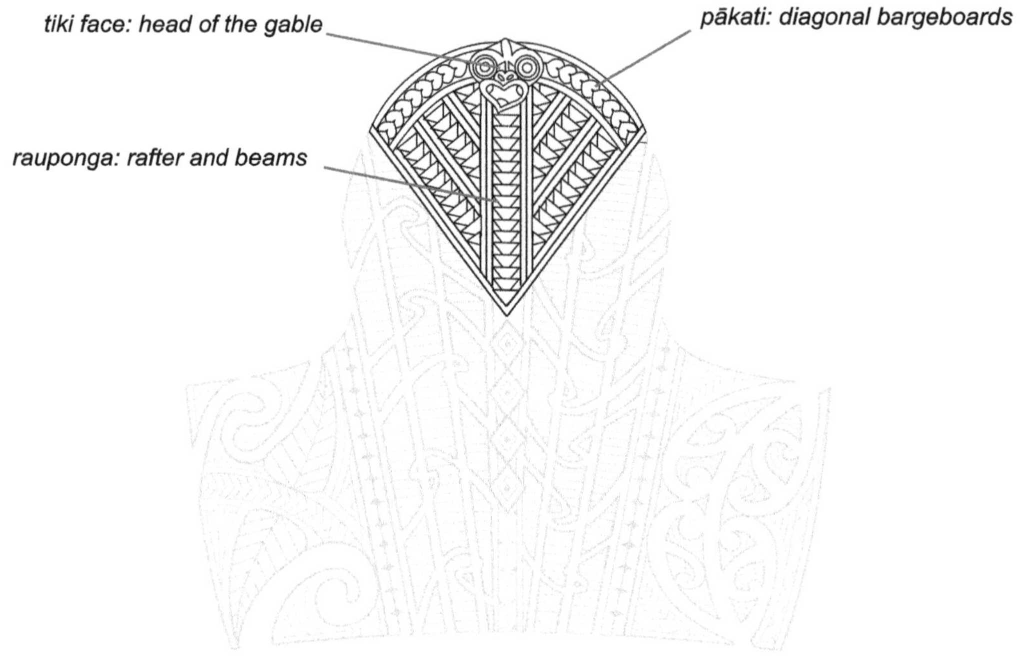

Fig. 7.13: Stylization of the community house.

The upper part of the shoulder was designed to recall the structure of a *whare whakairo*, the decorated house that is the place where the community members meet, the symbol of their ancestry, and of the place where they belong. The *tiki* face on top represents the founding ancestor, and the two patterns on its sides are a representation of the bargebords, while the *rauponga* motif below them, symbolizing community, also mimics the structure of the main rafter and of its side beams.

Below the *whare whakairo*, two parts inlaid with the *puhoro* motif represent the two voyages taken by the family, one placed on the back of the arm, related to the past and symbolizing going away, and the other on the front to represent coming back in the future (fig. 7.14).

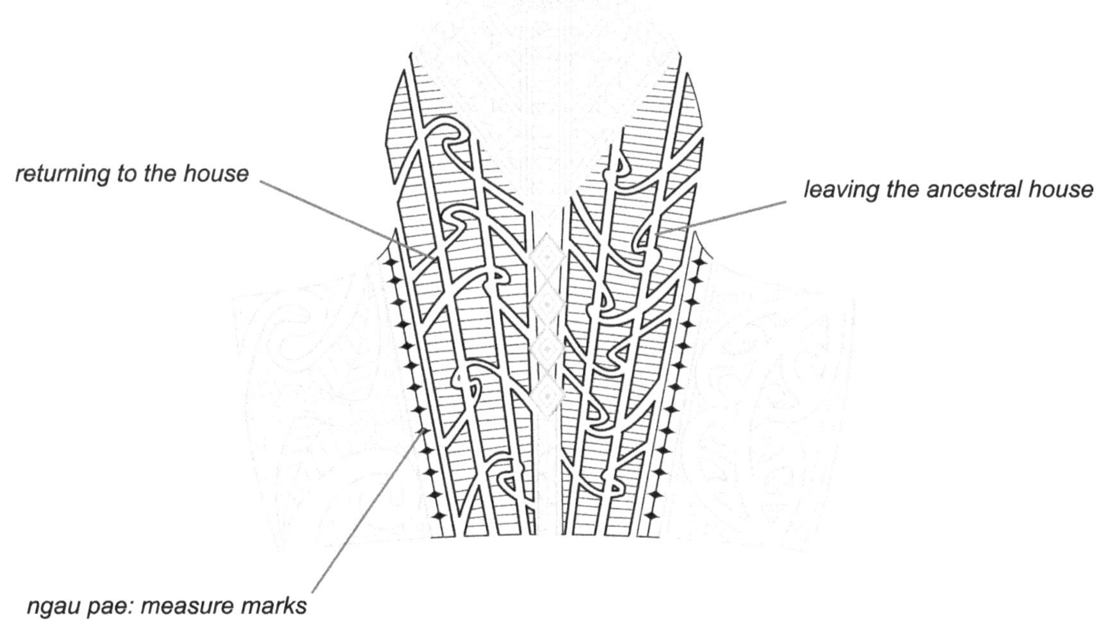

Fig. 7.14: Two challenging voyages, going away and coming back.

The row of marks along the voyages represent the achievements of the family, all the steps taken in order to finally find prosperity, symbolized by the flounder motif that connects the *ritorito* pattern of the family to the house of the ancestors.

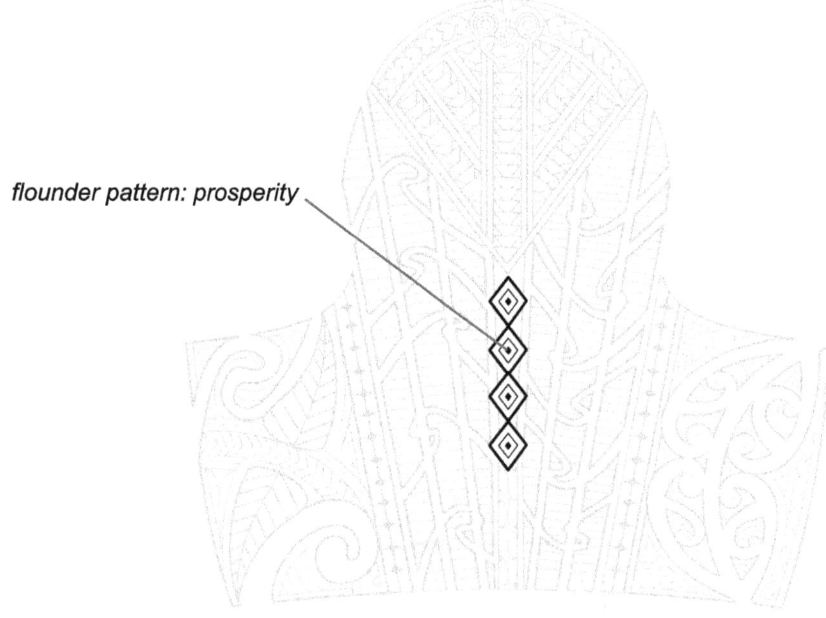

Fig. 7.15: Prosperity as the goal of the voyage.

Band

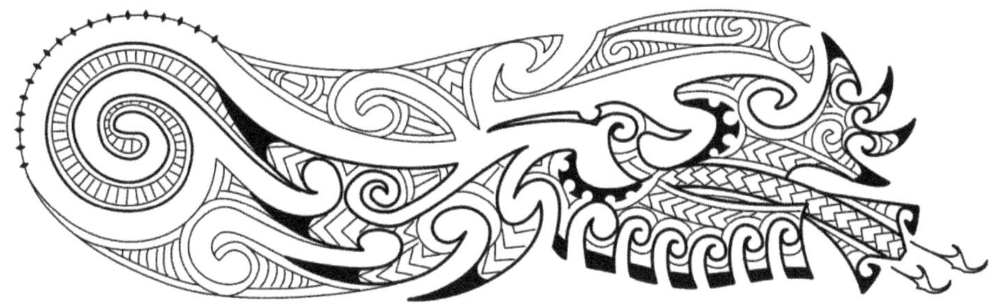

Request: *ankle band for a woman representing protection and tenacity to pursue and achieve every goal in life.*

This band was designed in a less traditional way, including a naturalistic representation of a flying *kotuku* ("white heron") in the band. We chose the white heron because it is a bird rarely seen, whose feathers were sought after and kept for the highest chieftains. It symbolizes here the woman who rose above every difficulty in order to achieve her goals.

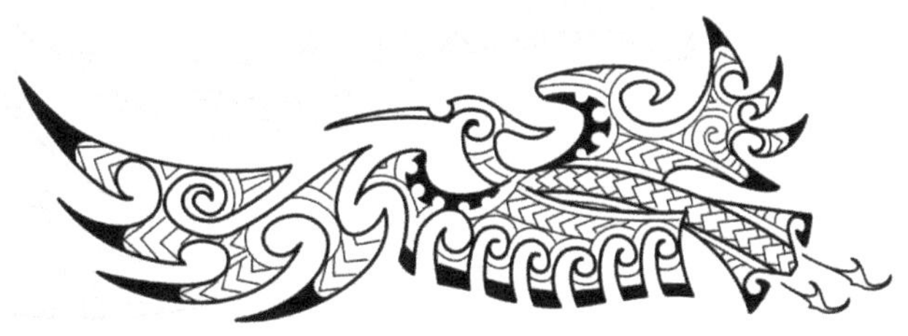

Fig. 7.16: Flying white heron.

The spiral in front of the heron symbolizes growth, and it is made of a *ahuahu o Mataora* pattern which represents the challenges faced along the way, while the circle of marks around it symbolizes achievements and shapes a sun as a symbol of success.

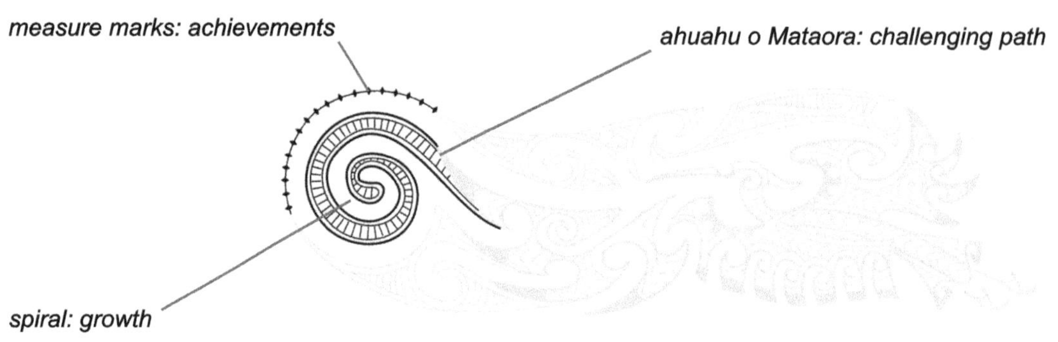

Fig. 7.17: A challenging path to personal growth and success.

To complete the band around the heron, *koru* elements were added to symbolize new beginnings, hammerhead shark motifs for tenacity, and Maui's fish hook for prosperity.

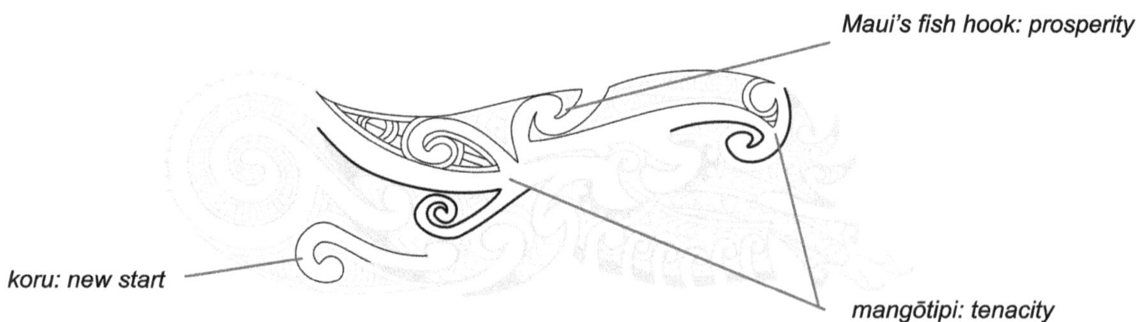

Fig. 7.18: Tenacity brings a new beginning, a fresh start.

The wings of the heron incorporate black parts to symbolize the balance between darkness and light, feminine and masculine, the union of opposites that allows one to reach every goal. The edges of the wings and tail include a row of *koru* to symbolize the evolution in life and all the new beginnings that arose along the path. The motif on the back of the heron, called *hikuaua*, represents prosperity, and it is flanked by stylized dog-tooth patterns on both sides for protection.

The two *kape* elements on the wings symbolize fierceness, and they represent the will to never give in to any difficulty.

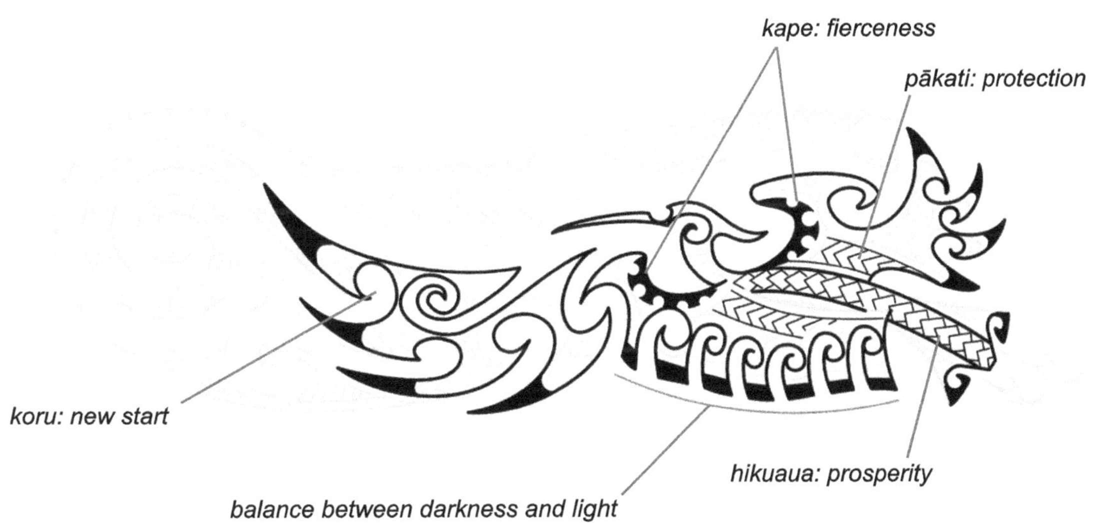

Fig. 7.19: Prosperity, protection, and new life.

'O le fogava'a e tasi
"One single canoe deck."

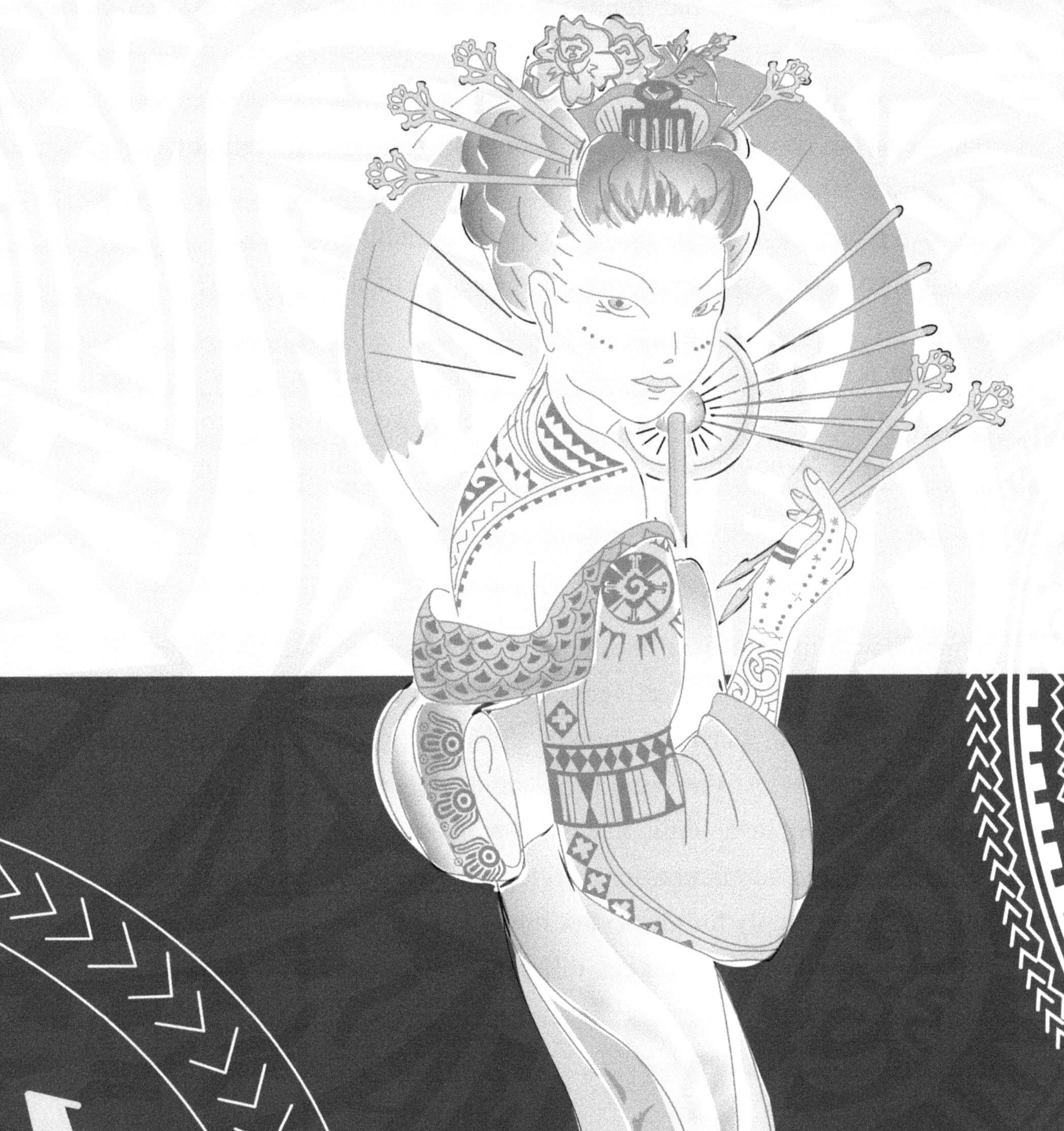

" 'O le fogava'a e tasi."
—***One single canoe deck*:**
We all are one family.

This chapter deals with two questions often asked in relation with Polynesian tattoos:

- Is it proper for non-Polynesians to receive traditional tattoos?
- Is it proper to incorporate non-Polynesian elements into them?

There is not a single correct answer to them, but many possible ones depending on what we mean by "proper". We consider proper any approach to Polynesian cultures and traditions, including tattooing, when it's based on respect.

We have explained the difference between *tapu* and *noa*, and the existence of symbols with very particular cultural significance, as well as symbols with more general meaning. We therefore consider it proper for natives to use any traditional symbol related to their lineage and family, both *tapu* and *noa*, when the symbols are strongly connected to their own roots and origins. At the same time, anyone should be entitled to wear tattoos designed in a traditional way with *noa* symbols as a sign of appreciation and admiration for a culture that they can relate to, whether by ancestry or simply for likeness of mind.

We also believe that mixing different styles should be allowed for various reasons: a peaceful union of different cultures always results in an enrichment for all of them (as shown by the example designs of this chapter); and also, genetic studies show that most people possess genes from several different ethnic backgrounds. Our society becomes each day more multicultural and the very idea of an unmixed "race" is meaningless in a world where moving around is easier than ever before.

Polynesian peoples have mixed over the centuries, and it is fair to let their tattoos reflect this, and to have more than one style side by side in the same tattoo. Polynesian tattoos themselves suggest this concept, as their styles evolved from a simpler, original one, into several artistically different variants, also thanks to contacts with other cultures.

Moreover, tattoos have always been a mirror of the society they belong to. They remind us of where we come from, but they should not stop us from undertaking new journeys. This is probably the meaning of Sulu'ape Petelo's words when asked about the new designs produced by contemporary artists: "We didn't have that sort of art before. We only knew of the traditional *pe'a* and traditional *malu*, but now these people have come in with fancy ideas of having their arms and legs done, you know. We can't stop it." In a world where everything is quickly forgotten and aesthetics often impose themselves over contents, would it be wise to forbid different styles to be mixed or non-Polynesians to receive them, knowing that maybe we are losing a chance to plant a little seed, a chance to allow someone to get closer to an art and a culture that are so much more than just pretty designs and amusing stories? Wouldn't we do more good to these traditions and to their values by teaching them to the people while allowing them to receive such tattoos?

After all, Polynesian traditions are now enjoying an unprecedented revival because one man decided that by reaching beyond his own culture, sharing what had been closely guarded knowledge, he could possibly save it from extinction. This man was Mau Piailug, the person who first taught the traditional seafaring techniques of his people to foreigners, setting the foundations for the first voyage of the Hōkūle'a double-hulled canoe in 1975, and showing that his ancestors knew how to sail the open ocean without modern technology, and that they actually did. He was right, and he drew new interest in Polynesian cultures, bringing them a renewed respect and a new dignity.

Polynesian navigators knew their way on the ocean because they always knew very clearly where they came from and where they were at during each stage of their voyages. Knowing the origin, the path traveled, and the surrounding environment were the keys to reaching the destination. In a similar way, a community must remember its origins and history to avoid losing its identity. Honoring our origins is never a matter of considering our culture superior though; it means instead to honor the achievements of our ancestors, committing to doing our best to uphold their example. It means receiving strength from our roots, for the whole plant, the whole family to prosper. Tattooing is important in this sense, as a constant reminder of our course, and it should be shared with anyone who can understand and appreciate its value. Education, and not prohibition, should be the rule.

The tattoos shown in this chapter were prepared for people of mixed descent, or people strongly passionate about Polynesia, and they represent some examples of how different traditions can coexist in one design, adding to its personal meanings as well as to its aesthetics.

Each element used to prepare them was chosen to complement the others in achieving the desired result of telling someone's personal story.

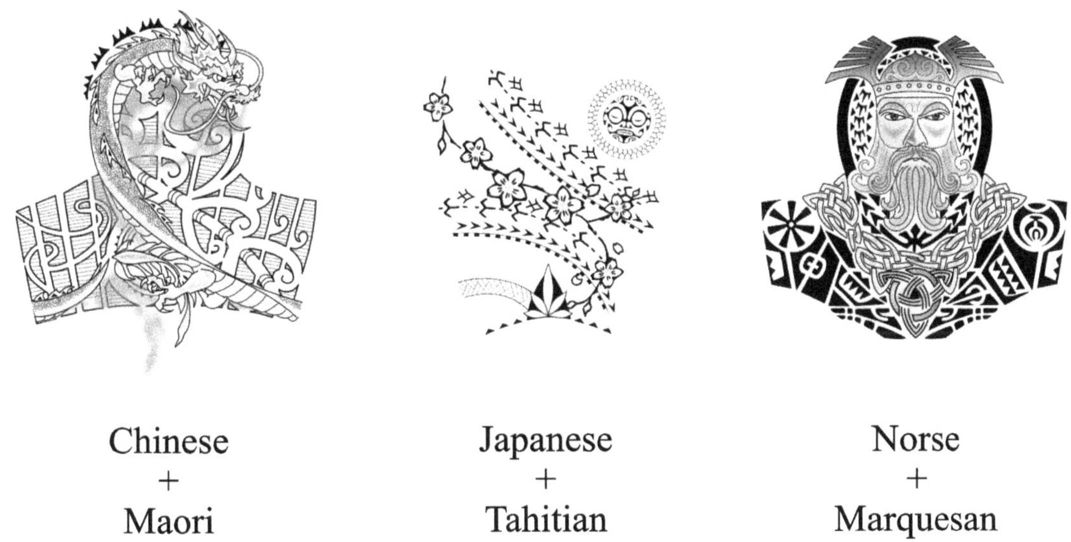

Chinese + Maori

Japanese + Tahitian

Norse + Marquesan

Chinese + Maori

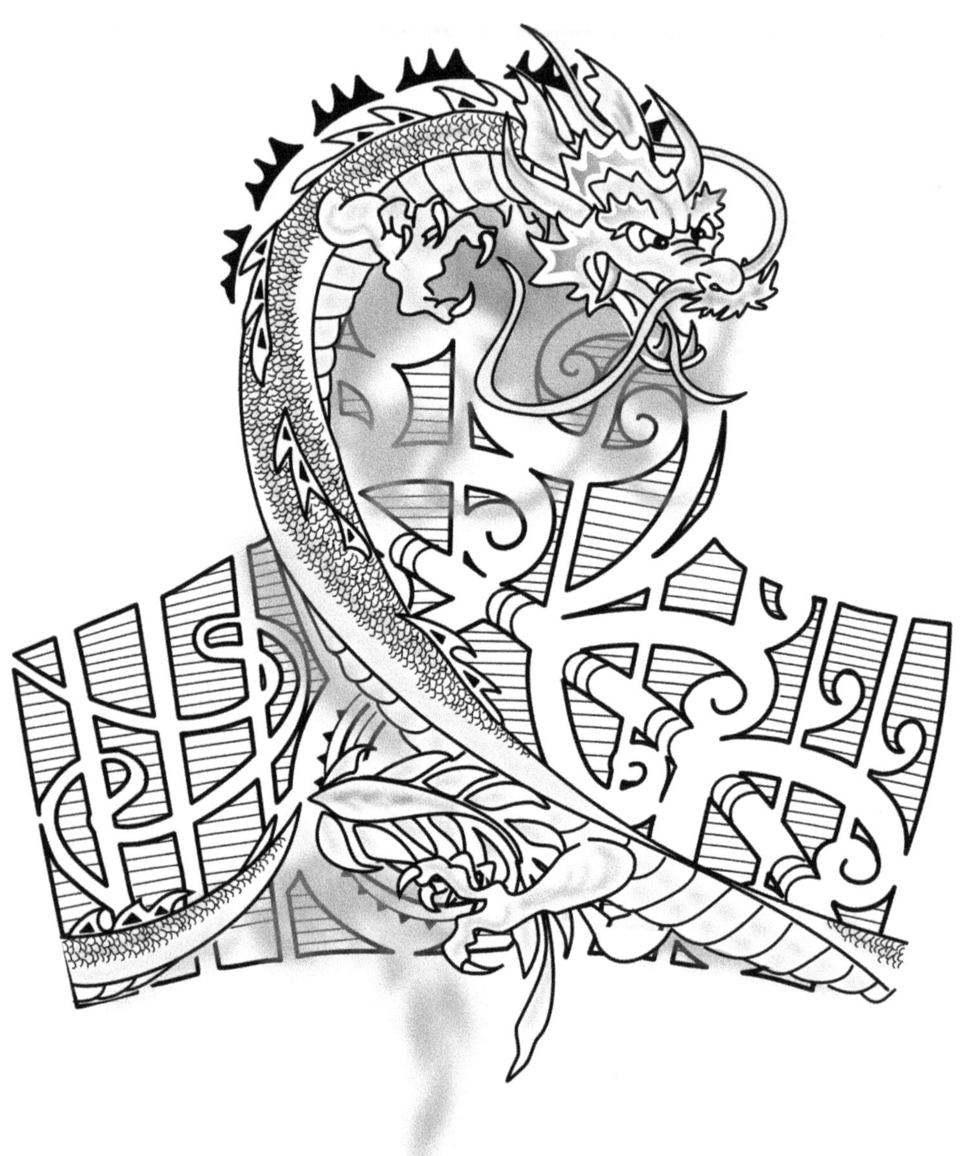

This half sleeve tattoo was designed to represent Chinese and Maori ancestry.

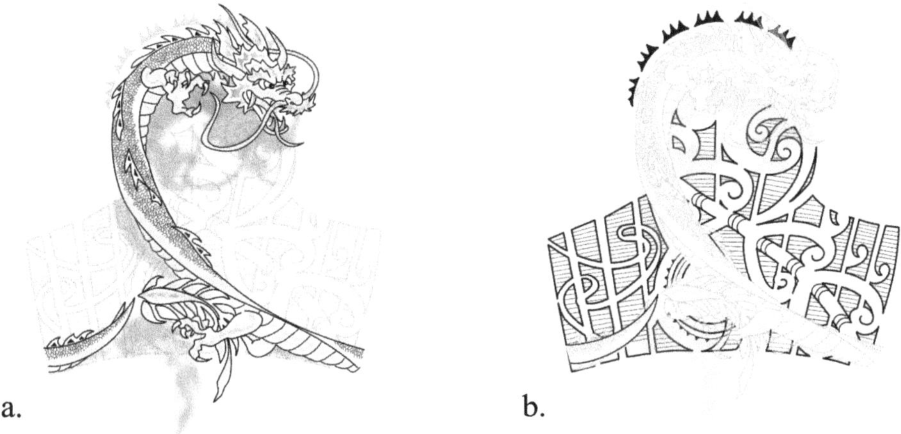

Fig. 8.1: (a) Chinese and (b) Maori elements.

The dragon symbolizes a warrior spirit, firmly chasing one's goals. The *puhoro* pattern in the background represents a difficult path and the success achieved by facing every challenge with perseverance. Perseverance and strength are symbolized by the hammerhead shark motif behind the body of the dragon.

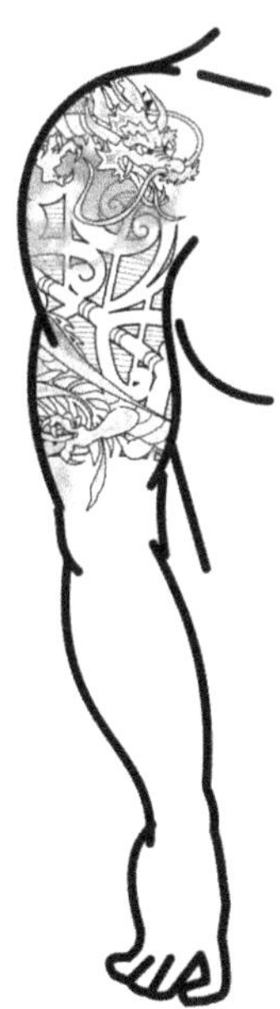

The shadow left by the dragon on the underlying Maori pattern gives it a three-dimensional look. The mountains on top following the design of the dragon's back crests contribute to linking and blending the two styles together.

Japanese + Tahitian

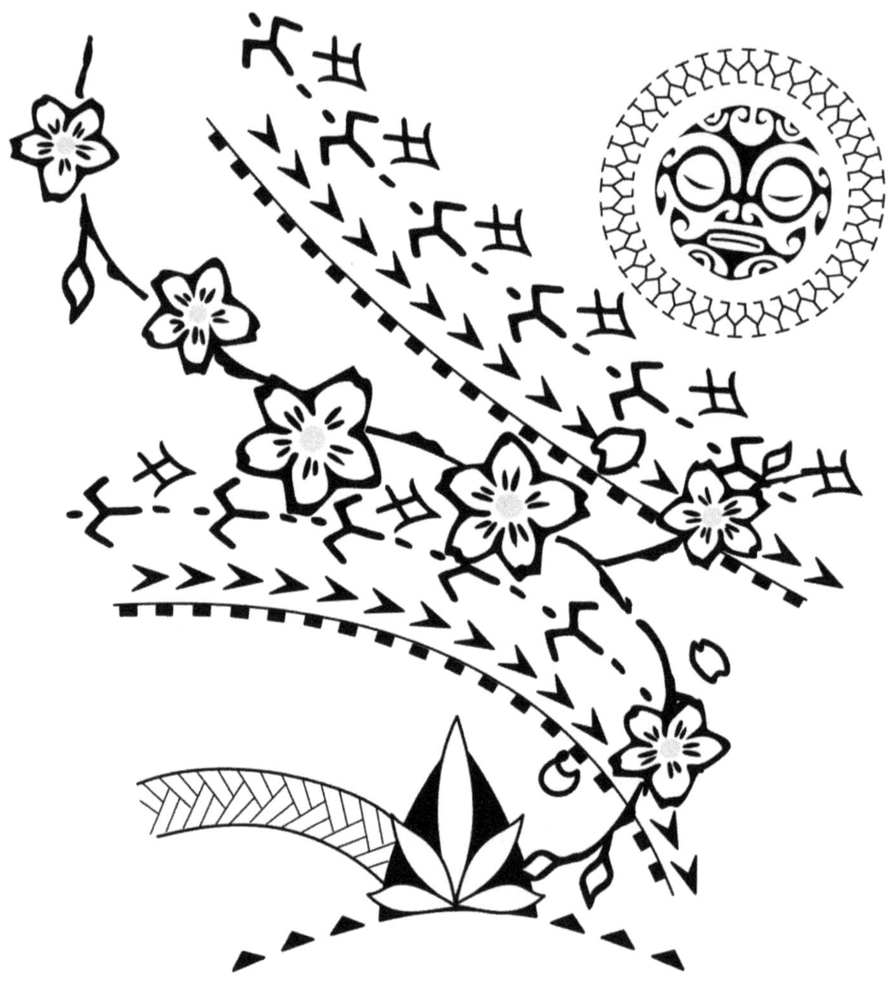

This forearm wrap tattoo was designed for a woman to represent her Japanese and Tahitian ancestry.

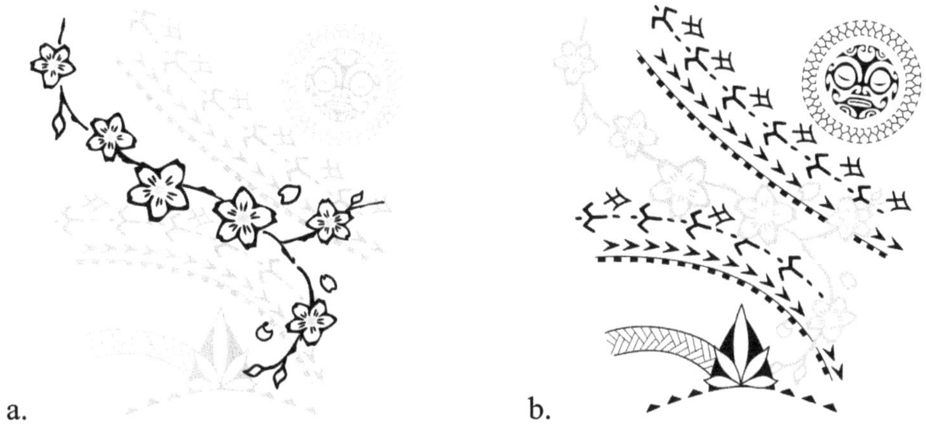

Fig. 8.2: (a) Japanese and (b) mixed Polynesian elements.

The branch of cherry blossoms is characteristic of Japanese designs, where cherry flowers symbolize beauty and seizing the moment (carpe diem), as their flowers bloom all at once in a glorious display of magnificence despite their short life.

The central elements that embrace them symbolize life as a voyage, a challenging path full of moments to be lived and trials to be faced with courage. Family and unity are at the base of everything while ancestors give protection from above.

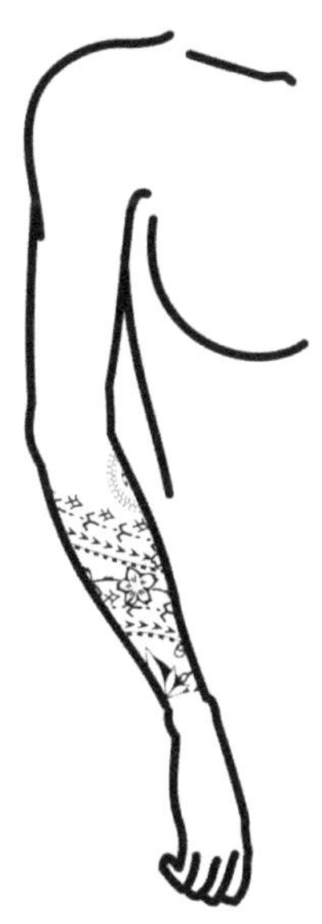

Norse + Marquesan

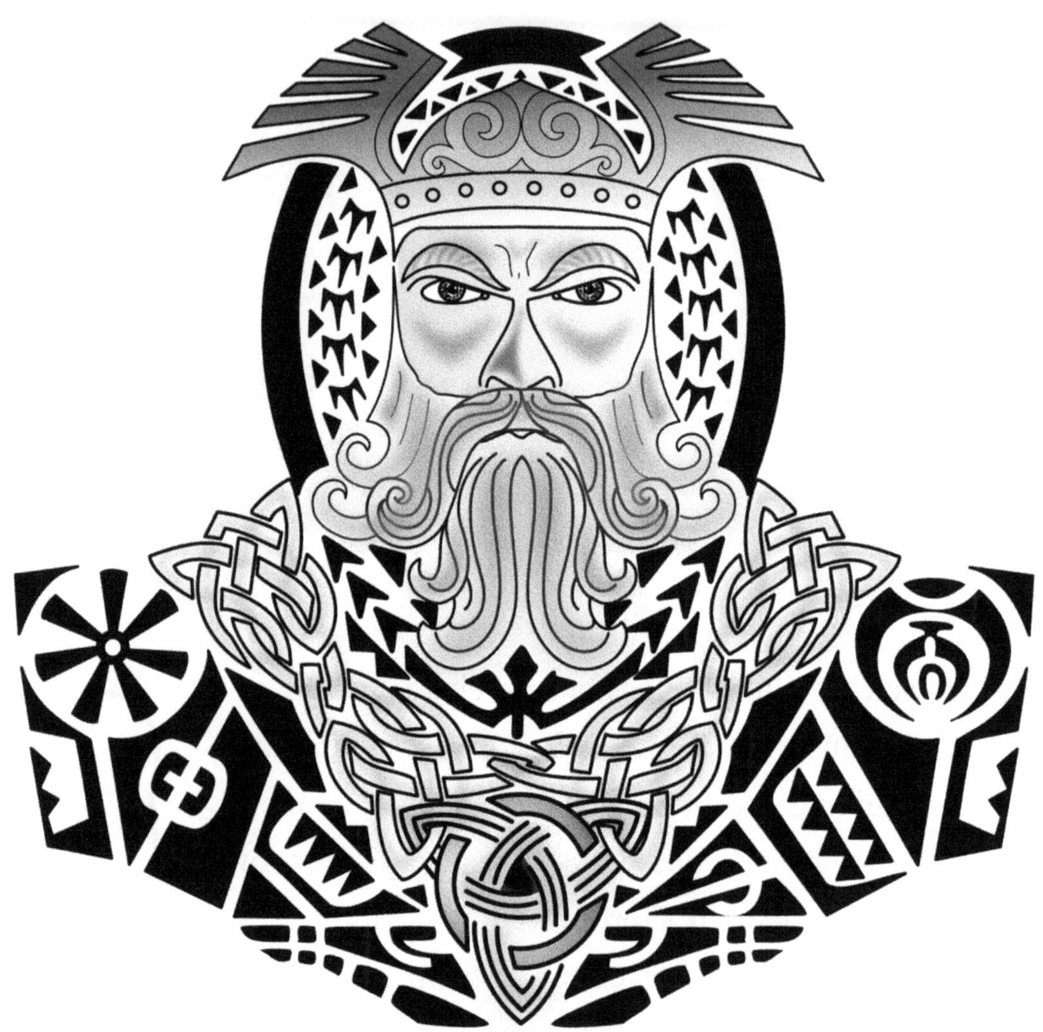

This half sleeve tattoo was designed to represent Norse ancestry paired with a passion for the "vikings of the sunrise", as Polynesian navigators have been called by the Maori historian Te Rangi Hiroa.

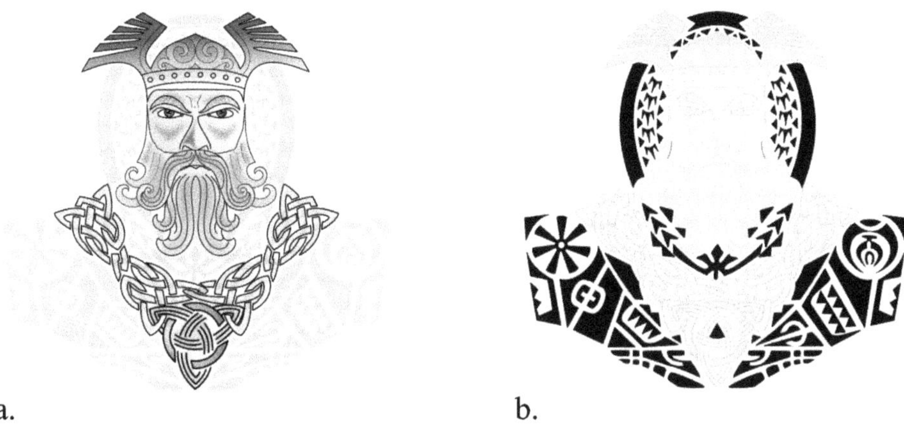

Fig. 8.3: (a) Norse and (b) Marquesan elements.

Vikings and Polynesians share many common traits, such as their ability as navigators, voyaging beyond the known limits of their time, and their fighting spirit.

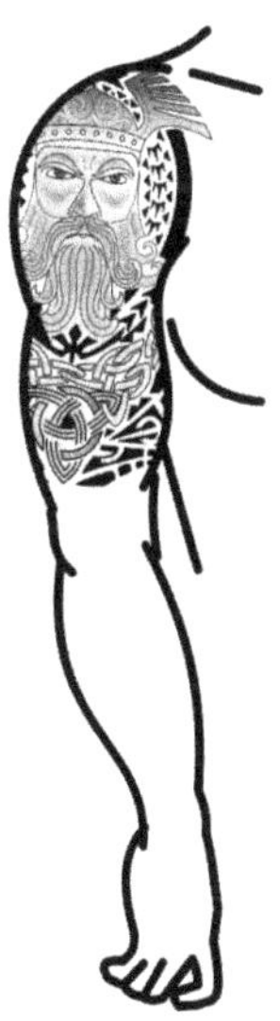

We decided to place a viking centrally to represent the lineage of the man for whom this tattoo was prepared, coupled with Marquesan elements to enhance its bold look and to reinforce the warrior symbolism.

The two round elements placed at the joints of the shoulders are a star and an all-seeing eye to represent someone who is favored by the gods, and to give him protection. Shark teeth also symbolize protection, strength, and tenacity. The stepping stones at the base symbolize all the achievements and lessons learnt along his life journey (the rows of birds and *mōlina* lines around the viking's head), which are now the foundations of his life. Right below the viking, an *enata* and two rows of spearheads represent the warrior.

The tattoos in this chapter are not traditional designs in a strict way, but they resonate with the lives of those for whom they were prepared, as we believe that anyone should be able to receive a tattoo that tells their story and reflects their beliefs and passions.

If you have read this far, you now know that Polynesian tattoos have a deeper meaning that is always personal. Each design is created for a specific person and it relates to their life. Polynesian tattoos always include details that are disclosed to their wearers only. They give *mana* to that person because they resonate with their life. Hence, the right tattoo can increase a person's *mana*, but the wrong one could affect it in a negative way. Choose wisely. You have now the tools to understand their symbolism and to prepare them in a way that is respectful of their nature, purpose, and message.

The Coming of the Maori. Te Rangi Hiroa (Peter H. Buck), 1949.

'Cureous Figures': European Voyagers and Tatau/Tattoo in Polynesia, 1595-1800. Douglas Bronwen, 2005.

'A Curious Document': Ta Moko as Evidence of Pre-European Textual Culture in New Zealand: BSANZ Bulletin. Sarah K. J. Gallagher, 2003.

A Dictionary of the Hawaiian Language. Lorrin Andrews, 1865.

A Journal of a Voyage to the South Seas in His Majesty's Ship, the Endeavour. Sydney Parkinson, 1773.

JPS - The Journal of Polynesian Society. Several numbers from 1892–2018.

L'Art du Tatouage aux Îles Marquises. K. v. d. Steinen (1928), trad. par Denise et Robert Koenig, 2007.

The Lapita People. Patrick Vinton Kirch, 1997.

The Material Culture of the Cook Islands (Aitutaki). Te Rangi Hiroa (Peter H. Buck), 1927.

Moko or Maori Tattooing. H. G. Robley: Chapman and Hall Ltd, 1896.

On the Road of the Winds: An Archæological History of the Pacific Islands before European Contact. Patrick Vinton Kirch, 2000.

Parlons Marquisien. Edgar Tetahiotupa, 2009.

Samoan House Building, Cooking and Tattooing. E. S. Craighill Handy and W. C. Handy, 1924.

Samoan Material Culture. Te Rangi Hiroa (Peter H. Buck), 1930.

South Sea Folk: A Handbook of Maori and Oceanic Ethnology. Archey Gilbert, 1967.

Tatauing the Post-Colonial Body. Albert Wendt, 1996.

Tattooing in the Marquesas. W. C. Handy: B. P. Bishop Museum Bulletin no. 1, 1922.

The Tattooing of Both Sexes in Samoa. Carl Marquardt, 1984.

The Three Famous Voyages of Captain James Cook Round the World. J. Cook and J. King, 1889.

Vikings of the Sunrise. Te Rangi Hiroa (Peter H. Buck), 1938.

Voyages Autour du Monde. M. De Krusenstern, 1821.

Wrapping in Images: Tattooing in Polynesia. A. Gell, 1993

A Year among the Maoris: Study of Their Arts and Customs. Frances Del Mar, 1924.

TattooTribes.com
2018

www.ingramcontent.com/pod-product-compliance
Ingram Content Group UK Ltd.
Pitfield, Milton Keynes, MK11 3LW, UK
UKHW061701190726
13853UKWH00008B/2340